What is Morphology?

Fundamentals of Linguistics

Each book in the Fundamentals of Linguistics series is a concise and critical introduction to the major issues in a subfield of linguistics, including morphology, semantics, and syntax. The books presuppose little knowledge of linguistics, are authored by well-known scholars, and are useful for beginning students, specialists in other subfields of linguistics, and interested non-linguists.

What is Morphology?
Mark Aronoff and Kirsten Fudeman

What is Meaning? Fundamentals of Formal Semantics
Paul H. Portner

What is Morphology?

Mark Aronoff and
Kirsten Fudeman

Blackwell
Publishing

BLACKWELL PUBLISHING
350 Main Street, Malden, MA 02148-5020, USA
9600 Garsington Road, Oxford OX4 2DQ, UK
550 Swanston Street, Carlton, Victoria 3053, Australia

First published 2005 by Blackwell Publishing Ltd

7   2009

Library of Congress Cataloging-in-Publication Data

Aronoff, Mark.
  What is morphology? / Mark Aronoff and Kirsten Fudeman.
    p. cm. — (Fundamentals of linguistics 1)
  Includes bibliographical references and index.
  ISBN 978-0-631-20318-6 (hardcover : alk. paper) — ISBN 978-0-631-20319-3 (pbk. : alk. paper)
  1. Grammar, Comparative and general—Morphology.
  I. Fudeman, Kirsten Anne. II. Title. III. Series.

  P241.A699 2005
  415'.9—dc22

                                                              2004010915

A catalogue record for this title is available from the British Library.

Set in 10/12½ pt Palatino by Graphicraft Ltd, Hong Kong
Printed and bound in Singapore by Utopia Press Pte Ltd

The publisher's policy is to use permanent paper from mills that operate a sustainable
forestry policy, and which has been manufactured from pulp processed using acid-free and
elementary chlorine-free practices. Furthermore, the publisher ensures that the text paper
and cover board used have met acceptable environmental accreditation standards.

For further information on
Blackwell Publishing, visit our website:
www.blackwellpublishing.com

Contents

Preface

This little book is meant to introduce fundamental aspects of morphology to students with only a minimal background in linguistics. It presupposes only the very basic knowledge of phonetics, phonology, syntax, and semantics that an introductory course in linguistics provides. If, having worked through this book, a student has some understanding of the range of basic issues in morphological description and analysis; can appreciate what a good morphological description looks like, how a good morphological analysis works and what a good theory of morphology does; can actually do morphological analysis at an intermediate level; and most importantly understands that linguistic morphology can be rewarding; then the basic goal of the book will have been met.

The book departs from a trend common among current linguistics textbooks, even at the elementary level, which tend to be quite theoretical in orientation and even devoted to a single theory or set of related theories. We have chosen instead to concentrate on description, analysis, and the fundamental issues that face all theories of morphology. At the most basic level, we want to provide students with a grasp of how linguists think about and analyze the internal structure of complex words in a representative range of real languages. What are the fundamental problems, regardless of one's theoretical perspective? We therefore dwell for the most part on questions that have occupied morphologists since the beginnings of modern linguistics in the late nineteenth century, rather than on more detailed technical points of particular theories.

Of course, this means that we assume that there are general questions, but in morphology, at least, the early modern masters were grappling with many of the same questions that occupy us to this day. Descriptions and analyses that Baudouin de Courtenay wrote in the 1880s are not merely understandable, but even interesting and enlightening to the modern morphologists. The same is true of the work of Edward Sapir and Roman Jakobson from the 1920s and 1930s. Yes, the terminology and theories are different, but the overall goals are much the same. That is not to say that no progress has been made, only that the basic issues about word-internal structure have remained stable for quite a long time.

One of the fundamental assumptions that go back to the beginnings of modern linguistics is that each language is a system where everything holds together ("la langue forme un système où tout se tient et a un plan d'une merveilleuse rigueur": Antoine Meillet). More recent linguists have stressed the importance of universal properties that all languages have in common over properties of individual languages, but not even the most radical universalists will deny the systematicity of individual human languages. It is therefore important, from the very beginning, that a student be presented, not just with fragmentary bits of data from many languages, as tends to happen with both morphology and phonology, but with something approaching the entire morphological system of a single language. To that end, we have divided each of the chapters of this book up into two parts. The first part is the conventional sort of material that one would find in any textbook. Here our focus is often on standard American English, although we present data from many other languages, as well. The second part describes in some detail part of the morphology of Kujamaat Jóola, a language spoken in Senegal. For each chapter, we have tried to select an aspect of Kujamaat Jóola morphology that is close to the topic of the chapter. By the end of the book, the student should have a reasonable grasp of the entire system of Kujamaat Jóola morphology and thus understand how, at least for one language, the whole of the morphology holds together. Of course, no one language can be representative of all the world's languages, and morphology is so varied that not even the most experienced analyst is ever completely prepared for what a new language may bring. But students certainly will benefit from a reasonably complete picture of how a single language works.

The Kujamaat Jóola material complements the material in the main portion of the chapter, but it is not meant to mirror it exactly. Our inclusion of particular Kujamaat Jóola topics was dictated in part by the data that was available to us. Our primary sources were J. David Sapir's *A Grammar of Diola-Fogny*, his 1967 revisions to the analysis of the Kujamaat Jóola verb (Thomas and Sapir 1967), and his unpublished dictionary. In a number of cases, we have used the Kujamaat Jóola section of each chapter to delve into topics not treated in the main portion, or treated only superficially. Thus chapters 2 and 7 contain detailed examinations of Kujamaat Jóola noun classes and verb morphology, respectively, and in chapter 3 we address its rich interactions between vowel harmony and morphology.

We chose Kujamaat Jóola for this book because its morphology, though complex and sometimes unusual, is highly regular, which makes it an excellent teaching vehicle. Some might question this choice, preferring a language with a higher degree of morphological fusion. Such a language might have led to theoretical issues, for example, that we do not explore in any detail here. However, we felt that in a book of this type, aimed at the beginning or intermediate-level morphologist, Kujamaat Jóola was an ideal choice.

One value of presenting beginning students with the largely complete morphological description of a single language is that descriptive grammars (which more often than not concentrate on morphology and phonology) form a mainstay of linguistic research, not only at more advanced levels of study, but throughout a researcher's career. The ability to work through a descriptive grammar is not innate, as many of us assume, but an acquired skill that takes practice. The Kujamaat Jóola sections taken together comprise an almost complete descriptive morphology of that language, so that by the end of the book students will have had the experience of working through an elementary morphological description of one language and will be somewhat prepared to tackle more complete descriptions when the time comes.

This brings us to the topic of how we intend the Kujamaat Jóola sections of this book to be used. Because of their inherent complexity, it is crucial that the instructor not simply assign these sections as readings. Instead, each must be gone over carefully in class until the students have a good grasp of the material in it. Otherwise, students are not likely to extract full value from the Kujamaat Jóola sections. Although we feel that these sections will be both useful and rewarding, it is also the case that the main portions of the chapter are freestanding, and an instructor who prefers not to do some or all of the Kujamaat Jóola sections does not have to.

Each chapter closes with a set of problems that are cross-referenced with the text, and we expect that the solutions to these problems will be discussed in detail in class. Some simpler exercises are integrated into the text itself, with answers provided. We feel that some exercises, particularly open-ended questions, are especially well suited to class discussion, and so instructors may decide not to assign them in written form. Most chapters also contain Kujamaat Jóola exercises designed to get students to apply the data we have provided creatively and analytically.

Chapter 1 contains two sample problem sets with answers (section 1.5.3). We suggest that instructors assign these separately from the rest of the chapter reading and that they ask students to write them out as they would a regular assignment, without reading the explanation and analysis that go with them. Then students can check their work on their own. This should prepare them for doing some of the other analytical problems in the text.

Another feature of this book is a glossary. The terms in it appear in **bold** the first time they are used or explained in the text.

Ideally, each class session will be divided into three parts, corresponding to the division of the chapters: exposition of new pedagogical material; detailed discussion of Kujamaat Jóola; and finally discussion of solutions for the homework problems of the day (we assume that problems will be assigned daily and that students' performance on them will comprise a good part of the basis of their grades in the course).

We close with a warning to both the instructor and the student: this book does not pretend to cover all of morphology, but rather only a number of general topics drawn from the breadth of the field that are of special interest to its authors. We have purposely not gone deeply into the aspects of morphology that interact most with other central areas of linguistics (phonology, semantics, and syntax), because that would require knowledge of these areas that beginning students might not have. Thus there is little discussion of clitics, for example. We have also provided scant coverage of the exciting new work using experimental and computational methods that is bound to be more central in the future. But please permit us to remind the user in closing that our ambitions in writing this volume are quite modest. We do not expect students who have worked through this book to have a full understanding, but to have developed a lasting taste for morphology that, with luck, will sustain them as it has us.

We owe a debt of thanks to the many people who helped us as we worked on this project. We are especially grateful to the various people who read drafts of the manuscript and made suggestions on how to make it better. These include Harald Baayen, Donald Lenfest, Lanko Marušič, and two anonymous Blackwell reviewers. We give special thanks to Phil Baldi and Barbara Bullock, who tested the manuscript in a morphology class at the Pennsylvania State University, and to five anonymous student reviewers. Their comments were particularly thorough and helped us to improve this book on many different levels. Harald Baayen and some of our anonymous student reviewers also suggested a number of excellent exercises, which we incorporated into the current version.

Peter Aronoff read the manuscript over his winter break and still took a linguistics course the next semester. For their input and discussion, we thank Bill Ham, Alan Nussbaum, and Draga Zec. We are also grateful to Jane Kaplan, who shared her collection of language-related cartoon strips, advertisements, and other magazine and newspaper clippings with us.

J. David Sapir generously gave us permission to reproduce copious amounts of Kujamaat Jóola data from his published and unpublished work, and Eugene Nida allowed us to include exercises first published in his classic textbook on morphology. We are pleased that his exercises will be introduced to a new generation of students.

This book owes a great deal to the guidance and particularly the patience of the editors at Blackwell over the years: Philip Carpenter, Sarah Coleman, Tami Kaplan, Beth Remmes, and Steve Smith. Thanks also to our desk editor, Fiona Sewell. Writing the book has been a joint effort, and we would like to emphasize that the order of the authors' names given on the title page is alphabetical.

Mark Aronoff and Kirsten Fudeman

Acknowledgments

The authors and publisher wish to acknowledge the copyright material used in this book:

p. xviii: The International Phonetic Alphabet. Courtesy of the International Phonetic Association (c/o Department of Linguistics, University of Victoria, British Columbia, Canada).

p. 13: Digital DNA™ advertisement. Copyright of Motorola, used by permission.

p. 42: *Wizard of Id*. By permission of John L. Hart FLP, and Creators Syndicate, Inc. Creators Syndicate, 5777 W. Century Blvd., Suite 700, Los Angeles, CA 90045.

p. 129: *Foxtrot*. Universal Press Syndicate, AMU Permissions Department, 4520 Main Street, Kansas City, MO 64111-7701.

The publisher apologizes for any errors or omissions in the above list and would be grateful if notified of any corrections that should be incorporated in future reprints or editions of this book.

Abbreviations

A, adj	adjective
abs	absolutive
acc	accusative
act	active
agr	agreement
an	animate
apass	antipassive
app	applicative
Ar.	Arabic
ASP	aspect
C	consonant
caus	causative
cl	noun class
ct	combining with a circumstantial topic
d	declarative
def	definite
DEM	demonstrative
dir	directional
du	dual
emph	emphatic
erg	ergative
excl	exclusive
f	feminine
Fr.	French
FUT	future
gen	genitive
hab	habitual
imp	imperfective

inan	inanimate
inc	dubitive-incompletive
incl	inclusive
ind	indicative
inf	infinitive
irr	irrealis
LOC	locative
m	masculine
Mdk.	Mandinka
n, N	noun
ne	noun emphasis
neg	negative
nom	nominative
nonfut	non-future
nonhum	non-human
NP	noun phrase
nts	combining with a non-topical subject
obj	object
part	participle
partic	particulizer
pass	passive
perf	perfective
pl	plural
Port.	Portuguese
poss	possessive
pres	present
PROG	progressive
PRTC	particle
ps	past subordinate
qm	question marker
redup	reduplicative
refl	reflexive
rel	relativizer
res	resultative
sg	singular
stat	stative
sub	subject
subord	subordinating morph
tns	tense
tri	trial
v, V	verb; vowel; theme vowel

Remarks on Transcription

Modern linguistics has been struggling with the problem of phonetic and phonological transcription since its inception. The International Phonetics Association was founded in 1886 with the goal of providing for linguistics a worldwide standard system for naming sounds, the International Phonetic Alphabet (IPA), akin to that universal standard language used in chemistry and physics since the mid-nineteenth century to name the elements and their compounds. But linguists have long resisted this standardization, especially for phonological transcription, much to the dismay of students over the generations. There are many reasons for this resistance. The phonological transcription of a language is often driven by the desire to develop a practical orthography, in which phonetic accuracy and consistency take a back seat to ease of use. Also, phonological theorists since the beginning of that field have enjoyed a love–hate relationship with phonetics, arguing over the true nature of the connection between a phoneme and its various phonetic realizations, leading them to downplay the importance of consistency for phonological transcription across languages, since each language has its own unique phonological system. Leonard Bloomfield, for example, one of the great linguists of the twentieth century, used the symbol U for schwa (IPA ə) in his Menomini grammar, largely for typographical convenience.

In this book, we have made a compromise. Wherever possible or practicable, we have used the IPA, a copy of which is included facing p. 1. We have deviated from the IPA chiefly in our representation of the English approximant rhotic, choosing to use instead the symbol <r> for simplicity. (For more on the International Phonetics Association and the International Phonetic Alphabet, visit the website of the Association at http://www.arts.gla.ac.uk/IPA/ipa.html.) But many languages have well-established orthographies or systems of phonological transcription, which we have not disturbed. Most prominently, in transcribing Kujamaat Jóola, we have adopted wholesale the system used by J. David Sapir in the grammar from which our data and description are adapted. We have endeavored, though, in all cases where transcription departs from the IPA, to give the IPA equivalent for non-standard symbols.

This lack of consistency may be a little confusing for the student at first, but we hope that it will teach students to be careful, because the symbols used in phonological transcription may sometimes be used in arbitrary and even capricious ways, so that it is important to pay close attention to the phonetic description that accompanies the symbols at their introduction. Reading Bloomfield's Menomini grammar without knowing that U stands for schwa can lead to serious misunderstanding.

THE INTERNATIONAL PHONETIC ALPHABET (revised to 1993, updated 1996)

CONSONANTS (PULMONIC)

	Bilabial	Labiodental	Dental	Alveolar	Postalveolar	Retroflex	Palatal	Velar	Uvular	Pharyngeal	Glottal
Plosive	p b			t d		ʈ ɖ	c ɟ	k ɡ	q ɢ		ʔ
Nasal	m	ɱ		n		ɳ	ɲ	ŋ	N		
Trill	ʙ			r					ʀ		
Tap or Flap				ɾ		ɽ					
Fricative	ɸ β	f v	θ ð	s z	ʃ ʒ	ʂ ʐ	ç ʝ	x ɣ	χ ʁ	ħ ʕ	h ɦ
Lateral fricative				ɬ ɮ							
Approximant		ʋ		ɹ		ɻ	j	ɰ			
Lateral approximant				l		ɭ	ʎ	ʟ			

Where symbols appear in pairs, the one to the right represents a voiced consonant. Shaded areas denote articulations judged impossible.

CONSONANTS (NON-PULMONIC)

Clicks	Voiced implosives	Ejectives
ʘ Bilabial	ɓ Bilabial	ʼ Examples:
ǀ Dental	ɗ Dental/alveolar	pʼ Bilabial
ǃ (Post)alveolar	ʄ Palatal	tʼ Dental/alveolar
ǂ Palatoalveolar	ɠ Velar	kʼ Velar
ǁ Alveolar lateral	ʛ Uvular	sʼ Alveolar fricative

VOWELS

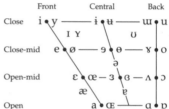

Where symbols appear in pairs, the one to the right represents a rounded vowel.

OTHER SYMBOLS

ʍ Voiceless labial-velar fricative

w Voiced labial-velar approximant

ɥ Voiced labial-palatal approximant

ʜ Voiceless epiglottal fricative

ʢ Voiced epiglottal fricative

ʡ Epiglottal plosive

ɕ ʑ Alveolo-palatal fricatives

ɺ Alveolar lateral flap

ɧ Simultaneous ʃ and x

Affricates and double articulations can be represented by two symbols joined by a tie bar if necessary.

k͡p   t͜s

DIACRITICS   Diacritics may be placed above a symbol with a descender, e.g. ŋ̊

̥ Voiceless	n̥ d̥	̤ Breathy voiced	b̤ a̤	̪ Dental	t̪ d̪		
̬ Voiced	s̬ t̬	̰ Creaky voiced	b̰ a̰	̺ Apical	t̺ d̺		
ʰ Aspirated	tʰ dʰ	̼ Linguolabial	t̼ d̼	̻ Laminal	t̻ d̻		
̹ More rounded	ɔ̹	ʷ Labialized	tʷ dʷ	̃ Nasalized	ẽ		
̜ Less rounded	ɔ̜	ʲ Palatalized	tʲ dʲ	ⁿ Nasal release	dⁿ		
̟ Advanced	u̟	ˠ Velarized	tˠ dˠ	ˡ Lateral release	dˡ		
̠ Retracted	e̠	ˤ Pharyngealized	tˤ dˤ	̚ No audible release	d̚		
̈ Centralized	ë	̃ Velarized or pharyngealized ɫ					
̽ Mid-centralized	e̽	̝ Raised	e̝ (ɹ̝ = voiced alveolar fricative)				
̩ Syllabic	n̩	̞ Lowered	e̞ (β̞ = voiced bilabial approximant)				
̯ Non-syllabic	e̯	̘ Advanced Tongue Root	e̘				
˞ Rhoticity	ɚ a˞	̙ Retracted Tongue Root	e̙				

SUPRASEGMENTALS

ˈ   Primary stress

ˌ   Secondary stress

ˌfoʊnəˈtɪʃən

ː   Long   eː

ˑ   Half-long   eˑ

̆   Extra-short   ĕ

ǀ   Minor (foot) group

ǁ   Major (intonation) group

.   Syllable break   ɹi.ækt

‿   Linking (absence of a break)

TONES AND WORD ACCENTS

LEVEL			CONTOUR		
e̋ or	˥	Extra high	ě or	˩˥	Rising
é	˦	High	ê	˥˩	Falling
ē	˧	Mid	e᷄	˦˥	High rising
è	˨	Low	e᷅	˩˨	Low rising
ȅ	˩	Extra low	e᷈	˧˩˧	Rising-falling
ꜜ	Downstep		↗	Global rise	
ꜛ	Upstep		↘	Global fall	

1 Thinking about Morphology and Morphological Analysis

mor·phol·o·gy: a study of the structure or form of something
Merriam-Webster Unabridged

■ 1.1   What is Morphology?

The term **morphology** is generally attributed to the German poet, novelist, playwright, and philosopher Johann Wolfgang von Goethe (1749–1832), who coined it early in the nineteenth century in a biological context. Its etymology is Greek: *morph-* means 'shape, form', and *morphology* is the study of form or forms. In biology *morphology* refers to the study of the form and structure of organisms, and in geology it refers to the study of the configuration and evolution of land forms. In linguistics *morphology* refers to the mental system involved in word formation or to the branch of linguistics that deals with words, their internal structure, and how they are formed.

■ 1.2   Morphemes

A major way in which morphologists investigate words, their internal structure, and how they are formed is through the identification and study of **morphemes**, often defined as the smallest linguistic pieces with a grammatical function. This definition is not meant to include all morphemes, but it is the usual one and a good starting point. A morpheme may consist of a word, such as *hand*, or a meaningful piece of a word, such as the *-ed* of *looked*, that cannot be divided into smaller meaningful parts. Another way in which morphemes have been defined is as a pairing between sound and meaning. We have purposely chosen not to use this definition. Some morphemes have no concrete form or no continuous form, as we will see, and some do not have meanings in the conventional sense of the term.

You may also run across the term **morph**. The term 'morph' is sometimes used to refer specifically to the phonological realization of a morpheme. For example, the English past tense morpheme that we spell *-ed* has various morphs. It is realized as [t] after the voiceless [p] of *jump* (cf. *jumped*), as [d] after the voiced [l] of *repel* (cf. *repelled*), and as [əd] after the voiceless [t] of *root* or the voiced [d] of *wed* (cf. *rooted* and *wedded*). We can also call these morphs **allomorphs** or **variants**. The appearance of one morph over another in this case is determined by voicing and the place of articulation of the final consonant of the verb stem.

Now consider the word *reconsideration*. We can break it into three morphemes: *re-*, *consider*, and *-ation*. *Consider* is called the **stem**. A stem is a base morpheme to which another morphological piece is attached. The stem can be **simple**, made up of only one part, or **complex**, itself made up of more than one piece. Here it is best to consider *consider* a simple stem. Although it consists historically of more than one part, most present-day speakers would treat it as an unanalyzable form. We could also call *consider* the root. A **root** is like a stem in constituting the core of the word to which other pieces attach, but the term refers only to morphologically simple units. For example, *disagree* is the stem of *disagreement*, because it is the base to which *-ment* attaches, but *agree* is the root. Taking *disagree* now, *agree* is both the stem to which *dis-* attaches and the root of the entire word.

Returning now to *reconsideration, re-* and *-ation* are both **affixes**, which means that they are attached to the stem. Affixes like *re-* that go before the stem are **prefixes,** and those like *-ation* that go after are **suffixes**.

Some readers may wonder why we have not broken -*ation* down further into two pieces, -*ate* and -*ion*, which function independently elsewhere. In this particular word they do not do so (cf. **reconsiderate*), and hence we treat -*ation* as a single morpheme.

It is important to take very seriously the idea that the grammatical function of a morpheme, which may include its meaning, must be constant. Consider the English words *lovely* and *quickly*. They both end with the suffix -*ly*. But is it the same in both words? No – when we add -*ly* to the adjective *quick*, we create an adverb that describes how fast someone does something. But when we add -*ly* to the noun *love*, we create an adjective. What on the surface appears to be a single morpheme turns out to be two. One attaches to adjectives and creates adverbs; the other attaches to nouns and creates adjectives.

There are two other sorts of affixes that you will encounter, **infixes** and **circumfixes**. Both are classic challenges to the notion of morpheme. Infixes are segmental strings that do not attach to the front or back of a word, but rather somewhere in the middle. The Tagalog infix -*um*- is illustrated below (McCarthy and Prince 1993: 101–5; French 1988). It creates an agent from a verb stem and appears before the first vowel of the word:

(1) Root   -um-
     /sulat/   /s-um-ulat/   'one who wrote'
     /gradwet/   /gr-um-adwet/   'one who graduated'

The existence of infixes challenges the traditional notion of a morpheme as an indivisible unit. We want to call the stem *sulat* 'write' a morpheme, and yet the infix -*um*- breaks it up. Yet this seems to be a property of -*um*- rather than one of *sulat*. Our definition of morphemes as the smallest linguistic pieces with a grammatical function survives this challenge.

Circumfixes are affixes that come in two parts. One attaches to the front of the word, and the other to the back. Circumfixes are controversial because it is possible to analyze them as consisting of a prefix and a suffix that apply to a stem simultaneously. One example is Indonesian *ke . . . -an*. It applies to the stem *besar* 'big' to form a noun *ke-besar-an* meaning 'bigness, greatness' (MacDonald 1976: 63; Beard 1998: 62). Like infixes, the existence of circumfixes challenges the traditional notion of morpheme (but not the definition used here) because they involve discontinuity.

We will not go any more deeply here into classical problems with morphemes, but the reader who would like to know more might consult Anderson (1992: 51–6).

■ 1.3   Morphology in Action

We would like to explore the idea of morphology more deeply by examining some data. These are examples of morphology in action – morphological facts of everyday life.

■ 1.3.1   Novel words and word play

If you had been walking down the street in Ithaca, New York, a few years ago, you might have looked up and seen a sign for the music store "Rebop," a name that owes its inspiration to the jazz term *rebop*.[1] *Rebop* was originally one of the many nonsense expressions that jazz musicians threw into their vocal improvisations, starting in the early 1920s. In the 1940s, *rebop* became interchangeable with *bebop*, a term of similar origin, as the term for the rhythmically and harmonically eccentric music played by young black musicians. By the 1950s the name of this musical style was quite firmly established as simply *bop*.[2] Today, the original use of *rebop* is known only to cognoscenti, so that most people who pass by the store will be likely to interpret the word as composed of the word *bop* and the prefix *re-*, which means approximately 'again'. This prefix can attach only to verbs, so we must interpret *bop* as a verb here. *Rebop* must therefore mean 'bop again', if it means anything at all. And this music store, appropriately, specialized in selling used CDs. There's something going on here with English morphology. Of course, *rebop* is not a perfectly well-formed English word. The verb *bop* means something like 'bounce', but the prefix *re-* normally attaches only to a verb whose meaning denotes an accomplishment. The verb *rebop* therefore makes little sense. But names of stores and products are designed to catch the consumer's attention, not necessarily to make sense, and this one does so by exploiting people's knowledge of English in a fairly complex way and breaking the rules so as to attract attention, as verbal art often does.

Consider now the following phrases, taken from a Toni Braxton song: *Unbreak my heart, uncry these tears.*

We have never seen anyone *unbreak* something, and you certainly can't *uncry* tears, but every English speaker can understand these words. We all know what it means to unbreak somebody's heart or to wish that one's heart were unbroken. If we asked somebody, "unbreak my heart," we would be asking them to reverse the process of having our heart broken. We can visualize "uncry these tears," too – we just think of a film running backwards. We can understand these words because we know the meaning of *un-*, which basically reverses or undoes an action. The fact that these particular actions, breaking a heart and crying tears, cannot be reversed only adds poignancy to the song.

All human beings have this capacity for generating and understanding novel words. Sometimes someone will create an entirely new word, as J. R. R. Tolkien did when he coined the now-familiar term *hobbit* (which, despite its popularity, is still not listed in the 2000 edition of the *American Heritage Dictionary*). But more often than not, we build new words from pre-existing pieces, as with *unbreak* and *uncry*. We could easily go on to create more words on this pattern.

Novel words are all around us. Jerry Seinfeld has talked about the *shushers*, the *shushees*, and the *unshushables* in a movie theater. Morley Safer was dubbed *quirkologist* – expert on quirky people – on a special episode of *60 Minutes*. For those who hate buffets, the TV character Frasier Crane came up with the term *smorgsaphobia*. Finally, the longest novel morphologically complex word we have been able to find on our own in the daily press is *deinstitutionalization*, from the *New York Times*.

These are everyday morphological facts, the kind you run across every day as a literate speaker of English. What these words – *rebop, unbreak, uncry, hobbit, quirkologist, smorgsaphobia,* and *deinstitutionalization* – have in common is their newness. When we see or hear them, they leap out at us, for the simple reason that we have probably never seen or heard them before. It is interesting that novel words do this to us, because novel sentences do not. When you hear a new sentence, you generally don't realize that this is the first time that you've heard it. And you don't say to yourself, "What a remarkable sentence," unless it happens to be one from Proust or Joyce or some other verbal artist. Many people have made the observation before that morphology differs from syntax in this way. **[Exercises 1–3]**

Morphological challenge

As you work through this book, keep an eye – or an ear – out for novel or otherwise striking words, on television, in magazines and newspapers, in books, and in conversations. Keep a running list of them, then e-mail your list to the authors: mark.aronoff@stonybrook.edu.

■ 1.3.2   Abstract morphological facts

Now let's move to some more abstract morphological facts. These are the kind of morphological facts that you don't notice every day. They are so embedded in your language that you don't even think about them. They are more common than the ones we have just looked at, but at the same time deeper and more complex.

If you speak English and are concerned about your health, you might say:

(2)   I eat one melon a day.

Let's imagine that we are even more concerned about our health than you are. We don't just eat one melon a day, rather:

(3)   We eat two melons a day.

It is a fact about standard American or British English that we cannot say:

(4)   *We eat two melon a day.

However, if we were speaking Indonesian or Japanese, we would say the equivalent of *two melon* (*three melon*, *four melon*, etc.) because these languages don't use morphological plurals in sentences like this.

(5)   Indonesian:
      Saiga makan dua buah semangka (se) tiap   hari
      I   eat   two fruit melon   every day
      'I eat two melons every day.'

      Japanese:
      mainichi futatsu-no meron-o   tabemasu
      every.day two-   GEN melon-OBJ eat.IMPERF
      'I eat two melons every day.'

The morphological grammar of English tells us that we have to put an -*s* on *melon* whenever we are talking about more than one. This fact of English is so transparent that native speakers don't notice it. If we happen to be speakers of a language without obligatory plural marking, however, we will notice it because we are going to have a lot of trouble with it.

We have now observed something about English morphology. If a word is plural, it takes the suffix -*s*. Living creatures don't eat only melons, however:

(6)   The evil giant at the top of the beanstalk eats two melons, three fish, and four children a day.

Everyone agrees that *fish* is plural, but there is no plural marker. *Children* is also plural, but it has a very unusual plural suffix, *-ren*, plus an internal change: we say [ʧɪld-] instead of [ʧajld]. In other words, it's not always the case that we mark plural words with an *s*-like thing; there are other ways in which we can mark plurals. Native speakers of English know this, and they do not need to think about it before making a plural. **[Exercise 4]**

Consider the following:

(7)   Today they **claim** that they will fix the clock tower by Friday, but yesterday they **claimed** that it would take at least a month.

In this example, we use two different forms of the verb *claim*. One is present tense, and the other is past. Again, this is not true for all languages. If we were speaking Vietnamese, for example, we wouldn't make any distinction between *claim* and *claimed* – we wouldn't mark the verb at all. If we were speaking Chinese, we would not distinguish between *claim* and *claimed* in a sentence like this, because the adverb *zuótiān* 'yesterday' is sufficient to indicate past tense:

(8)   jīntiān tāmen shuō tāmen xīngqī wǔ ké yǐ xiū hǎo zhōnglóu,
      today they   say   they   Friday   can fix well clock.tower
      kě shì zuótiān tāmen què   shuō zhì shǎo xū yào yíge yuè
      but yesterday they however say at least need   a   month
      'Today they claim that they will fix the clock tower by Friday, but yesterday they claimed that it would take at least a month.'

If we were to leave out *zuótiān* 'yesterday', we would need to use the particle *le* after the verb to show that the action took place in the past. In other words, whether or not a speaker must indicate past tense in Chinese depends on context.

Notice what happens in English when we use some other verbs besides *claim*:

(9)   Today they **say** ... but yesterday they **said** ...
            tell us   **told** us
            know   **knew**

That these verbs and others do not add *-t*, *-d*, or *-əd* to make their past tense is an elementary fact about English morphology. We'll talk more about verbs like these later in the chapter.

The next observation about English morphology has to do with pronouns. The following is a real exchange between an American mother and her 6-year-old son:

(10)   Who just threw a pool ball through the basement window?
       Not me.

In this context, the 6-year-old (who was indeed guilty) would never have responded *Not I*. But if he were to answer with a sentence, the response would be *I didn't*, not *Me didn't*. In that case, the object form of the pronoun would be ungrammatical. Without formally knowing anything at all about subjects and objects, English-speaking 6-year-olds (and children even younger) master the pronoun system of their language. **[Exercise 5]**
    Given the following sentence, how many children does Joan have?

(11)   All of Joan's children are brilliant and play musical instruments surpassingly well.

From this statement you cannot know how many children Joan has, but one thing is certain: she has more than two. If Joan had only two children, we would normally say *both of Joan's children*, because it is a fact about English that there is a morphological distinction among universal quantifiers between the one designating all of two (*both*) or all of more than two (*all*) of a particular type of entity. In some other languages, marking for dual is even more pervasive. This is the case in Ancient Greek, as shown by the following examples:

(12)   ho   stratiô:tes   lambánei tous   híppous
       the.NOM.SG soldier.NOM.SG take.3SG the.ACC.PL horses.ACC.PL
       'The soldier takes the horses.'

       to: stratió:ta   lambáneton tous   híppous
       the.NOM.DU soldier.NOM.DU take.DU   the.ACC.PL horses.ACC.PL
       'The two soldiers take the horses.'

       hoi   stratiô:tai lambánousi tous   híppous
       the.M.PL soldier.PL take.3PL   the.ACC.PL horses.ACC.PL
       'The soldiers (three or more) take the horses.'

While English does not have special affixes to mark the dual, it keeps track of the distinction through words like *all* and *both*. There are actually languages in the world like Manam (Papua New Guinea: Gregersen 1976) and Larike (Central Maluku, Indonesia: Laidig and Laidig 1990) that distinguish not only singular, dual, and plural, but trial as well. The use

of singular, dual, trial, and plural second person subject prefixes in Larike
is illustrated below:

(13) **Ai-**   rala   iter-   lawa   peʔa- o ?
     2SG.SUB- chop.down 1PL.INCL.SUB- garden finish- QM
     'Did you (sg.) finish clearing our garden?'

     Kalu au-   ʔanu, **irua** musti   **iruai-**   ʔanu siʔu.
     if   1SG.SUB- eat   2DU certainly 2DU.SUB- eat   also
     'If I eat, certainly you both will eat too.'

     Kalu **iridu-**   ta- ʔeu, au-   na- wela.
     if   2TRI.SUB- NEG- go   1SG.SUB-IRR- go.home
     'If you three don't want to go, I'm going home.'

     Memang iri-   hise tapi **imi-**   ta- ʔariʔi-
     truly   3PL.NONHUM- exist but 2PL.SUB-NEG- see-
     ri.
     3PL.NONHUM.OBJ
     'They really do exist, but you (plural) didn't see them.'

■ 1.4   Background and Beliefs

This book is a general introduction to morphology and morphological
analysis from the point of view of a morphologist. The purpose is
not to advocate any particular theory or to give the truth (whatever that
is), but rather to get you, the reader, to where you can look for it by
yourself. Still, it is inevitable that some of our remarks will be colored
by our own beliefs and background. We would therefore like to present some of our foundational beliefs about linguistics and linguistic
methodology.

First, we believe that **languages differ from one another**. You might
be thinking, "Of course they do!" But we mean this in a very special way.
Some linguists are always looking for ways that languages are similar,
and at times, we do that, too. But we believe that if you focus only on the
similarities between languages, you miss out on all of the exciting ways
in which they differ. What's more, you may find parallels and similarities
where none really exist. We try to approach linguistic analysis with as
open a mind as possible, and to do this, it is first necessary to appreciate
the uniqueness and diversity of the world's languages.

Our second foundational belief is that *languages*, **which we can write
with a small *l*, are different from** *Language*, **with a capital *L*.** There are

thousands of individual languages in the world. But we may also speak of language in general to mean the general phenomenon of Language that encompasses all individual languages. This Language is related to Noam Chomsky's notion of Universal Grammar, which posits that languages are all alike in basic ways. There is an important distinction between these two uses of the word *language* and each is equally important to linguistics. Individual languages have features that are not characteristic of Language in general. For example, one feature of English is that its regular way of forming plural nouns is to add /z/. We would never claim, however, that this is universally true, or that it is a property of Language. To tie this belief in with the preceding one, we strongly believe that morphological theory and morphological analysis must be grounded in morphological description. If we want to appreciate what morphology really is, it's best to have some idea of what the morphology of individual languages is like. At the same time, we must have a reasonably well-thought-out general theory of the morphology of Language, so that we can compare our descriptions of individual languages within a wider context. In short, linguists need to pay equal attention to both small-l language and capital-L Language.

Our next belief is that **morphology is a distinct component of languages or grammars**. If you are not already familiar with some of the controversy surrounding morphology, this needs an explanation. The fact that some languages, such as Vietnamese, do not have morphologically complex words has led some people to conclude that morphology should not be a separate branch of linguistics. The reasoning is that linguistics is generally understood to deal with properties of all languages – more precisely, Language with a capital L. If there are languages that don't have morphology, then morphology is not a property of all languages, and morphological phenomena should be treated in **syntax** or **phonology**. We disagree. It has been shown elsewhere (e.g., Aronoff 1994) that there are aspects of morphology that cannot be attributed to syntax or phonology, or anything else.

One piece of evidence that morphology is separate from syntax, phonology, and other branches of linguistics is that words in some languages are grouped into largely arbitrary classes that determine their forms in different environments. Latin nouns fall into five distinct classes, called declensions, which have little or nothing to do with syntax or phonology, and certainly cannot be explained by either. They are purely morphological in their significance. The uniquely morphological nature of these classes is truly brought home by the fact that Latin nouns also fall into syntactic agreement classes (usually called genders) and the two systems cross-cut one another: two nouns may belong to the same gender but to different declensions and vice versa. We'll examine cases like these in later chapters, but their mere existence in many languages shows that morphology must be given some independent status in linguistics. Of course, morphology, probably more than any other component of language, interacts with all the rest, but it still has properties of its own.

We also believe that **morphologies are systems**. This is a very old observation. Because of it, it is impossible to talk about isolated facts in a language – everything holds together. This belief together with the second one, above, are the reasons why we'll be looking carefully at the morphology of a particular language, Kujamaat Jóola, throughout this book. Considering the morphology of Kujamaat Jóola in close to its entirety will give us a valuable perspective that we would never gain if we only focused on isolated facts from several languages.

So far, we have given you our beliefs about the nature of language and morphology. We also have some that pertain to methodology. The first is that we should **take an attitude of skeptical realism**. Albert Einstein said that a physicist must be both a realist and a nominalist, a realist in the sense that you must believe that what you ultimately find will be real, but a nominalist in the sense that you must never believe that you've found what you're looking for. Martin Joos made a similar statement about linguistics. On the one hand, you should always believe that what you are looking for is God's truth, but on the other, you should consider all that you have found so far as hocus-pocus. We believe strongly in the value of having a linguistic theory, but we believe equally strongly that you should never trust it completely.

Our other methodological belief can be summed up as a motto: **Anything goes**. This methodological belief is associated with the Against Method of Paul Feyerabend, a twentieth-century philosopher who felt that if we insisted on a single rule of scientific methodology, one that would not inhibit progress, it would be "Anything goes." We take a no-holds-barred approach to linguistics. We'll use any tool or method that will tell us how language works. This attitude stems in part from our skepticism about particular theories. People who are wedded to individual theories tend to believe in using tools that are rooted in that theory. Our tools are not theory-based in that way. If a tool does the job, we are happy to use it, whether it is a traditional linguistic tool (e.g., native speaker consultants, dictionaries, written grammars), an experimental tool (e.g., imaging technology), or a statistical tool.

■ 1.5   Introduction to Morphological Analysis

■ 1.5.1   Two basic approaches: analysis and synthesis

There are two complementary approaches to morphology, analytic and synthetic. The linguist needs both.

The analytic approach has to do with breaking words down, and it is usually associated with American structuralist linguistics of the first half of the twentieth century. There is a good reason for this. These linguists were often dealing with languages that they had never encountered before, and there were no written grammars of these languages to guide them. It was therefore crucial that they should have very explicit methods of linguistic analysis. No matter what language we're looking at, we need analytic methods that will be independent of the structures we are examining; preconceived notions might interfere with an objective, scientific analysis. This is especially true when dealing with unfamiliar languages.

The second approach to morphology is more often associated with theory than with methodology, perhaps unfairly. This is the synthetic approach. It basically says, "I have a lot of little pieces here. How do I put them together?" This question presupposes that you already know what the pieces are. So in a sense, analysis in some way must precede synthesis.

Say that you've broken a clock and taken it apart, and now you have to put all the little pieces back together. There's a catch: you don't know how. You could always go by trial and error. But the most efficient way would be to have some theory of how the clock goes together. Synthesis really involves theory construction.

From a morphological point of view, the synthetic question you ask is, "How does a speaker of a language produce a grammatically complex word when needed?" This question already assumes that you know what kinds of elementary pieces you are making the complex word out of. We think that one of the real problems of a morphological theory is that we don't always have a good idea of what the pieces are. Syntacticians can supply us with some tools: case and number, for example, are ancient syntactic notions that we can use in our morphology. But the primary way in which morphologists determine the pieces they are dealing with is by examination of language data. They must pull words apart carefully, taking great care to note where each piece came from to begin with.

We have described analysis and synthesis in terms of the morphologist studying language, but the two notions are equally applicable to speakers themselves. Speakers apply morphological analysis when they read or hear a complex word that they have never encountered before. In order to understand it, they pull it apart and ask themselves whether they recognize any of the pieces. Speakers use synthesis whenever they create new forms from pre-existing pieces.

Read the caption in the following Motorola ad carefully. It contains an example of morphology in action – a striking morphological fact. Comment on it, relating it to the discussion of analytic and synthetic approaches to word-formation.

Who'd of thought that an electronic chip inside your car could help you avoid curbs, other cars, and best of all, Earl in repair.

■ **1.5.2   Analytic principles**

Before we encounter any actual problems, we would like to give you some basic analytic principles used in morphology. They are taken from Eugene Nida's (1949; revised edition 1965) textbook *Morphology*.[3]

The first principle is given in (14):

(14)   **Principle 1**
       Forms with the same meaning and the same sound shape in all their occurrences are instances of the same morpheme.

Step one in morphological analysis is to look for elements that have the same form and the same meaning. This is the basic type-token problem. Let's say that we have a bunch of coins. Each is a **token**, a form. If we look at them carefully, we see that three of them look very much the same (they are all nickels), and two of them are identical – they both say 1997. These two coins are tokens of exactly the same type: they have identical forms and identical values. We may further say that the three coins are all tokens of a larger type that includes all nickels, not just those minted in 1997. But five pennies, though they have the same value as a nickel, do not together comprise the same type as the nickel, because, although identical in value to the nickel, they are different in form.

Divide the following forms into morphemes. (For answers, turn the page.)

a.   password
b.   sprayable
c.   childhoods
d.   autobiography
e.   co-educational

   To apply this distinction between types and tokens to the morphological analysis of words, consider the Spanish words *buenísimo* 'very good' (< *bueno* 'good'), *riquísimo* 'very delicious' (< *rico* 'delicious'), and *utilísimo* 'very useful' (< *útil* 'useful'). In each case, the suffix *-ísimo* contributes the same superlative meaning, and it has the same shape. We logically conclude that the suffix is the same for all three words. Note that we presented three words, all with the same suffix. It is not enough to look at one form when attempting to break it up into its smaller parts. One thing that makes a morpheme a morpheme is that it recurs, and thus speakers are able to identify it and give it a meaning. **[Exercises 6–8]**

This isn't the whole story, as Principle 2 tells us:

(15) **Principle 2**
Forms with the same meaning but different sound shapes may be instances of the same morpheme if their distributions do not overlap.

In Kujamaat Jóola, for example, the stem /baj-/ has two possible shapes, [baj-] and [bəj-], but their distributions don't overlap. [bəj-] occurs in the presence of a morpheme with an underlyingly tense vowel, but [baj-] does not. This non-overlapping distribution allows us to conclude that the two forms are instances of the same morpheme. When two or more instances of a given morpheme occur with different shapes, we call them allomorphs. Allomorphs were introduced above in section 1.2.

The regular plural marker in English has several allomorphs – voiceless alveolar fricative /s/, voiced alveolar fricative /z/, schwa plus voiced alveolar fricative /z/, syllabic alveolar nasal /n/, and Ø – as shown in (16):

(16) seat-/s/
      shade-/z/
      hedg-/əz/
      ox-/n̩/
      fish-Ø

As in the previous example, the distributions of these forms do not overlap, and they all have the same meaning. We can infer that they are instances of the same morpheme.

(17) **Principle 3**
Not all morphemes are segmental.

Normally, when we think of morphemes, we think of forms that can be pronounced in some sense, e.g., *chicken*, *the*, *un-*, *-ize*. But some morphemes can't be pronounced on their own. They are dependent on other morphemes for their realization. In English, for example, vowel alternations may serve to differentiate basic and past forms of the verb. We refer to these alternations as **ablaut** (as in 18):

(18) run   ran
      speak spoke
      eat   ate

We know that there is a past tense marker distinguishing the words in the second column from those in the first. But what is it? It is not the /æ/

Answers to morpheme-breakup exercise:

a. pass/word
b. spray/able
c. child/hood/s
d. auto/bio/graph/y
e. co-/educ/at/ion/al

of *ran* or the /o/ of *spoke* but rather the difference between these vowels and the vowels of the basic verb, which is not segmental at all. We must look at both the present and past tense forms of these verbs, because it is the contrast between them that is important. Another type of non-segmental morpheme in English is shown in (19):

(19)   breath$_N$ breathe$_V$
        cloth$_N$ clothe$_V$
        house$_N$ house$_V$

In each pair, the noun ends in a voiceless fricative ([θ, s]), while the verb ends in a voiced fricative ([ð, z]). Assuming that the noun is basic, we say that the morpheme that marks the verbs consists of the phonological feature [+voice]. **[Exercise 9]**

Although Principle 3 says that we can apply the term morpheme to the non-segmental alternations seen in (18) and (19), it is nonetheless the case that doing so is awkward. Pairs like *run~ran* or *breath~breathe* are more easily explained as processes than as concatenation of morphemes. In the next chapter we will further address this issue. In section 1.2 we briefly mentioned classical problems with morphemes in the context of infixation and circumfixation. The existence of non-segmental alternations such as those in (18) and (19) is another classical problem.

The contrast between forms was crucial in (18) and (19). The notion of contrast can be further extended, leading to Principle 4:

(20)   **Principle 4**
        A morpheme may have zero as one of its allomorphs provided it has a non-zero allomorph.

Fish is an example of a word with a zero plural: one fish, two fish-Ø. We can say that it has a zero plural, and that this zero plural is an allomorph of the usual plural [z], because other words in the language, like *frogs*, have non-zero plurals. This is an analytic procedure, not a theoretical point. We cannot posit a zero unless it contrasts with some non-zero variant. In Japanese, where *sakana* means both 'fish (sg)' and 'fish (pl)', we cannot posit a zero plural (*sakana-Ø*) because nowhere in the language does -Ø_PL contrast with a non-zero allomorph. **[Exercises 10–11]**

1.5.3 Sample problems with solutions

Now that you have been introduced to some principles of morphological analysis, let us examine a data set. This one comes from the Veracruz dialect of Aztec, spoken in Mexico, and is taken from Nida (1965: 11):

(21) Aztec

a.	ikalwewe	'his big house'		i.	petatci·n	'little mat'
b.	ikalsosol	'his old house'		j.	ikalmeh	'his houses'
c.	ikalci·n	'his little house'		k.	komitmeh	'cooking-pots'
d.	komitwewe	'big cooking-pot'		l.	petatmeh	'mats'
e.	komitsosol	'old cooking-pot'		m.	ko·yameci·n	'little pig'
f.	komitci·n	'little cooking-pot'		n.	ko·yamewewe	'big male pig'
g.	petatwewe	'big mat'		o.	ko·yameilama	'big female pig'
h.	petatsosol	'old mat'		p.	ko·yamemeh	'pigs'

Our task is to list all the morphemes and to give the meaning of each. Before reading the following discussion, try this out on your own. Then, if you run into trouble or want to check your answers, read on.

We begin by looking for recurring pieces that have a consistent meaning or function. In this, the English glosses of each form are very useful. Consider (21a–c, j). All have something to do with 'house', and more specifically, 'his house(s)'. Examining the forms carefully we find that they all contain the piece *ikal-*, but have nothing else in common. We deduce from this that *ikal-* means 'his house'. We include a hyphen after *ikal-* because since it never appears on its own, we cannot know if Aztec requires that it be suffixed. The data set does not contain any other examples with an English gloss of 'his' or another possessive pronoun; nor does it contain any examples meaning 'house' without the possessor 'his'. This means that we cannot break *ikal-* up further.

Form (21a) *ikalwewe* 'his big house' contains the additional piece *-wewe*. Looking over the rest of the data, we find that *-wewe* also occurs in (21g) *petatwewe* 'big mat', (21d) *komitwewe* 'big cooking-pot', and (21n) *ko·yamewewe* 'big male pig'. All of these also contain the meaning 'big'. We conclude that *-wewe* means 'big'. Again we use the hyphen because in this particular data set, *-wewe* always appears attached to the stem.

One form contains the meaning 'big' but not the morpheme -*wewe*. This is (21o) *ko·yameilama* 'big female pig'. We recognize the piece *ko·yame-* 'pig', which also appears in (21m–n, p). Based on the minimal data we have, we can only deduce that like -*wewe*, -*ilama* means 'big', but that it attaches only to a certain class of noun. Both (21o) *ko·yameilama* 'big female pig' and (21n) *ko·yamewewe* 'big male pig' appear to have the same stem, but since one refers to a female animal and the other to a male animal, such a situation would not be unprecedented.

Based on (21b–c) *ikalsosol* 'his old house' and *ikalci·n* 'his little house' we isolate the pieces -*sosol* 'old' and -*ci·n* 'little'. This analysis is affirmed when we look at other words in the data set, such as (21e–f) *komitsosol* 'old cooking-pot' and *komitci·n* 'little cooking-pot', which contain the same pieces. We can also isolate *komit-* 'cooking-pot'.

In all, we can isolate the following morphemes:

(22)   ikal-   'his house'
       komit-   'cooking-pot'
       ko·yame-   'pig'
       petat-   'mat'
       -ci·n   'little'
       -sosol   'old'
       -ilama   'big' (occurs with stem meaning 'female pig')
       -wewe   'big' (occurs with stems meaning 'his house', 'cooking-pot', 'mat', 'male pig')
       -meh   plural marker

This exercise was fairly simple in the sense that there were no allomorphs, and the morphology was entirely morphemic – it did not interact with any non-segmental phenomena. However, there were a few difficulties. One was the fact that we did not have enough data to break up *ikal-* 'his house', and yet, since the English gloss clearly has two parts, you may have been tempted to break it into two parts, too. A second difficulty was the presence of both -*ilama* and -*wewe* 'big'. Again, we did not have enough data to understand fully what their difference is. Occasionally uncertainty is something that morphologists have to accept when working with published data sets and written grammars. Sometimes there are gaps in what is presented. Morphologists doing field research have the advantage of native speaker consultants whom they can ask. But in order to ask the right questions, it is important that morphologists alternate data collection with data analysis and not wait to get back home to analyze their findings.

A final observation is that this data set was not presented in the IPA. For example, you probably were not familiar with Nida's convention for marking long vowels: a raised dot, as in -ci·n 'little'. This fact in itself should not have posed any problems. It is often possible to isolate morphemes, particularly when there are no allomorphs or phonological interactions between them, whether or not we fully understand the transcription system. That was the case here. However, the use of a non-standard transcription system may make a problem set seem more daunting.

As explained in the prefatory remarks to this book, we chose to retain non-standard transcription systems despite the difficulties they present because as a linguist you will be faced with them time and time again. We hope that the experience you gain in this book will help you deal with such systems in your own research.

Our next sample problem set comes from French. It addresses different issues than the Aztec data discussed above. The French adjectives in the first column are masculine, and those in the second are feminine. Your task is to determine how masculine and feminine adjectives are differentiated and to outline a possible analysis. You may ignore changes in vowel quality.

(23) | | Masculine | Feminine | |
|---|---|---|---|
| a. | gros [gʁo] | grosse [gʁos] | 'fat' |
| b. | mauvais [movɛ] | mauvaise [movɛz] | 'bad' |
| c. | heureux [øʁø] | heureuse [øʁøz] | 'happy' |
| d. | petit [pəti] | petite [pətit] | 'small' |
| e. | grand [gʁɑ̃] | grande [gʁɑ̃d] | 'big' |
| f. | froid [fʁwa] | froide [fʁwad] | 'cold' |
| g. | soûl [su] | soûle [sul] | 'drunk' |
| h. | bon [bõ] | bonne [bɔn] | 'good' |
| i. | frais [fʁɛ] | fraîche [fʁɛʃ] | 'fresh' |
| j. | long [lõ] | longue [lõg] | 'long' |
| k. | premier [pʁœmje] | première [pʁœmjɛʁ] | 'first' |
| l. | entier [ɑ̃tje] | entière [ɑ̃tjɛʁ] | 'entire' |
| m. | gentil [ʒɑ̃ti] | gentille [ʒɑ̃tij] | 'kind' |
| n. | net [nɛt] | nette [nɛt] | 'clean' |

As with the Aztec set, you should limit yourself to the data provided, although some of you may know French.

One way to begin is to see whether there is a single morpheme, which may or may not have allomorphs, that signals the difference between masculine and feminine. There is not. Masculine and feminine adjectives are differentiated by an alternation between Ø and [s] in (23a), Ø and [z] in (23b–c), Ø and [t] in (23d), Ø and [d] in (23e–f), Ø and [l] in (23g), Ø and [n] in (23h), Ø and [ʃ] in (23i), Ø and [g] in (23j), Ø and [ʁ] in (23k–l), and Ø and [j] in (23m). The masculine and feminine forms of [nɛt] 'clean' are identical. (It is important to focus on pronunciation and not spelling. Spelling conventions are not part of the mental grammar.) We cannot consider the many final sounds of the feminine forms to be allomorphs of one another. Phonetically, they are extremely varied. Their distribution overlaps, too. For example, we find both [ʃ] and [z] after [ɛ], in (23i) *fraîche* 'fresh' (f) and (23b) *mauvaise* 'bad' (f), respectively. There is no apparent reason why (23n) *net, nette* 'clean' should behave differently from the other words in the list in having only one form [nɛt].

You may be thinking that the spelling can account for the final sound of the feminine forms. However, spelling often reflects the history of a word and not its synchronic analysis. Therefore, we cannot base our analysis on it.

So far it appears as if the final sound of the feminine forms of the adjectives is arbitrary. And yet, it cannot be wholly arbitrary, or speakers would not know which form the feminine takes. We have been treating this problem until now as if the feminine form is derived from the masculine one. A second possibility is that the opposite is true. We can form a hypothesis: perhaps the masculine form results when we remove the final sound of the feminine. This accounts for (23a–m). (Recall that we asked you to ignore changes in vowel quantity.) But this hypothesis fails when we apply it to (23n) *net, nette* 'clean'. Both are pronounced [nɛt]. Our current hypothesis, that we arrive at the masculine form by subtracting the last segment of the feminine form, cannot account for this fact.

At this point in the problem, you need to make a new hypothesis. There is room for more than one. One is that in French, adjectives have more than one stem, and both the masculine and feminine stems need to be memorized. This would mean that for (23b) *mauvais, mauvaise*, speakers memorize that the first is pronounced [movɛ] and the second [movɛz]. A second reasonable hypothesis is that we were on the right track earlier, and that speakers arrive at the masculine form by dropping the final segment of the feminine form. The feminine form is the only one that needs to be memorized, then, since the masculine can be derived from it by a regularly applying rule. Under this hypothesis, (23n) *net, nette* 'clean', both pronounced [nɛt], is an exception that speakers must memorize. Many would consider the fact that, based on our data set, this hypothesis requires speakers to memorize fewer forms to be an advantage.

We may not have arrived at a single, neat solution to the French data, but we have analyzed them and presented the hypotheses that they suggest carefully. Presentation is important whenever you undertake to solve a linguistics problem. We close this section with a few tips for writing one up. First, when you include examples from a data set in the text of your analysis, set them off by underlining them or using italics, as we have done. Second, whenever you present a foreign-language form, provide its gloss, or definition. The most standard linguistic practice is to put the gloss in single quotation marks, like this: 'definition'. Finally, be sure you know what the problem is asking. If the problem asks for a list of morphemes, for example, that is all you need to provide (but don't forget to give their glosses, as well). If the problem asks for your analysis, present it carefully, as we have done above. In order to make your answer more compelling, you may need to explore analyses that do not work, as well. This is what we did in examining the French data. **[Exercises 12–14]**

■ 1.6 Summary

We have given a whirlwind introduction to the field of morphology and to some of the phenomena that morphologists study. We introduced a key notion, that of the morpheme, but acknowledged that there are problems with its traditional formulation. We presented some basic beliefs of ours that underlie this and other chapters of the book, as well as four principles that will help the reader undertake morphological analysis. Finally, we led the reader through two sample problems in order to illustrate the steps a morphologist must take when analyzing data, as well as possible stumbling blocks that he or she might encounter.

We next turn to an introduction to Kujamaat Jóola, the language we have chosen to examine and analyze throughout this volume.

■ Introduction to Kujamaat Jóola

The Kujamaat Jóola people (who call themselves Kujamaat and their language Kujamutay) live in the Basse-Casamance region of Senegal, West Africa. Jóola is a cluster of dialects, of which Kujamaat, sometimes called Foñy, and Kasa are the most important.[4] The total number of speakers in 1998 was about 186,000 (Grimes 2002). Kujamaat Jóola belongs to the Atlantic (sometimes called West Atlantic) language family, of which the best-known languages are Wolof, the national language of Senegal, and Fula. Looked at in terms of linguistic history, the Atlantic languages form a branch descending from the most widespread language family in Africa, Niger-Congo, which is also one of the largest language families in the world. Kujamaat Jóola has a number of features – most particularly its intricate system of **noun classes** and agreement – which are remarkably similar to those of the distantly related but much larger and better-known subfamily of Niger-Congo, the Bantu languages.

The most pervasive and characteristic morphological features of Kujamaat Jóola are (i) a simple and elegant vowel harmony system, (ii) an extensive noun class or gender system, (iii) rich agreement morphology, and (iv) agglutinative verbal morphology. Over the course of this book we will be exploring these and other topics in Kujamaat Jóola morphology as they relate to issues raised in individual chapters.

We have chosen Kujamaat Jóola for this book because its morphology, though complex and sometimes unusual, is highly regular, which makes it an excellent teaching vehicle. The morphology is also spread out across nouns, verbs, and adjectives. The inflection includes some of the most common types that one is likely to find: nominal gender, agreement, and verbal tense and aspect. Finally, there is J. David Sapir's superb grammar, from which most of the Kujamaat Jóola data in this book are drawn, which provides a wonderfully lucid description of the language and especially of the morphology. The grammar has also stood the test of time: it speaks to us as clearly today as it did when it was written almost forty years ago.

Of all the distinct aspects of language, morphology is the most deeply entwined with the others. There is no way to talk about morphology without also talking about phonology, syntax, **semantics**, and **pragmatics**. Phonology is especially important, for there is no way to get at the morphology of a language without first stripping away the effects of phonology on the forms of words. For that reason our introduction to

Kujamaat Jóola morphology must be preceded by a brief overview of its phonology. Treatment of Kujamaat Jóola vowel harmony can be found in chapter 3.

The phonemic inventory of Kujamaat Jóola is given in (1) and (2).[5] Kujamaat Jóola has a set of voiceless and voiced stops in three places of articulation – bilabial, alveolar, and velar – and nasal consonants in four – bilabial, alveolar, palatal, and velar. It has voiceless and voiced postalveolar affricates /ʧ/ and /ʤ/, transcribed here as <c> and <j> (following Sapir 1965), voiceless labiodental and alveolar fricatives /f/ and /s/, two liquids /l/ and /r/, and labiovelar and palatal glides /w/ and /y/. The voiceless glottal fricative /h/ rarely occurs.

(1) Consonants

labial	alveolar	palatal	velar	glottal
p	t		k	
b	d		g	
m	n	ɲ	ŋ	
	c			
	j			
f	s			h
	l			
	r			
(w)		y	(w)	

Vowels occur in tense–lax pairs and may be short or long; what Sapir represents as schwa is realized as "a tense unrounded high-mid central vowel" under stress (Sapir 1965: 6), and is the tense counterpart to /a/. Tense high vowels are underscored (i̱ and u̱). The lax counterparts of tense /e/ and /o/ are /ɛ/ and /ɔ/ respectively:

(2) Vowels (all may be either long and short)

```
i  i̱              ʊ  u̱
   e      ə      o
      ɛ       ɔ
         a
```

The organization of this vowel chart follows standard linguistic practice. It reflects the position of the tongue during articulation and resonance, with the high vowels [i, i̱, u, u̱] at the top of the triangle, and the low vowel [a] at the bottom. Vowels on the left are articulated toward the front of the vocal tract, and those on the right farther back.

Kujamaat Jóola words showing all of the vowels are listed in (3):

(3) bəsi̱kən   'mortar'
     kəsi̱:t   'feather'
     gis   'tear'
     i:s   'show'
     ebe   'cow'
     -fe:gi̱r   'three'
     ɛfɛl   'to untie'
     ɛfɛ:l   'to annoy'
     ekəl   'type of antelope'
     ekə:l   'to be partially ripe'
     kafa:lɛn   'to continue'
     ɛgɔl   'stick'
     ɛgɔ:l   'corner'
     fu̱ko   'head'
     fu̱ko:k   'wall'
     ɛkuk   'to take big handfuls'
     ɛku:ku   'mouse'
     kəku̱ku̱l   'to cultivate in dry ground'
     kəku̱:ku̱:l   'type of tree'

Nasal–nasal and nasal–consonant clusters are very common. Of these, only /mb/ and /nd/ occur freely, including at the beginning of a word; /nn/, /mf/ (transcribed here as <nf>, following Sapir), and /ns/ clusters occur only word-internally. The remaining clusters can occur in either internal or final position in a word. In all cases the two consonants have the same place of articulation. Both /lt/ and /rt/ occur in word-internal position, as well, though very rarely. There are no other consonant clusters. Some examples are given in (4):[6]

(4) kəgu̱:mp   'ashes'
     mba   'or'
     nimammaŋ   'I want'
     -buntɛn   'cause to lie'
     nicɛɲcɛŋ   'I asked'
     -maɲj   'know'
     aŋkaŋk   'hard'
     emu̱ŋgu̱no   'hyena'
     fanfaŋ   'lots'
     ndaw   'a man's name'
     -saltɛ   'be dirty'
     -ərti̱   'negative suffix'

Kujamaat Jóola syllables are generally of the shape C(onsonant) V(owel), although V, VC, CVC, and CVNC (where N represents any nasal) syllables occur as well. Vowels may be long or short. Stress is stem-initial.

The most salient feature of Kujamaat Jóola phonology is its pervasive vowel harmony. Vowel harmony is the agreement among vowels in a word with respect to a given feature, such as height, rounding, or backness. We will explore Kujamaat Jóola vowel harmony in depth in chapter 3. Until then, keep an eye out for how certain morphemes influence the shape of Kujamaat Jóola stems, and, more often, vice versa.

Exercises

1. Create five new words – in English or your native language, if different. Give their definitions if they are not obvious.

2. Many product names are novel English forms coined by marketers. Look at the following list of product names and make hypotheses about how people came up with their names. Possibilities include, but are not limited to, the following: (i) combination of elements already occurring in English; (ii) combination of Latin or Greek morphemes – even without knowing Latin or Greek, you might be able to recognize a few; (iii) new use for a term already existing in English; (iv) use of a proper name. This is meant to be a fun exercise, ideally one to be discussed in class. It should not be graded.
   a. pHisoderm   A pH-balanced cleanser
   b. Nescafé   Coffee made by Nestlé
   c. Ajax   A strong household cleanser
   d. Eucerin   Moisturizing lotion
   e. Friskies   Cat food
   f. Tums   Antacid tablets
   g. Trident   Chewing gum
   h. Life savers   Hard candy shaped like a donut
   i. Spam   Canned meat similar to ham

3. New technology creates a need for new words. You may not consider the TV remote control new, but relative to other examples of modern technology, it is. Besides "remote control," it is called by many other names. What do you call it? In class, compile a list of words that your classmates and instructor use to refer to it. Comment on the morphological form of the various words.

4. Choose a language other than English. It may be one you know or have studied, or one that you would like to learn more about by using library resources. How are nouns marked for plural in that language? Are they marked at all? Make a comprehensive list of plural types in the language, with examples.

5. We choose the example "Not me" and have it coming out of the mouth of a child (someone unlikely to have been exposed to much prescriptive grammar) on purpose. While some English speakers

may consider "Not I" to be more correct, many would agree that "Not me" sounds more natural. Can you think of other instances where "I" is considered to be more correct, at least by traditionalists, but where "me" sounds more natural, at least to you? What does this have to do with morphology, in your opinion?

6. Etymologically, the following words contain more than one morpheme. Break each of them up into its constituent morphemes, then list at least one other word that contains each morpheme. When identifying morphemes, it is always useful to identify other forms that contain them, and this exercise is to encourage you to begin doing so.

Example:

morphemic	morph-	amorphous, polymorphic, metamorphic
	-em-	phoneme, hypoglycemia, academy
	-ic	tonic, sonic, academic

a. monologue
b. predispose
c. receive
d. phonology

e. decline
f. television
g. circumscribe
h. bibliophile

7. Rewrite the following forms and then separate them into morphemes using a slash or a hyphen. If a form consists of only one morpheme, call it **monomorphemic**.
   a. Danny
   b. theorists
   c. multifaceted
   d. weather

   e. monkey
   f. partnerships
   g. hysterical
   h. children

8. Should -*ful* be analyzed as one morpheme or two different morphemes (*ful*$_1$ and *ful*$_2$) in the following examples? Explain your answer and bring in further examples if necessary.
   a. wrathful
   b. handful

9. English noun and verb pairs
   A. The following words can be used as nouns or verbs, but their pronunciation changes accordingly. How? State your answer as

a generalization that contrasts the pronunciation of all the nouns with that of the verbs.

a. import   g. transfer
b. contrast   h. convict
c. insult   i. project
d. insert   j. rebel
e. protest   k. conflict
f. convert

B. For many English speakers, the verb *protest* has two different pronunciations. One fits the pattern that you identified in part A as being characteristic of nouns; the other fits the pattern you identified as being characteristic of verbs. If you are familiar with the two pronunciations of the verb *protest*, first identify the two possibilities, then come up with a hypothesis that might explain their coexistence.

10. English *spit* has two past tense forms: *spit* or *spat*. The second is an example of ablaut, mentioned in the discussion of Principle 3. What about the first? Should we analyze it as a single morpheme, or as two morphemes, *spit* and $\emptyset$?

11. Organize the following set of German nouns into singular–plural pairs. Then determine the allomorphs of the plural ending. Ignore changes in the stem vowel.

Väter   'fathers'   Auge   'eye'
Kinder   'children'   Adler   'eagle'
Pferd   'horse'   Kind   'child'
Männer   'men'   Augen   'eyes'
Vater   'father'   Kuh   'cow'
Mann   'man'   Frauen   'women'
Adler   'eagles'   Auto   'car'
Kühe   'cows'   Autos   'cars'
Pferde   'horses'   Frau   'woman'

12. Etymologically, the following forms contain more than one morpheme. In your opinion, does your mental grammar treat them as such, or does it treat them as monomorphemic forms? Deal with each form separately, because your answer may not be the same for all. Explain.

a. holocaust
b. parade
c. presence

13. Zoque, Mexico (Nida 1965: 12)
     List all morphemes and give the meaning of each.

pən	'man'
pənta?m	'men'
pənkəsi	'on a man'
pənkotoya	'for a man'
pənhi?ŋ	'with a man'
pənkəsita?m	'on men'
pənkəsiʃeh	'as on a man'
pənʃeh	'manlike'
pənʃehta?m	'like men'
nanah	'mother'
nanahta?m	'mothers'
nanahkotoya	'for a mother'
?unehi?ŋ	'with a child'
?unehi?ŋta?m	'with children'
naka	'skin, leather'
nakapit	'by means of leather'
nakapitʃeh	'as if by leather'
yomo	'woman'
yomota?m	'women'
yomohi?ŋ	'with a woman'
yomotih	'just a woman'
yomo?une	'girl'
kahʃi	'hen'
kahʃi?une	'chick'
libru	'book'
libru?une	'booklet'
wetu	'fox'
wetu?une	'fox whelp'
te? pən	'the man'
maŋu te? pən	'the man went'
maŋpa te? pən	'the man goes'
maŋke?tpa te? yomo	'the woman also goes'
minpa te? ?une	'the child comes'
minu te? ?une	'the child came'
maŋke?tu	'he also went'
maŋutih	'he went (and did nothing more)'

14. Congo Swahili, Elisabethville dialect
     A. Identify as many morphemes as possible and give the meaning
         of each.

B. Imagine that you have the opportunity to do fieldwork on Congo Swahili. List a few sentences that you would elicit from consultants that might enable you to confirm or complete your morphological analysis.

Supplementary information:
a. The future -*taka*- and the negative -*ta*- are not related.
b. The final -*a* may be treated as a morpheme. Its meaning is not indicated in this set.
c. The passive morpheme may be described as having two forms, -*iw*- and -*w*-. Its form depends on what precedes it.

ninasema	'I speak'
wunasema	'you (sg) speak'
anasema	'he speaks'
munasema	'you (pl) speak'
wanasema	'they speak'
ninapika	'I hit'
ninanupika	'I hit you (pl)'
ninakupika	'I hit you (sg)'
ninawapika	'I hit them'
ananipika	'he hits me'
ananupika	'he hits you (pl)'
nilipika	'I have hit'
nilimupika	'I have hit him'
nitakanupika	'I will hit you (pl)'
nitakapikiwa	'I will be hit'
ninaona	'I see'
ninamupika	'I hit him'
tunasema	'we speak'
wutakapikiwa	'you (sg) will be hit'
ninapikiwa	'I am hit'
nilipikiwa	'I have been hit'
nilipikaka	'I hit (remote time)'
wunapikizwa	'you (sg) cause being hit'
wunanipikizwa	'you (sg) cause me to be hit'
wutakanipikizwa	'you (sg) will cause me to be hit'
sitanupika	'I do not hit you (pl)'
hatanupika	'he does not hit you (pl)'
hatutanupika	'we do not hit you (pl)'
hawatatupika	'they do not hit us'

NOTES

1 Conveniently, it also blended the first names of the two owners, Renee and Bob.

2 We thank Krin Gabbard for the etymology of *rebop*.

3 Nida has six principles; we present four here.

4 The Kujamaat Jóola data presented here comes almost exclusively from J. David Sapir's 1965 grammar, *A Grammar of Diola-Fogny*. We also used Sapir (1970, 1975; Thomas and Sapir 1967), Hopkins (1990), and Gero and Levinsohn (1993).

5 We choose to present the Kujamaat Jóola data in the transcription systems used by Sapir because being able to deal with different transcription systems is an essential skill for all linguists. Elsewhere in this book, we will generally use IPA transcription unless otherwise indicated.

6 In subsequent chapters nasal–consonant clusters will be written <nj>, <nc>, <ng>, and <nk>, respectively, following Sapir. In other words, we do not represent assimilation in place of the nasal to the following consonant (e.g., we write /nk/ for phonetic [ŋk]).

2   Words and Lexemes

A single word can have multiple uses and interpretations. Occasionally a headline-writer underestimates this fact and ends up writing side-splitting headlines where no humor was intended. Here are some oldies but goodies that have circulated widely by e-mail:

BRITISH LEFT WAFFLES ON FALKLAND ISLANDS
MINERS REFUSE TO WORK AFTER DEATH
EYE DROPS OFF SHELF
LOCAL HIGH SCHOOL DROPOUTS CUT IN HALF
REAGAN WINS ON BUDGET, BUT MORE LIES AHEAD
SQUAD HELPS DOG BITE VICTIM
JUVENILE COURT TO TRY SHOOTING DEFENDANT
KIDS MAKE NUTRITIOUS SNACKS

Did the British abandon breakfast pastries on the Falkland Islands? Are zombie miners acting up? No. While *waffles* tends to be interpreted more easily as a noun, it's used in the first headline as a verb. The last headline is horrifying until we realize that *make* is ambiguous in meaning here between two of its thirty-odd meanings: 'prepare' and 'be useful as'. The first sense is the one intended in the headline.

Words like **noun**, **verb**, **adjective**, and **adverb** refer to what linguists call **lexical category**. They are labels that tell us how a word is generally used in a sentence. A noun can be the subject of a sentence, but not so a verb. In many cases, identical-sounding or identical-looking words can belong to multiple categories, and that is what is going on in these sentences.

Lexical category is basic information about a word, but there is much more that, as linguists, we want to say. In this chapter we address the question of what a word is in detail. It will pave the way for the more advanced discussions of later chapters.

■ 2.1   What is a Word?

There are various ways to define a word, but no definition is entirely satisfactory. Scholars have acknowledged this fact over and over again. Here we present some of the reasons why what seems like a relatively simple task (we all think we know what a word is, right?) proves to be so problematic.

■ 2.1.1   Defining words syntactically

One way that people have attempted to define words is to call them the smallest unit of syntax. It seems reasonable: sentences are built by combining words according to particular patterns. But even this simple definition runs into problems. Take a sentence like the following:

(1)   Harry coughs every time he steps outside.

Everyone would agree that *Harry*, *every*, and *outside* are words, and that *-s* is not. But at the same time, some people (though not all) would argue that *-s* is indeed a unit of syntax and that it occupies a particular position in a syntactic tree. The following diagram illustrates how we might break *cough* off from *-s* syntactically:

(2)

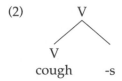

Another problem with calling words the minimal unit of syntax is that it raises the question, "What is syntax?" If we think of syntax as the component of the human grammar that governs the ordering of items, then *-s* should be a word. After all, it is subject to ordering principles. It must follow *cough*; we don't say *s-cough*. If we respond by saying that syntax governs the ordering of not just any item, but only words, then we are back where we started. What is a word?

Another characteristic of words is that they are the smallest unit of language that can stand alone:

(3)   When are you going to the store?   *Tomorrow.*
       What did the emperor wear to the procession?   *Nothing!*

We recognize the ability of words to stand alone by saying that they are **free forms**. Units that are incapable of standing alone, such as affixes, are correspondingly called **bound forms**. This characteristic of words also runs into problems. Certain forms that native speakers would identify as words are not capable of standing alone and therefore do not meet this definition:

(4)   Whose book is this?   *My.

My is a word, as we would all agree. But it generally does not stand alone.[1] The reasons why *my* cannot stand on its own have more to do with syntax than with morphology: it is a determiner, and it generally appears alongside a noun. Speakers would use *mine* in this context instead. Nevertheless, this example shows that a potential diagnostic for wordhood – can it stand alone? – is not universally reliable.

Furthermore, once in a while we get a supposedly bound form appearing on its own. In the musical *Camelot*, Queen Guenevere sings the following lines:

(5) It's May, it's May, the month of "yes, you may"
     The time for every frivolous whim, proper or *im-*
     . . .
     When all the world is brimming with fun, wholesome or *un-*

The prefix *im-* is used on its own to rhyme with *whim*, and *un-* is used to rhyme with *fun*. We are dealing with a creative word play here. Both *im-* and *un-* are stressed, which means that in some sense, the songwriter has turned them into words. We are not proposing otherwise. We present this example only as part of our argument that words are difficult to define, and that traditional notions such as bound and free are not always reliable.

■ 2.1.2 Defining words phonologically

One point we must make is that words tend to be an important unit phonologically as well as syntactically. The word is typically the domain of stress assignment, for example. In French, stress always falls on the last syllable of a word. In Cairene Arabic, stress falls on one of the three final syllables, depending on syllable weight. In Polish, main stress falls on the penultimate (next-to-last) or antepenultimate (third-to-last) syllable (Hayes 1995: 67–8). But even this generalization is not absolute. Clitics (from Classical Greek *klinein* 'to lean') are grammatical words that are unable to stand on their own phonologically, but must instead lean on another adjacent word. They must be incorporated into the prosodic structure of another word. This means that clitics often have an effect on the position of word stress. In Modern Greek, for example, stress is always on one of the last three syllables of a word. When a genitive clitic such as *mas* 'our' follows or leans on a word that is stressed on the third-to-last syllable, stress readjustment occurs (Nespor and Vogel 1986) and the stress shifts over one syllable:

(6)   a.   o ánθropos
          'the person'
      b.   o ánθropòs mas
          'our person'

We see in (6) that *ánθropos* 'person' is stressed on the third-to-last syllable. When followed by *mas*, a secondary stress is inserted on its final syllable. The shift is understandable, but only if we think of the sequence *ánθropòs mas* as a single word, for purposes of stress. In that case, the stress of *ánθropòs*, which was originally on the third-to-last syllable, would be on the fourth-to-last syllable with the addition of *mas*, but that would be impossible, since Greek stress can fall no further back than the third-to-last syllable, so it moves (to the second-to-last, which is the most common position). We thus see that the word-plus-clitic sequence functions as a single word as far as stress assignment is concerned in Modern Greek. (See the definition of *phonological word* below.)

■ 2.1.3   Grammatical words

Despite the elusiveness of a definition of word, speakers – literate and illiterate – have clear intuitions about what is and what isn't a word. Children readily learn to break utterances up into words when learning to write. There are even written languages, such as Chinese, that represent words with symbols called logograms. So for now, we are simply going to assume that we know a word when we see one.

The term **grammatical word** or **morphosyntactic word** is virtually synonymous with word, but it tends to be used to refer specifically to different forms of a single word that occur depending on the syntactic context. You would be justified in thinking, for example, that *rabbit* and *rabbits* are basically tokens of the same word. But they absolutely must be considered to be two different grammatical words. The first occurs in contexts appropriate for a singular noun, and the second in contexts appropriate for a plural noun. Even though forms like *and*, *into*, and *lovely* have only one form, they are also considered grammatical words.

■ 2.2   Empirical Tests for Wordhood

While it is difficult to come up with a definition that tells us whether something is a word, there are empirical tests that can tell us whether something *isn't* a word.

■ 2.2.1 Fixed order of elements

Our first empirical test has to do with the fixed order of elements within a word. Take a morphologically complex word like *unbreakable*. We can't say *breakableun* or *unablebreak*. The same doesn't hold for sentences. To use examples from the Mad Hatter and the March Hare in Lewis Carroll's *Alice in Wonderland*, "I see what I eat" is just as grammatical as "I eat what I see," and "I like what I get" and "I get what I like" are equally acceptable. When we change the order of words in a sentence, we generally also change the meaning. When we change the order of morphemes in a word, we generally end up with something completely ungrammatical.

Of course, in English we cannot change the order of words in a sentence any which way and still have a grammatical result. We don't say **get like I what I*, for instance. But there are languages such as Latin where you can order the words of particular sentences any possible way and still have a grammatical result. In contrast, there are no languages in which you can arrange morphemes any which way.

■ 2.2.2 Non-separability and integrity

Two more diagnostics that we will make use of here involve the notions of **non-separability** and **integrity**. Words differ from larger units, such as phrases, in that they cannot be broken up by the insertion of segmental or phrasal material. (For the moment, we'll ignore infixes.) This characteristic of words is called non-separability. Likewise, syntactic processes cannot apply to pieces of words. This is integrity. Adjectives and adverbs, for example, modify words, not morphemes. Words and phrases are often displaced to the beginning of a sentence or questioned, but not morphemes:

(7) a. That girl, I saw her sneaking around yesterday.
         Which girl did you see sneaking around?
     b. Possible, it's im-.
         Which school- did you see bus? (i.e., Which school's school bus did you see?)

Non-separability and integrity diagnostics tell us that **compounds** like *doghouse*, *greenhouse*, and *school bus* consist of a single word, rather than a pair of words.

Let's begin with *doghouse*. We know that this is a single word because we can't put anything inside it or modify the internal components in any way. We can't distinguish between a *doghouse* and a **dogshouse*, where a *doghouse* is a house for one dog, and a *dogshouse* for two or more.

The same restrictions hold for *greenhouse*. If we break up the components in any way (8a) or try to modify only a part (8b), the meaning 'warm glassed-in structure for growing plants' gets lost:

(8)　a.　　a green and blue house
　　　　　a greener house
　　　b.　　a very green house
　　　　　*a very greenhouse

It happens to be the case that the way we write *doghouse* and *greenhouse* reflects their status as single words. But orthography cannot always be relied upon as a diagnostic. *Deer tick* is also a compound, but it is generally written as two words. Modifiers must modify the whole compound, not just a part (so a brown deer-tick is not a tick that lives on brown deer, but is instead itself brown), and its components are non-separable (**deer brown tick* is impossible, though *brown tick* is perfectly acceptable, because we can't reach inside a compound and separate its components).

■ 2.2.3　Stress

The diagnostics given in the preceding section, non-separability and integrity, establish that *hot dog* (the edible kind) is a compound. If the hot dog you are eating is hotter than mine, you wouldn't say that you were eating a **hotter dog* or a **very hot dog*. Given this fact, compare the pronunciation of the sequence *hot dogs* in the following two sentences:

(9)　We ate two *hot dogs* each.
　　　The *hot dogs* ran for the lake.

In the first sentence, the stress in *hot dog* is on *hot*, while in the second, it is on *dog*. These two examples show that stress can also be used as a diagnostic for whether or not a sequence of words is a compound. In the first sentence, *hot dog* is a compound. English compounds are normally stressed on their first element. The same sequence, *hot dog*, is a phrase in the second sentence, with *hot* functioning as an adjectival modifier of *dog*. Phrases are normally stressed on their last element in English.

If you pay attention to the way people around you stress words and phrases, you will discover that certain sequences are compounds for some people, but not for others. Two examples are *ginger ale* and *chicken salad*. Say them aloud. If you say *gínger ale*, then it is a compound for you. If you say *ginger ále*, it is a phrase. **[Exercise 1]**

■ 2.3   Types of Words

As fluent readers of English, we tend to think only in terms of written words, probably because they are easily identified by the fact that they are separated by blank spaces. But words may be defined in different ways from different perspectives, with each perspective picking out a somewhat different object from the others. Linguists distinguish phonological words, grammatical words (discussed in 2.1.3), and lexemes. In this book, we will be concerned with grammatical words and lexemes, but we will begin with phonological words, just to make sure that we have made the proper distinctions.

■ 2.3.1   Phonological words

A **phonological word** can be defined as a string of sounds that behaves as a unit for certain kinds of phonological processes, especially stress or accent. For the most part, we don't have to distinguish phonological words from other kinds of words. It makes no difference for the words *morphology, calendar, Mississippi,* or *hot dog* whether we think of them as phonological words or morphological words. But sometimes we do need to separate the two notions. In English, for example, every phonological word has a main stress. Elements that are written as separate words but do not have their own stress are therefore not phonological words in English. Consider again the sentence *The hot dogs ran for the lake.* Think now in terms of word stress. The sentence has seven words, but only four word stresses, there being no stress on *the* or on *for.* In fact, the English written word *the* receives stress only under unusual circumstances, in exchanges like the following:

(10)   A: I saw Jennifer Lopez on Fifth Avenue last night.
         B: Not *the* Jennifer Lopez?

Prepositions like *for* sometimes have stress, but as often as not are also included in the stress domain of the following word. We therefore say that the string *for the lake,* which we write as three separate words, is a single phonological word.

As we noted in 2.1.2 above, items like *the* and *for,* which are phonologically dependent on adjacent words, are termed **clitics** (see Zwicky and Pullum 1983; Zwicky 1985). Syntactically, clitics pattern like distinct words, but they cannot usually stand alone phonologically and need to be incorporated into the prosodic structure of an adjacent word, the **host**.[2] **Proclitics** precede their host and **enclitics** follow it. Other well-known examples of clitics are the contracted form of the English auxiliary verb BE ('*m*, '*s*, and '*re*), as in *Mary's here* or *We're in this together*. We know that contracted auxiliaries function just like full words from the point of view of the syntax, because they alternate with full forms that have the same meaning (cf. *Mary is here*, *We are in this together*). But phonologically, these auxiliaries are wholly unable to stand on their own. [Exercise 2]

■ 2.3.2   Content words vs. function words

Another distinction that we need to make when talking about words is that between **content words** and **function words**. We think that Finegan (1994: 161) expresses the difference well. He writes that content words "have meaning in that they refer to objects, events, and abstract concepts; are marked as being characteristic of particular social, ethnic, and regional dialects and of particular contexts; and convey information about the feelings and attitudes of language users." Function words also have meaning, but in a different way.

Most nouns, verbs, adjectives, and adverbs are content words. Function words are often best defined by their function. Examples of function words are determiners, pronouns, conjunctions, and certain verbs – those with little or no meaning such as *be, should,* or *must*.

Paris
in the
the spring

If you are like many people, the first time you see the graphic above, you read, "Paris in the spring." But look again. In fact, it says, "Paris in the the spring." This is a well-known case of expectation affecting perception. You expect to read one "the," so you don't realize that the stimulus contains two. This trick doesn't work if we write "Paris Paris in the spring," or "Paris in the spring spring." The key is to repeat a function word – the – because we tend to take words like that for granted. A similar perception trick repeats the "a" of "Once upon a time." Again, it capitalizes on the fact that *a* is a function word.

Function words are like thumbtacks. We don't notice thumbtacks; we look at the calendar or the poster they are holding up. If we were to take the tacks away, the calendar and the poster would fall down. Likewise, if we took the function words out of speech, it would be hard to figure out what was going on:

took function words speech hard figure going on

This is what the previous sentence would look like if we took out all of the function words.

One generalization we can make is that while content words are an open class and it is possible to coin new ones, function words are a closed class. A person cannot easily invent a new preposition or conjunction, for example. Perhaps most telling is the long history of people trying to invent a gender-neutral singular pronoun for English. Suggestions have included *co, et, hesh, na, e,* and *thon*. Some linguists have recently proposed *tey* (on the analogy of plural *they*, which is gender-neutral), with further forms *tem* and *ter* (modeled on *them* and *her*). The point is that none of these novel words has caught on, while novel content words like *modem* and *cell phone* enter the language without any question. **[Exercises 3–5]**

Content words	Function words
Nouns: *baby, bargain, Josianne*	Pronouns: *I, him, our*
Verbs: *publicize, hurtle, sleep*	Verbs: *am, was, should*
Adjectives: *peaceful, quick, bright*	Determiners: *the, an, a*
Adverbs: *readily, carefully*	Demonstratives: *this, those*
	Adverbs:[3] *very, not*
	Prepositions:[4] *in, by*

■ 2.3.3 Lexemes

We need one more distinction, which will allow us to tell grammatical words apart from lexemes. Let's say we run across the word *dog* and notice that we have at least three tokens of the word:

(11) a. DOG₁: [noun], a canine
      b. DOG₂: [noun], a hooked or U-shaped device used for gripping heavy objects
      c. DOG₃: [verb], to follow closely and persistently

These three words sound alike: they are tokens of the same phonological word. Semantically, the meanings of (11a) and (11c) are related, and that of (11b) is not. Despite the semantic relatedness of (11a) and (11c), however, all three tokens can be said to have distinct meanings.

When we want to distinguish among phonologically similar forms on the basis of their differing meanings, we can do so by calling each a separate **lexeme**. A lexeme is a word with a specific sound and a specific meaning. Its shape may vary depending on syntactic context. Thus we have *dog* and *dogs*, distinct grammatical word forms of the same lexeme DOG. (For more on the definition of lexeme, see the box opposite.) We use the term **paradigm** to refer to the set of all the inflected forms that a lexeme assumes.

DOG$_1$ 'a canine' and DOG$_2$ 'a hooked or U-shaped device used for gripping heavy objects' happen to be **homophones** or **homonyms**, words that sound alike but have unrelated meanings. However, a word doesn't have to be a homophone in order to be or belong to a lexeme. All words either are lexemes or belong to a lexeme's paradigm. So TO, INTO, MUST, ROTATE, and MOON are all lexemes.

In order to talk about lexemes, morphologists give them each a name, and by convention, they put these names in capital or small capital letters. The name is generally the form by which a lexeme would be listed in a dictionary, and for this reason, we call it the **citation form**. The citation form is useful, but it does not necessarily have any mental status. Across languages, the citation form of a noun is most often the singular form. The citation form of a verb, however, varies widely. In English it is the bare infinitive (the infinitive minus "to": e.g., READ). In French and Spanish it is the infinitive (e.g., Fr. REGARDER, Sp. MIRAR 'to look at'). In Greek it is the first person singular form (e.g., MILO 'I speak').

In (11) each word had the same phonological shape but a different meaning. In (12) we see just the opposite. The verb *look* appears in several different forms, but with a consistent meaning:

What is a lexeme?

- A lexeme, such as BOOK, AND, EAT, is a word.
- It has a particular meaning or grammatical function (e.g., 'a set of written or printed pages fastened along one side and encased between two covers'; 'connects words, phrases, or clauses that have the same grammatical function').
- It is generally referred to by its citation form (e.g., BOOK, AND, EAT), but its shape may vary systematically according to the syntactic context in which it is used (e.g., one *book*, two *books*; I am *eating* right now, I *ate* a big dinner yesterday).

---

(12)   I *look*
       she *looks*
       we *looked*
       they were *looking*

Each of these forms is a distinct phonological word, for the simple reason that they do not all sound exactly alike. In addition, we can label them as different grammatical words (discussed in 2.1.3) because each plays a distinct grammatical role within a sentence. But at some level these different words are all tokens of the same type: they mean the same thing and no one would expect a dictionary to give them four separate entries. We must be dealing with a single lexeme, but one that happens to be realized in several different forms, depending on grammatical context. This example shows you that a lexeme is not a single form, but rather a set of forms. [**Exercises 6–7**]

We have already said that in order to talk about lexemes, morphologists give them each a name, and by convention, they put these names in small capital letters. In reality, though, the name of a lexeme is much more than a name. In English it also happens to be the lexeme's **lexical stem**. The lexical stem is the form of the lexeme that is most often used in the creation of new words.

To illustrate what we mean by lexical stem, let's look closely at the lexeme GO. This lexeme has five forms, two of them irregular: *go, goes, went, gone, going*. Of these forms, *go* has a different status from the rest. Lexemes formed from GO most often use it as their stem, as opposed to an inflected form. You have probably heard the word *church-goer*, but not *church-wenter*, someone who used to go to church. Likewise, there are *go-betweens* but not *gone-betweens*.

It would be a mistake to overgeneralize and say that the lexical stem is always used in creating new words. We could use the word *went-between* and people would understand what we meant to say. A quick glance at the dictionary reveals the forms *goner*, *going-over*, and *goings-on*, derived from the past and present participles *gone* and *going*. The last two examples are phrasal items – phrases that have been turned into words.

HAVE is the name of another lexeme that works the same way as GO. It has several distinct forms, some of them irregular: *have*, *has*, *had*, and *having*. But only one of them, HAVE, is generally used in forming new lexemes. The *haves and the have-nots* is a common expression, but not the *had-nots*, people who used to not have any money.[5] We generally do not make up words from the inflected forms *has*, *had*, or *having*. Exceptions, like *has-been*, are most likely to be phrasal items.

Nouns have two forms, a singular and a plural. The singular form is the lexical stem. It is therefore the form that most often appears in compounds. We say *apple-corer*, *boathouse*, *saber-tooth*, and *songwriter*, but never **apples-corers*, **boatshouse*, **saber-teeth*, or **songswriter*. This is only a generalization: occasionally we do find the plural form in a compound. Thus we have seen *antiques store*, *admissions office*, *customs house*, and *sports page*.[6]

Finally, so that you won't get away thinking that things are so simple, consider the case of Latin. Latin has the peculiarity of having words, notably verbs, with more than one lexical stem. One lexical stem of the verb 'sing'[7] is *can-*. This is the stem found in *cano*: 'I sing'. Another lexical stem is *cant-*, also called the participial stem. To form the word meaning 'singer', we take the participial stem *cant-* and the agentive suffix *-or*, giving the form *cantor*. The participial stem is always used in the formation of agentives.

To summarize, a lexeme is an abstract object, not a single concrete word, but a set of grammatical words. Cross-linguistically, one of those words is generally privileged to be the lexical stem from which other words are formed, although some languages permit more than one lexical stem. However, in morphology it is often safer to talk of tendencies than absolutes. Many phenomena are not categorical, but graded. So it is with the creation of new words from lexemes. Occasionally, particularly in the case of phrasal items like *has-been*, a form of a lexeme other than the lexical stem is used for creating new words. **[Exercise 8]**

■ 2.4 Inflection vs. Derivation

Once you understand the difference between words and lexemes, you can understand the distinction made by morphologists between **inflection** and **derivation**. We will discuss both of these more fully in later chapters of the book.

Inflection involves the formation of grammatical forms – past, present, future; singular, plural; masculine, feminine, neuter; and so on – of a single lexeme. The use of these grammatical forms is generally dictated by sentence structure. Thus *is*, *are*, and *being* are examples of inflected forms of the lexeme BE, which happens to be highly irregular not only in English, but in many other languages as well. Regular verb lexemes in English have a lexical stem, which is its bare form with no affixes (e.g., *select*) and three more inflected forms, one each with the suffixes *-s*, *-ed*, and *-ing* (*selects*, *selected*, and *selecting*). Noun lexemes in English have a singular and plural form. Adjectives, adverbs, prepositions, and other parts of speech typically have only one form in English.

As you can tell from the example of *select* given above, one way in which inflection is realized is through affixes. Further examples of affixal realization of inflection can be found in the following box.

Examples of words + *inflectional morphemes*

Nouns: wombat + *s*
        ox + *en*
Verbs: brainwash + *es*
        dig + *s*
        escape + *d*
        rain + *ing*

Derivation involves the creation of one lexeme from another, such as *selector* or *selection* from *select*. Compounding is a special type of derivation, since it involves the creation of one lexeme from two or more other lexemes. In the discussion of non-separability above, we had many instances of compounds (*doghouse*, *greenhouse*, *hot dog*, and *deer tick*), all of which are formed by combining two lexemes. Many processes can be involved with derivation, as we will see in chapter 4. In the box on the next page we give only examples of affixal derivation.

One question you may be asking yourself is how we distinguish inflection from derivation. This issue is addressed fully in chapter 6. For now, two criteria you might rely on are: (1) derivation generally results in a change in lexical meaning or the lexical category of a particular word, while inflection does not; and (2) the application or non-application of inflectional morphology generally depends on the syntactic context (e.g.,

Examples of words + *derivational affixes*

Nouns to nouns:	New York + *ese*
	fish + *ery*
	Boston + *ian*
	auto + biography
	vice + president
Verbs to verbs:	*un* + tie
	re + surface
	pre + register
	under + estimate
Adjectives to adjectives:	gray + *ish*
	a + moral
	sub + human
	il + legible
Nouns to adjectives:	hawk + *ish*
	poison + *ous*
	soul + *ful*
	iron + *like*
Verbs to nouns:	discombobulat + *ion*
	acquitt + *al*
	digg + *er*
Adjectives to adverbs:	sad + *ly*
	efficient + *ly*

what is the subject of the verb? is the noun singular or plural?), while the application of derivational morphology does not.

Readers will come across the terms **word formation** and **lexeme formation**, both referring to derivation, in the morphological literature. We prefer to avoid the term word formation, since it is used by some linguists to refer to inflection and derivation, or to morphology in general.

■ 2.5 Two Approaches to Morphology: Item-and-Arrangement, Item-and-Process

Hockett (1954) distinguishes between two approaches to morphology, which he calls **item-and-arrangement** and **item-and-process**. Both are associated with American structuralist linguistics, codified by Bloomfield (1933), but they continue to be important today. Item-and-arrangement and item-and-process represent two distinct points of view. Item-and-arrangement proceeds from a picture of each language as a set of elements and the patterns in which those elements occur. The item-and-process picture gives no independent status to the items, which arise instead through the construction of the patterns.

Item-and-arrangement grew out of the structuralists' preoccupation with word analysis, and in particular, with techniques for breaking words down into their component morphemes, which are the items. Morphology is then seen as the arrangement of these morphemes into a particular order or structure. For example, *books* results from the **concatenation** of the two morphemes *book* and *-s*.

Item-and-process, as its name suggests, is an approach to morphology in which complex words result from the operation of processes on simpler words. If we were working in an item-and-process framework, we might say that *books* results when the lexeme *book* undergoes the function 'make plural'. In regular cases, this function will add the segment /-z/ (cf. *photos*, *lions*), which is realized as /-s/ after most voiceless segments (cf. *giraffes*), and as /-əz/ after sibilants and affricates (cf. *roses*).

Item-and-arrangement and item-and-process are almost equivalent to one another mathematically. Everything that you can express in item-and-arrangement can be expressed in item-and-process, and almost anything that you can express in item-and-process can be expressed in item-and-arrangement. It just depends on what you regard as an item. For example, if you allow items to have a negative value (on the analogy of negative numbers like −1), then even subtractive morphology of the sort seen in the formation of the Papago (Uto-Aztecan) perfective (13) can count as item-and-arrangement (data from Zepeda 1983: 59ff., cited in Anderson 1992: 65):[8]

(13)

Imperfective			Perfective		
singular		plural	singular		plural
him	'walking'	hihim	hi:	'walked'	hihi
hi:nk	'barking'	hihink	hi:n	'barked'	hihin
gatwid	'shooting'	gagtwid	gatwi	'shot'	gagtwi
'elpig	'peeling'	'e'elpig	'elpi	'peeled'	'e'elpi

In (13) we see that the Papago perfective is generally formed by removal of the final consonant of the imperfective, regardless of what consonant it is. It might seem counterintuitive to think of this deleted consonant as a segment with some particular value, parallel to the English past tense marker *-ed*, but mathematically, such a negative entity is not very difficult to imagine. We could think of the affix as something like a negative final consonant.

Despite their mathematical similarity, there are many morphological phenomena that do not fit neatly into the item-and-arrangement model. Papago perfective formation is an example of one. While we can imagine a negative affix, its plausibility is nonetheless questionable.

■ 2.5.1 Affixation in the item-and-process and item-and-arrangement models

Let's look at a very simple English example of a lexical function within the item-and-process model, which we happen to be most comfortable with. The following function creates agent nouns from verbs:

(14)   X]$_V$ er]$_N$
       Examples: think]$_V$ er]$_N$, runn]$_V$ er]$_N$, fli]$_V$ er]$_N$, hunt]$_V$ er]$_N$

We generally think of lexeme-formation functions as having a phonological, a syntactic, and a semantic component. Phonologically, the function in (14) takes a pre-existing string of segments and adds the suffix /ɼ/. Syntactically, it produces a noun from a verb. Semantically, it produces an agent of the verb.

In the function in (14), the phonology, syntax, and semantics are additive. When we derive an agent noun from a verb via the suffix /ɼ/, we add phonological information in the form of an additional segment, syntactic information in terms of the lexical category noun, and semantic information (the fact that the new noun represents an agent). Furthermore, the old information is preserved, not lost: *worker* includes both the form and the meaning of the verb *work*, to which the suffix /ɼ/ has been added, as well as the fact that *work* is a verb, not a member of some other lexical category. The phonology, syntax, and semantics of most derivational functions are additive in this sense.

Additive functions like this one are easily recast in the item-and-arrangement model. To express (14) in item-and-arrangement, we also need to break agent nouns into two parts. Then we put them back together. One way we can show this is through a tree structure. There will be more on morphological trees in chapter 4:

(15)   Agent noun

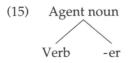

       Verb   -er

Worker, then, is represented as follows:

(16)   Noun

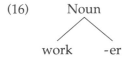

      work   -er

This tree illustrates how the affix *-er* attaches to the stem *work* to form the agent noun *worker*. **[Exercise 9]**

■ 2.5.2 Non-affixal phenomena and the item-and-process model

Many languages have morphological phenomena that are not affixal at all. These still make sense within the item-and-process model, though they do pose problems for some morphological frameworks based on the item-and-arrangement model, as we noted above.

2.5.2.1 English noun–verb pairs

An example of a non-affixal morphological phenomenon is illustrated in (17). English possesses a number of noun–verb pairs that are distinguished phonologically by the location of stress. Verbs are stressed on the final syllable, and nouns on the first syllable. The pattern is ancient; examples can be found in Old English and in other related Germanic languages, suggesting that the difference existed at least as far back as proto-Germanic times, over two thousand years ago:

(17)   *Verb*   *Noun*
       overflów   óverflow
       condúct   cónduct
       insért   ínsert
       rejéct   réject
       convíct   cónvict

It is possible to represent the shift in stress in these examples as an item, but the forms in (17) are more amenable to a processual analysis, where the appropriate function would be something like 'shift stress'.

2.5.2.2 Agar Dinka

Non-segmental phenomena make up only a small part of the morphology of English and related languages. But non-affixal morphology is widespread among the world's languages. For the Western Nilotic language Dinka, non-affixal morphology is the norm. Despite the fact that it is almost entirely monosyllabic, Dinka manages to have a very rich morphology by exploiting alternations in vowel quality, vowel length, voice quality, **tone**, and final consonants, as demonstrated by Andersen (1993) for the Agar dialect, spoken in Southern Sudan.

Agar Dinka is characterized by a rich set of vowel contrasts. Vowels come with two distinct voice qualities, creaky /v̰/ and breathy /v̤/, and may be long /vvv/, half-long /vv/, or short /v/. Furthermore, vowels might bear a high tone /v́/, low tone /v̀/, or falling tone /v̂/. Vowel quality plays a role as well. For example, the distinction between lèɛt 'insult (3sg)' and làat 'insult (1sg)' or dɔ́ɔk 'spin (3sg)' and dàak 'spin (1sg)' is one of vowel quality. The seven contrastive vowel qualities of Agar Dinka are given in the following table (Andersen 1993: 4).

Agar Dinka vowels

	Front unrounded	Central unrounded	Back rounded
High	i		u
Higher-mid	e		o
Lower-mid	ɛ		ɔ
Low		a	

Every transitive verb stem in Agar Dinka has 11 inflectionally distinct forms. This is illustrated in (18) for the stem bòk 'to throw at', preceded in each case by the declarative proclitic particle [à-]. Note that while some of the forms contain suffixes (18f–h, j), most of the morphological distinctions are expressed through non-affixal means. In all, there are seven forms of the verb stem:

(18)   Agar Dinka inflectional paradigm (Andersen 1993: 6)
    a. Ø   ḑɔ̀ɔk à-bòk   dít
                boy D-throw.at bird
                'The boy is throwing at the bird'
    b. NTS   dít à-bóok   ḑɔ̀ɔk
                bird D-throw.at:NTS boy
                'The boy is throwing at the bird'
    c. 1SG   dít à-bɔ̀ɔk
                bird D-throw.at:1SG
                'I am throwing at the bird'

d. 2SG   dí̱t à̱-bò̱k
           bird D-throw.at:2SG
           'You are throwing at the bird'

e. 3SG   dí̱t à̱-bò̱ok
           bird D-throw.at:3SG
           'He is throwing at the bird'

f. 1PL   dí̱t à̱-bó̱k-kù̱
           bird D-throw.at-1PL
           'We are throwing at the bird'

g. 2PL   dí̱t à̱-bɔ̱́k-kà̱
           bird D-throw.at-2PL
           'You are throwing at the bird'

h. 3PL   dí̱t à̱-bó̱k-kè̱
           bird D-throw.at-3PL
           'They are throwing at the bird'

i. PASS   dí̱t à̱-bó̱k
           bird D-throw.at:PASS
           'The bird is being thrown at'

j. PASS: dò̱̱ot à̱-bò̱̱ok-è̱   dí̱t
    CT   stone D-throw.at-PASS:CT bird
           'The bird is being thrown at with a stone'

The seven forms of the verb stem are schematized in (19) for easy inspection. Andersen (1993: 269ff.) argues that (19a) represents the inflectionally unmarked (i.e., default) case. It occurs with topic (preverbal) subjects and in the second singular. (19b) is used when there is a non-topical (postverbal) subject noun phrase in the clause, and differs from the unmarked case in having a lengthened vowel and high tone. The first singular form (19c) has a half-long low-mid back rounded vowel /ɔ/ in place of the short high-mid rounded vowel that we see in (19a). Other forms differ from (19a) in having a lengthened vowel (19d, g), high tone (19e, f), falling tone (19g), and contrasting vowel quality (19f):

(19) Stems of the verb 'to throw at'
      a. bò̱k   (inflectionally unmarked)   Ø, 2SG
      b. bó̱ok   NTS
      c. bɔ̱̀ɔk   1SG
      d. bò̱ok   3SG
      e. bó̱k   1PL, 3PL, PASS
      f. bɔ̱́k   2PL
      g. bò̱ok   PASS:CT

From the perspective of a speaker of English or most other European and Asian languages, Agar Dinka morphology is exotic, but it clearly is not from the perspective of speakers of the language. There is no evidence that these seemingly exotic processes are prone to disappear over time or that the children of the community have any difficulty learning to speak the language. We must conclude that these non-segmental processes are just as normal for human languages as the run-of-the-mill affixation that we are used to, and that a theory of morphology should be able to treat them in the same way as it treats affixation. Item-and-arrangement theories can be made to accommodate morphology of the sort that we see in Agar Dinka, but only awkwardly. This fact is one of the primary arguments that proponents of item-and-process morphology use in support of their general framework, which does not give affixation any special pride of place. A fascinating question that comes to mind is why one language should use a certain type of morphology and another language should not, but this is a question we will not be able to delve into here.

■ 2.6   The Lexicon

Our discussion of words and lexemes would not be complete without a brief introduction to the **lexicon**. Etymologically, lexicon refers to a list of words, and linguists use the term in particular to refer to the mental dictionary. Within linguistics, lexicon has taken on multiple definitions. This complicates matters, particularly because linguists are not always careful to specify which definition of lexicon they assume.

There are two widely accepted views of the lexicon. According to one, the lexicon is a list of the indivisible morphological units, or morphemes, in a language. This definition comes from Baudouin de Courtenay (b. 1845 in Radzymin, Poland; d. 1929 in Warsaw), who, despite his French name and his relation to the Belgian royal family, was a Polish linguist of the middle to late nineteenth century and a very influential theorist at the time.

The second view of the lexicon, due more or less to Bloomfield (1933), is a list of irregular or arbitrary forms. Because they are irregular or arbitrary, they must be memorized. For example, a speaker of French must know that the sound sequence [aʁbʁ] refers to a tree, and a speaker of English has to know that the word *slide* refers to a small square object that we put in a slide projector to project an image onto a screen or wall.

The error many people make, including many morphologists, is to assume that the first definition is equivalent to the second. In other words, many linguists assume that the list of irregular forms is a list of morphemes, which is to say a list of indivisible units. If we spoke a perfect language, then that would be true. Every irregular form in the language would be indivisible. But where natural language is concerned, we know that this position is too extreme. There is a great deal of evidence that even morphologically complex forms are present in a speaker's lexicon.

One morphologically complex word that must be considered to be listed in the lexicon is *representative*. If it were enough to say that *re-*, *present*, and *-ative* are stored in the lexicon, we would expect the meaning of *representative* to be a function of its parts, which it is not. A representative is always a person who represents something, but in the United States, the word most commonly refers to an elected member of a specific state or federal legislative body. Senators may represent us, and thus they are representatives, but a United States Senator is not a *Representative*. (If you doubt us, perform the simple experiment of referring to a senator as a representative in conversation, and see what happens.)

Digging a little deeper, we find that most words ending in *-ative* are adjectives. *Representative* can be an adjective, but in this specific sense it is a noun, again an idiosyncrasy that must be listed in the lexicon along with the special meaning it has come to have in the context of United States government. In this and many other cases, we are tempted to think that the meaning of a complex word is the sum of the meaning of its parts, because the difference between the meaning that we expect a word to have based on the meanings of its parts and the meaning that it actually has is quite subtle. Still, there is no way out. If we want to know the meaning of the word *representative*, we must somewhere have a list in which we store the whole word and its very specific meaning. The lexicon is just such a list.

It turns out that almost anything can be in the lexicon. Affixes, such as English *re-*, can be assumed to be in the lexicon. We say this because speakers know and understand such affixes, and readily attach them to new stems.

Some affixed inflected forms, like *says*, must also be in a lexicon. We know this because *says* is an exception to the general rule "Add /-z/ to the basic stem of a verb to form the third person singular present." Say *say* and *says* out loud: *say* [sej] has a tense vowel, but *says* [sɛz] has a lax one. A speaker of English must therefore memorize the fact that the third person singular of *say* does not follow the normal rules of English. In other words, a speaker must store it in his or her lexicon. Is *says* a simple form or a complex form? We can safely assume that it is complex because it has two parts, a stem and a recognizable third person ending /-z/. So this tells us that complex forms may be stored in the lexicon.

Now consider a famous complex word, *antidisestablishmentarianism*, in which we can easily recognize the pieces *anti-*, *dis-*, *establish*, *-ment*, *-ary*, *-an*, and *-ism*. However, these pieces together tell us very little about the meaning of the word, 'opposition to denying special state recognition of a particular religion' (it was used in Irish political discussion in the mid-nineteenth century). If you are a speaker of English who happens to know and use this word, then it must live in your lexicon, because its meaning cannot straightforwardly be determined from the meaning of its parts.

We have established the need to list inflected forms and complex lexemes like *representative* in the lexicon. We need to list some compounds, too. Some people might argue that you don't need to list *doghouse* in the lexicon. (We would disagree: see exercise 1, chapter 4). However, there is no doubt that the compound *cathouse* is listed there, because its meaning, 'brothel', is not predictable from its form. Fixed phrases (*with respect to . . .* , *butterflies in my stomach*), phrasal verbs (*run up a bill*, *catch up with Tom*), people's names (*Audrey Hepburn*, *Gulf of Mexico*), and proverbs (*Don't count your chickens before they're hatched*) all need to be memorized, too, and are arguably in the lexicon. There have even been psycholinguistic studies that have shown that perfectly regular complex forms, if frequent enough, are listed in the lexicon.

In sum, the most accurate conception of the lexicon is as a list of forms that you know. The lexicon is in some sense equivalent to your linguistic memory. It cannot be just a list of indivisible morphological elements. Instead, it contains irregular forms, forms that are in some way unpredictable. Some of these are indivisible or unanalyzable morphologically, and others are not.

We would like to close this section by mentioning a third use of lexicon among linguists. Some linguists equate the lexicon with the morphological component of the grammar as a whole. We believe that this is a mistake, and that the mental dictionary should be considered separately from the internal mechanisms involved in the formation and analysis of words.

■ 2.7 Summary

We began this chapter by looking at syntactic and phonological definitions of word, and we found that many definitions of word are problematic.

Nevertheless, speakers have firm intuitions about what is a word and what isn't, and we were also able to present several empirical tests of wordhood involving the order of internal elements, non-separability, integrity, and stress. We presented key terms used in the discussion of words, particularly grammatical word, phonological word, and lexeme. The notion of lexeme in turn led to an introduction to inflection and derivation, which will be discussed more fully in chapters 4 and 6. We then looked at two approaches to morphology, item-and-arrangement and item-and-process, noting that the latter is better able to account for non-affixal phenomena. Finally, we looked at the lexicon, a mental list of forms that you know.

The Kujamaat Jóola portion of this chapter picks up on the word – the focus of the first portion – by examining how nouns are organized into classes.

■ Kujamaat Jóola Noun Classes

Kujamaat Jóola is like other Atlantic languages – indeed, most languages of the Niger-Congo family – in having a complex gender, or noun class, system. Linguists use the word *gender* in a different sense from most people, for whom gender is tied to sex, and consequently for whom there can be only two (masculine and feminine) or perhaps three, if we include neuter. For linguists, genders are agreement classes of nouns and pronouns, and a language has as many genders as the agreement system of the language distinguishes. While Indo-European languages like English, French, German, Greek, Russian, or Spanish may have two or three genders, Kujamaat Jóola has a whopping 19. And it is not unusual in this regard. Within West Atlantic we can name Gombe Fula with 25 noun classes, Serer with 16, Wolof with 10, Manjaku with 14, and Balanta with seven (Sapir 1971).

The observations that all words of a language, even borrowings, are assigned to genders and that speakers of languages with genders rarely make mistakes in their use indicate that gender systems are structured (Corbett 1991: 7). In other words, it is not wholly arbitrary that one noun belongs to one gender, and a second noun to another.

One way that gender or noun class systems may be organized is semantically. The Dravidian language Tamil, spoken in Sri Lanka and Southeastern India, is an example of a language with a highly regular semantically based gender system. Human nouns are assigned to the so-called male rational and female rational genders, and non-human nouns to the non-rational gender.

Indo-European gender systems are also organized partially on semantic grounds. In French, for example, *femme* 'woman' is feminine and *homme* 'man' is masculine. In English, too, although we find gender only in pronouns, gender distinctions are largely semantic and sex-based: *he* usually refers to males, *she* to females, and *it* is usually used where there is either no sex distinction or it is unimportant.

But describing gender assignment on the basis of semantics will often take us only so far. In describing French, we begin to run into problems when we encounter words like *personne* 'person', which is always feminine, or *professeur* 'teacher, professor', which is always masculine, at least in the standard language. (The clipped form *prof* can be masculine or feminine.) Words like *raisin* 'grape' (masculine) or *chaise* 'chair' (feminine) have gender that is utterly arbitrary from a semantic point of view.

The same is true of other noun class systems. You might not think of grouping women, fire, and dangerous things together on semantic grounds, but they all belong to a single noun class in the Australian language Dyirbal (Dixon 1972). In Algonquian languages, which distinguish between an **animate** and an **inanimate gender**, people and animals fall into the animate class as expected, but then so do large trees and a number of objects including tobacco, apples, kettles, and snowshoes. Some body parts, such as the calf and stomach, have animate gender, while others, such as the thigh, are inanimate (Bloomfield 1946: 94).

[Exercise 10]

As we go through the Kujamaat Jóola noun class system, you will see that semantic classes play a central role in noun class assignment, but that at the same time, noun classes can be semantically diverse. Even in English, where gender seems to be perfectly predictable, we run into some peculiarities: ships and cars are often treated as feminine in gender (also neuter, but never masculine): *she won't start; let's get her under sail.* For some (primarily British) varieties of English, the word *baby* is neuter, but not babies in general, since once the baby is called by name, the baby must be male or female: *it kept on crying, so I fed it ~ Lucinda kept on crying, so I fed her/*it.*

In order to talk about the gender or noun class systems of a language, linguists give them names or numbers. Each of Kujamaat Jóola's 19 classes is assigned a number. Speakers of the language do not make use of such numbers. They are able to use the noun classes correctly without a need for any such system.

Noun class in Kujamaat Jóola is marked by singular and plural prefixes of the shape (C)V-. Every noun generally has a noun class prefix in both singular and plural and is said to belong to both a singular and a plural class. For instance, the singular word *asɛk* 'one woman' is in class 1, as indicated by the prefix *a-*, but its plural, *kusɛk* 'more than one woman', is in class 2, as indicated by the prefix *ku-*. Looked at another way, we can say that the lexeme *sɛk* 'woman (neither singular nor plural)' falls into one of two classes, depending on whether it is singular or plural. This type of system, in which we speak of a particular singular class and a matching plural class as forming a pair, so that genders are characterized by pairs of classes, is characteristic of the entire Niger-Congo family, including the Bantu languages, which are the best known. Together, classes 1 and 2 form what we might call the personal gender, since they contain most words with human referents. Examples of other class 1/2 nouns are given in (1):

(1) Class 1 *a-* (sg.)   Class 2 *ku-* (pl.)
     asɛf   'chief' (< Fr. *chef*)   kusɛf   'chiefs'
     əku̱   'thief'   ku̱ku̱   'thieves'
     ajɔla 'Jóola person'   kujɔla 'Jóola people'

Although personal names bear no class prefix, we know that they belong to class 1 because they trigger class 1 agreement on adjectives, verbs, and so on, as we will see in chapter 6.

The gender consisting of classes 3 and 4 is semantically very diverse. Words for most animals are assigned to this gender, as are terms for various concrete objects. Furthermore, as pointed out by Sapir (1965: 62), "most loan words that are not persons, fruits, trees, containers, or bony objects" are assigned to this pair:

(2) Class 3 *ɛ-* (sg.)   Class 4 *si-* (pl.)
     ɛgɔl   'stick'   sigɔl
     ɛyɛn   'dog'   siyɛn
     emu̱ngu̱n   'hyena'   simu̱ngu̱n
     elu̱:p   'house'   silu̱:p
     emoːn   'trunk of body'   si̱moːn
     ɛsɛntur   'belt' (< Fr. *ceinture*)   sisɛntur
     ɛbandɛlɛ   'flag' (< Port. *bandeira*)   sibandɛlɛ
     ɛfɛːrɛ   'means, affair' (< Fr. *affaire*)   sifɛːrɛ
     edu̱:liːne   '(peanut) oil' (< Fr. *d'huile*)

Classes 3 and 4 contain some nouns with human referents, which *a priori* might have been expected to be assigned to classes 1 and 2. A few plural personal nouns, such as *siɲaːy* 'mother's sisters', belong to class 4 although, in this case at least, the singular is marked by the class 1 prefix (*aiɲaːy*). Furthermore, at least two forms that refer to "substandard people" are marked as belonging to classes 3 and 4: *ɛsɔŋ/sisɔŋ* 'fool, psychotic' and *egət/sigət* 'stupid person'. Placing humans in a non-human gender is a standard technique across languages for expressing disrespect or derogation, and is seen, for example, in Grebo (Kru), Tsova-Tush (Caucasian), and Yao (Bantu) (Head 1978: 175–7; Corbett 1991: 322–3). In Kujamaat Jóola the opposite is possible, as well. A storyteller may endow an animal with human qualities by marking it as belonging to class 1.

A number of class 3 nouns do not take a class marker, or take one only optionally. The former include *mbur* 'bread' and *dakar* 'Dakar'. Note that all place names belong to this type. Examples of nouns that take a class marker optionally are *(e)ji̱mu̱kor* 'lion' and *(ɛ)bɛkan* 'bicycle', the latter from French *bécane*. As with personal names, which belong to class 1, we know that these words belong to class 3 because they consistently trigger class 3 agreement on adjectives, verbs, and other words with which they enter into an agreement relation.

The gender consisting of classes 5 and 6 includes most words for fruit, including borrowings, and most words referring to periods of time or to events involving large crowds (Sapir 1965: 63). As usual, other semantic types are represented as well:

(3) Class 5 *fu-* (sg.)   Class 6 *ku-* (pl.)

fumang	'mango' (< Port. *manga*)	kumang
fulimən	'orange (fruit)' (< Fr. *limon*)	kulimən
fufimbar	'tomato'	kufimbar
funak	'day'	kunak
furi	'food, mealtime'	kuri
futamp	'circumcision festival'	kutamp
fuburə	'duck'	kuburə
fuko	'head'	kuko

Classes 5 and 6 have a derivational role as well: they may be used to form **augmentatives** or augmentative plurals of nouns from other classes. So we have *ɛgɔl* 'stick' (class 3) and *sigɔl* 'sticks' (class 4), but also *fugɔl* 'big stick' (class 5) and *kugɔl* 'big sticks' (class 6). Likewise, *asɛk* 'woman' can be placed into class 5 to produce *fusɛk* 'big woman'. Note again how the two classes are paired in a single gender, even when quite a different meaning is involved.

The next pair, classes 7 and 8, contains words referring to bones, bony objects (such as a fish's fin), and limbs of the body. It also includes most words for containers, including borrowings. However, they also contain the word for at least one type of frog and for language:

(4) Class 7 *ka-* (sg.)   Class 8 *u-* (pl.)

kɔːl	'bone'	wɔːl
kaŋag	'fin (of fish)'	uŋag
kəsinsiŋ	'(type of) basket'	usinsiŋ
kapɔt	'pot' (< Port. *pote*)	upɔt
kajata	'(type of) frog'	ujata
kasankɛn	'language'	usankɛn

"[W]ords for trees and for objects hollowed out from tree trunks and large limbs" are remarkably consistent in mapping onto the 9/8 pair, with only one recorded exception (Sapir 1965: 63). This is not to say that the 9/8 pair is semantically homogenous, however. As seen below, it contains words meaning 'road', 'spitting cobra', 'corpse', and 'fertilizer':

(5)   Class 9 *bu-* (sg.)   Class 8 *u-* (pl.)
      buḅəːr   'general word for tree'   uḅəːr
      busaːna   'silk cotton tree, dugout canoe'   usaːna
      buruŋ   'road'   uruŋ
      bulun   'spitting cobra'   ulun
      buyiŋ   'corpse'   uyiŋ
      buɲulɛn   'fertilizer'

The fact that two singular classes, 7 and 9, both make their plural in class 8 shows the necessity of putting singular and plural nouns of the same apparent gender in separate classes in languages like Kujamaat Jóola. In Indo-European languages there is generally a one-to-one mapping between singular and plural noun classes, with one plural type for every singular type, and vice versa.

We turn now to the pair of classes 10 and 11. A number of nouns, especially those that denote small animals, consistently appear with marking for classes 10 and 11. But these classes serve to form diminutives as well, corresponding to the way in which the 5/6 class pair is used to form augmentatives in addition to having a more specific use. Stems that typically appear in other classes, such as *-ko* 'head' (5/6) and *-ɲil* 'child' (1/2), form singular and plural diminutives by taking class 10 and 11 prefixes. Which familiar nineteenth-century novel might you translate into Kujamaat Jóola as *mu-sɛk*?

(6)   Class 10 *ji-* (sg.)   Class 11 *mu-* (pl.)
      jịko   'small head'   mụko
      jiɲil   'small child'   muɲil
      jịbəːr   'small tree'   mụbəːr
      jịkịt   'type of small antelope'   mụkịt
      jimandulit 'type of snake'   mumandulit

Taking the same two stems, *-ko* 'head' (5/6) and *-ɲil* 'child' (1/2), with which we formed diminutives above, we can form augmentatives by placing them into the pairs 9 and 12 and 5 and 12 respectively. These examples show that a single class, 5 in this instance, can be basic for some nouns (here *-ko* 'head'), but form an augmentative for others (here *-ɲil* 'child'):

(7)   Class 5 *fu*-; Class 9 *bu*- (sg.)   Class 12 *ɲi*- (pl.)
    fuɲil   'large child'   ɲiɲil
    buko   'large head'   ɲiko

There are no nouns that belong specifically to the 9/12 or 5/12 pairs.

    Mass nouns are generally assigned to class 11. Class 11 is otherwise a plural and it is odd to English speakers that mass nouns should be placed in a class that is normally plural. But we should keep in mind that what truly sets off mass nouns semantically is that they do not distinguish between singular and plural, so whether we use an otherwise singular or plural class is not material, and indeed diminutives of mass nouns fall into class 10, which is normally singular:

(8)   Class 11 *mu*-   Class 10 *ji*-
    mumɛl   'water'   jimɛl   'a little bit of water'
    miːl   'milk'   jimiːl   'a little bit of milk'
    musis   'salt'   jisis   'a little bit of salt'
    musana(y)   'news'   jisanay   'a little bit of news'

Sapir observes that there are also a few recorded instances of other class prefixes, including ɛ- (class 3), *si*- (class 4), *bu*- (class 9), or *fa*- (class 14) marking mass nouns. Some examples are given below:

(9)   Class 3:   erus   'wind'
                     eful   'cotton'
    Class 4:   sambun   'fire'
    Class 9:   bunuk   'palm wine'
    Class 14:   fəsim   'blood'
                     fakɔr   'smoke'

    Kujamaat Jóola also has a diminutive collective, which means 'little bunch of, little collection of'. This is formed by assigning a noun stem from just about any class to class 13:

(10)   Class 13 *ba*-
    bakikit (cf. ɛkikit 'pit, seed')   'small bunch of seeds'
    bajaŋata (cf. fujaŋata 'peanut')   'small bunch of peanuts'

So far we have encountered very few abstract nouns. These are scattered over a number of classes, some of which we have already seen. Many of them, including all color words, fall into class 15. Among the forms in (11), note the borrowing *bulore* 'blue', from French *bleu*. It has been assigned to class 15 because of the important role of semantics in the organization of the Kujamaat Jóola noun class system:

(11)   Class 15 *ma-*

majilayet	'yellow'
malaɛnɛ	'black'
məbulore	'blue' (< Fr. *bleu*)
malɛgɛn	'truth'
majɔl	'rapidity'
marapet	'stubbornness, insolence'

Some abstract nouns occur in classes 12, 13, or 14. As we have learned to expect, exceptions are possible, and thus we find *ɲikul* meaning 'funeral':

(12)   Class 12 *ɲi-*:

	ɲikul	'funeral'
	ɲiŋɔnk	'coldness'
Class 13 *ba-*:	bacar	'hunger'
	bərir	'right (direction)'
	batiay	'brotherhood, sisterhood'
Class 14 *fa-*:	falamat	'nonsense, bad act'
	falɛːt	'sulkiness'

Classes 16 (*ja-*), 17 (*wa-*), 18 (*ti-*), and 19 (*ri-*) are rare, and no examples are presented here.

Infinitives, like nouns, take a noun class prefix. The class prefix is generally predictable, and depends on the number of syllables in the stem. This fact is certainly worth a comment. We have seen a rough correspondence between noun classes and semantics, with each noun class having an association, admittedly not consistent, with some semantic class. Here we see a purely phonological criterion at work. Though not common, this sort of phonological conditioning is fairly widespread throughout the languages of the world. In Latin, for example, though the genders are correlated to some extent with sex, some nouns are assigned to genders purely on phonological grounds. Returning to our Kujamaat Jóola infinitives, we see that the phonological conditioning of the noun class membership of infinitives is highly regular: monosyllabic stems take the class 3 prefix *ɛ-*, while stems of more than one syllable take the class 7 prefix *ka-*:

(13)   a.

	ɛga	'to throw'
	ɛis	'to show'
b.	katundo	'to lose consciousness, to be in a coma'
	kətikər	'to be without'

Taking a monosyllabic verb and making it polysyllabic by adding a derivational affix results in a class 7 infinitive, as seen in the following pairs:

(14) a. *ɛgaːj* 'to smear something with a gooey substance'
kagaːjɛn (*gaːj* + causative *-ɛn*) 'to slander someone, to befoul something'

b. *eyem* 'to be red, to redden'
kəyemen (*yem* + causative *-ɛn*) 'to make red'

c. *ɛkɔf* 'to scratch someone lightly'
kakɔfɔɔr (*kɔf* + reflexive *-ɔr*) 'to scratch oneself'

Before we conclude, it is worth pointing out something that we touched on above. This is that noun class systems can be powerful inflectional and derivational mechanisms. We have seen that by changing a noun's class marker, not only can Kujamaat Jóola speakers make important number distinctions – singular, plural, mass, or collective – but they can also create diminutives or augmentatives, personify non-humans, or dehumanize humans. Two examples of stems that take on a variety of meanings by moving from one noun class to another are given below:

(15) a.
-sɛk	'woman'	
a-sɛk	'woman'	(class 1)
ku-sɛk	'women'	(class 2)
ji-sɛk	'small woman'	(class 10)
mu-sɛk	'small women'	(class 11)
ba-sɛk	'many small women'	(class 13)
fu-sɛk	'big woman'	(class 5)
ɲi-sɛk	'big women'	(class 12)

b.
-bəːr	'wood'	
bu̱-bəːr	'tree'	(class 9)
u̱-bəːr	'trees'	(class 8)
ji̱-bəːr	'small tree'	(class 10)
mu̱-bəːr	'small trees, underbrush'	(class 11)
e-bəːr	'stick'	(class 3)
si̱-bəːr	'sticks'	(class 4)

The facts that we have seen in this chapter suggest a possible analysis of the Kujamaat Jóola noun class system. It is plausible that some noun stems, such as *-sɛk* 'woman' (1/2), *-mu̱ngu̱n* 'hyena' (3/4), *-mang* 'mango' (5/6), and *-bik* 'large pot with wide mouth' (7/8), are not marked for any noun class in the lexicon, and are assigned to the appropriate classes by semantic rules. For example, nouns with human referents are automatically assigned to class 1 in the singular and class 2 in the plural, nouns referring to animals to classes 3 and 4, nouns referring to fruits to classes 5 and 6, and containers to classes 7 and 8. Other nouns must be lexically marked for a particular noun class. For example, we would expect -*tunguɲ* 'taciturn person' to be assigned to the 1/2 pair since it has a human referent. The fact that it belongs to class 13 is due to its being marked as belonging to class 13 in the lexicon. Lexical specification for noun class overrides assignment by semantic rule.

The behavior of **loanwords**, or words borrowed from other languages, in Kujamaat Jóola suggests that in the absence of lexical specification or an appropriate semantic rule, nouns are assigned to a default gender, which appears to be the gender consisting of class 3 in the singular and class 4 in the plural. As shown below, most loanwords are assigned to these two classes, with the exception of words that refer to persons, fruits, trees (no examples available), containers, or bony objects:

(16) Kujamaat Jóola loanwords

    3/4 pair:

εsεntur	'belt' (< Fr. *ceinture*)	sisεntur
εbandεlε	'flag' (< Port. *bandeira*)	sibandεlε
εfεːrε	'means, affair' (< Fr. *affaire*)	sifεːrε
εharijε	'talisman' (< Ar. *hirz*, Mdk. *harijéo*)	siharijε
εkɔnsε	'vacation' (< Fr. *congé*)	sikɔnsε

    1/2 pair (humans):

abaːriŋ	'kin (general term)' (< Mdk. *bariŋ*)	kubaːriŋ
amaːnsa	'king, rich man' (< Mdk. *manso*)	kumaːnsa

    5/6 pair (fruits):

fumang	'mango' (< Port. *manga*)	kumang
fuli̱mən	'orange (fruit)' (< Fr. *limon*)	kuli̱mən
fu̱nəːnə	'banana' (< Fr. *banane*)	ku̱nəːnə

    7/8 pair (containers and bony objects):

kapɔt	'pot' (< Port. *pote*)	upɔt
kajaːm	'leg and foot' (< Fr. *jambe*)	ujaːm

Because the 3/4 pair is the default gender, it is also the most semantically diverse, although historically, the opposite may have been true: because 3/4 happened to be the largest or most diverse gender pair, it may have become the default gender.

These three types of noun class assignment – default assignment to classes 3 and 4, lexical specification, and semantic rule – can all be overridden by the derivational mechanism illustrated by some of the nouns in (15). Therefore, almost any noun can be assigned to class 10 (*ji-*) to form a diminutive or to class 5 (*fu-*) to form an augmentative. **[Exercises 11 and 12]**

Exercises

1. We have said that speakers use adjectives to modify a compound as a whole and not to modify only one of its members. Thus a *brown deer tick* is a brown tick, not a tick that lives on brown deer. However, morphological generalizations are often not absolute. We heard the first of the following compounds on television, and read the second in *The Economist* (July 11, 2002):

   a. German car dealership (a dealership that sells German cars)

   b. rich-country club (the OECD, an international organization made up primarily of rich countries)

   Should these be considered counterexamples to the generalization that adjectives cannot modify part of a compound? Explain your answer. Then come up with two more examples that are parallel to these.

2. One English clitic is the possessive morpheme *'s*. Is the host of *'s* a word or a phrase? Present data to support your answer.

3. Identify each of the underlined words as a function or content word.

   <u>Row</u>, row, row <u>your</u> boat

   Gently <u>down</u> <u>the</u> <u>stream</u>

   <u>Merrily</u>, merrily, merrily, merrily

   Life <u>is</u> <u>but</u> a <u>dream</u>.

4. Some speakers of English always pronounce the words in column A with the vowel [ɛ], even when the words are stressed. They pronounce the words in column B with the vowel [æ]. This means that for them, *can* 'be able' and *can* 'metal container' are never homophones, as they sometimes are for other English speakers. Make two generalizations about the words in column A, one phonological and the other morphological, that accounts for their patterning together with respect to the shift from [æ] to [ɛ]. The fact that they consist of only a single syllable does not matter.

A	B
can 'be able'	can 'metal container', can't, cat, camera
am	yam, at, allergy
an	Ann, ant
than	cranberry, thatch

5. Some English speakers use *they* as a third person singular pronoun, as in (a). Using the examples in (a–d), describe the function of singular *they* and describe contexts in which an English speaker might choose to use it.
    a. If it's part of how a person defines *themself*, *they* should be allowed to wear it, even if it causes controversy. [High school student quoted in the *Ithaca Journal*]
    b. We *did* see somebody hanging around the dumpster. *They were/He was* wearing a jean jacket and a black cap.
    c. There was only one guy at the party. *He/*They* looked pretty amused.
    d. I ran into Cheryl after the play. *She was/*They were* really pleased about *her/*their* performance.

6. Are the following sets of boldfaced words forms of a single lexeme, or examples of different lexemes?
    a. **roast** (verb), **roast** (noun)
    b. **roaster** 'piece of equipment used for roasting', **roaster** 'chicken packaged and purchased for roasting'
    c. **roast** (verb), **roasting** (participle of verb: *We were roasting chicken halves for the fire station fundraiser*), **roasting** (adverb used to modify 'hot': *roasting hot*)
    d. **roast, roasts, roasted** (all verbs)
    e. **book, books** (both nouns)
    f. **book, bookie, booklet** (all nouns)

7. Read the following sentences out loud. Can you find phonological evidence that what we spell *have* in (a) and (b) corresponds to two different lexemes? (In (a), *have* is a content word meaning 'possess', and in (b), it is a function word meaning 'be obligated'.) This task may be difficult for non-native speakers of English.
    a. I **have** twelve cats.
    b. I **have** to go.

8. How many phonological words are there in the following set? Put all the forms that represent the same phonological word together in a list. How many grammatical words are there? List them. Finally, how many lexemes are there? List them as well, remembering to write them in capital letters.

flour (n), flour (v), flours (n), flours (v), floured, flower (n), flower (v), flowers (n), flowers (v), flowered

9. How might you analyze *civilization* in an item-and-arrangement-based model? in an item-and-process-based model?

10. If you know a language that has noun classes or genders, what is it? How many noun classes or genders are there? List them, with at least two examples for each. Can the noun class or gender of any words be predicted on the basis of their meaning? Explain.

11. Universal Grammar is the hypothesis that all languages are alike on some level of analysis. Implicit in this formulation is the idea that at other levels of analysis, languages are different. (See the discussion of *language* vs. *Language* in chapter 1.) Discuss the Kujamaat Jóola noun class system in this context. You may want to bring in examples of other gender systems, if you are familiar with any. How is it reflective of *language* and what does it tell us about *Language*?

12. Chichewa, Malawi (Nida 1965: 141–2)
The forms below can be divided into several noun classes. Describe the forms by (i) setting up the classes and (ii) describing each by means of a composite statement, as best you can given the limited number of data. (As a model, you can look again at the section on Kujamaat Jóola noun classes. For example, Kujamaat Jóola class 9 was described as containing the singular forms of words for trees and objects made by hollowing out tree trunks or large limbs.) Explain the distribution of any allomorphs that you encounter.

Supplementary information:
- Differences of tone should not be considered in analyzing this set. Tones are basic to the stem.
- The penultimate (next-to-the-last) syllable is always long in these forms. This is true of these nouns in isolation, but not necessarily in context.
- Certain phonologically defined allomorphs occur:
  mw- and *vj-* occur before vowels
  m- and *a-* occur before polysyllabic stems
- The stem of forms (c) and (d) is *-ána*.

a.	mu:nt^{h}u	'man'
b.	βa:nt^{h}u	'men'
c.	mwá:na	'child'
d.	βá:na	'children'
e.	mú:p^{h}wa	'man's sister's child'
f.	βá:p^{h}wa	'man's sister's children'
g.	mná:si	'neighbor'
h.	aná:si	'neighbors'
i.	mza:mba	'midwife'
j.	aza:mba	'midwives'
k.	dá:mbɔ	'marsh'
l.	madá:mbɔ	'marshes'
m.	fu:nɔ	'wish, need'
n.	mafu:nɔ	'wishes, needs'
o.	pɛmp^{h}ɛ:rɔ	'prayer'
p.	mapɛmp^{h}ɛ:rɔ	'prayers'
q.	bwɛ́:zi	'friend'
r.	mabwɛ́:zi	'friends'
s.	ʧá:ka	'year'
t.	vjá:ka	'years'
u.	ʧiβá:lɛ	'coconut tree'
v.	viβá:lɛ	'coconut trees'
w.	ʧipa:nda	'calabash'
x.	vipa:nda	'calabashes'
y.	ʧisɔ́:ŋga	'wooden arrow point'
z.	visɔ́:ŋga	'wooden arrow points'
aa.	ʧitsú:rɔ	'iron'
bb.	vitsú:rɔ	'pieces of iron'

NOTES

1 One exception is in first-language acquisition. Some children use *my* in this context before acquiring *mine*.

2 Single-syllable prepositions in English are normally clitics, except at the end of a sentence (e.g. *What did you do that for?*), a position which is regarded as unacceptable by prescriptive grammar.

3 Our use of "adverb" here mirrors that of traditional grammar. Some modern linguists would give *very* and *not* different labels.

4 In modern syntax, prepositions are considered a lexical category. This does not make them content words.

5 As an exercise, though, do an online search for *had-nots*. What sorts of examples do you find?

6 An interesting morphological fact pointed out to us by Donald Lenfest is that Ohio has switched from *driver's license* to *driver license*. Want to see it for yourself? Just check out the Ohio Bureau of Motor Vehicles web page, www.state.oh.us/odps/division/bmv/bmv.html at the time of this writing.

7 The citation form of Latin verbs is the first person indicative singular.

8 The perfective and imperfective are two forms of the verb. As a first approximation, we may say that the perfective expresses an action as being complete, while the imperfective expresses an action as being incomplete.

3 Morphology and Phonology

This chapter explores some of the many interactions that take place between morphology and phonology. These interactions and the grammar that describes them are often called **morphophonology** or **morpho-phonemics**. We begin by looking at phonological processes such as assim-ilation and the effect they have on the shapes of morphemes. We then consider limitations on the phonological shape of morphological entities such as words and stems. From there we will move on to two general types of affixes that are distinguished, in part, by phonological criteria. Their phonological behavior reveals details about their underlying structure and the point at which they attach to their bases. We conclude the chapter with a look at secret languages in which morphology and phonology interact to disguise the shapes of words.

We wrote in the introduction that we expect our readers to have the rudimentary knowledge of linguistics that comes from taking an introductory course. To understand the discussion in this chapter, you need to know three terms that are often not introduced in such courses. They are **onset**, **nucleus**, and **coda**. The onset of a syllable is made up of the first consonant or consonants. The nucleus is the syllable's core, usually a simple vowel or a diphthong. The coda is made up of the consonant or consonants that follow the nucleus. All syllables must have nuclei. Onsets and codas are optional, though some languages require the former.

■ 3.1 Allomorphs

The term 'allomorph' was introduced in the first chapter, in two contexts. In Kujamaat Jóola, we noted that the stem /baj-/ has two possible shapes, [baj-] and [bəj-], with [bəj-] occurring in the presence of a morpheme with an underlyingly tense vowel, and [baj-] elsewhere. In English, we observed that plural marker comes in several shapes, among them [s] as in *lips*, [z] as in *balls*, [əz] as in *roses*, [n̩] as in *oxen*, and null, as in *sheep*. In this chapter we will be most interested in alternations based purely on phonological context, as with the Kujamaat Jóola facts. In the English data, only the first three allomorphs of the plural suffix depend on phonological context. The last two, as in *oxen* and *sheep*, are lexical, and so we will not be concerned with them here.

Like the English plural suffix -s, the English past tense suffix has three forms: [d], [t], and [əd]:

(1)   [d]: blamed [blejmd], triggered [tɪɪgərd], realized [rijəlajzd], sighed [sajd], rubbed [rʌbd]
[t]: jumped [dʒʌmpt], yakked [jækt], shushed [ʃʌʃt], quaffed [kwɑft], itched [ɪtʃt]
[əd]: aided [ejɾəd], knighted [nʌjɾəd]

The distribution of the three allomorphs is predictable, and parallel to the distribution of the three allomorphs of the English plural suffix. [d] is found on verbs ending in a vowel or a voiced consonant, with the exception of alveolar stop [d]. [t] is found on verbs that end with a voiceless consonant, with the exception of alveolar stop [t]. In verbs that end with [t] or [d], we find [əd]. But we can formulate the distribution of the allomorphs in even simpler terms. We can say that the English past tense suffix is /d/, period. Where we find [t], the /d/ has **assimilated** to the preceding segment in voicing. Where we find [əd], we can say that the [ə] has been added by an automatic phonological rule of **epenthesis** (i.e., insertion of a phonological segment or segments) that is triggered by the fact that the final segment in the verb and the suffix itself agree in both place and continuancy. We can call /d/ the basic form or the basic allomorph of the English past tense suffix.

It is not always easy, or even possible, to determine the basic form of a morpheme. To do so, we must decide which form of a morpheme best accounts for the full range of data. Consider the two words from Classical Greek given below. The forms on the left are in the nominative case, used for subjects, and those on the right are in the genitive case.

(2)   aitʰiops   'Ethiopian'   aitʰiopos   'of an Ethiopian'
      pʰleps   'vein'   pʰlebos   'of a vein'

On the basis of these two forms, we can hypothesize that the nominative in Greek is formed by the addition of -s, and the genitive is formed by the addition of -os. What then are the basic forms of the stems meaning 'Ethiopian' and 'vein'? With respect to the first, the answer seems simple: comparing the nominative and genitive forms, we can isolate aitʰiop-. Finding the basic stem meaning 'vein' is more difficult. It might be pʰlep-, the stem of the nominative, or pʰleb-, the stem of the genitive (cf. *phlebotomist*). Theoretically, it could also be neither. However, we want the basic form of the allomorph to be one that speakers would be able to posit on their own given the available evidence, and when given a problem set we have to assume that we, too, have all of the relevant data.

If the basic form of the stem were pʰlep-, we would have no explanation for why Greek speakers did not simply add -os, as with aitʰiopos, yielding *pʰlepos. Positing an underlying stem of pʰleb- instead makes the genitive form pʰlebos understandable, and with an additional step of assimilation in voicing, it also allows us to explain the nominative form, pʰleps. **[Exercises 1 and 2]**

(3)   Formation of Classical Greek pʰleps
      a.   Stem + nominative suffix: pʰleb + s
      b.   Voicing assimilation: pʰleps

Allomorphs are often the product of assimilations like the one that takes /d/ to [t] in words like *jumped*, *baked*, or *kissed*, or that takes *pʰleb-s to pʰleps. In the case of the English past tense suffix, the voicelessness of the final consonant in the verb spreads forward to the suffix in what we call **progressive assimilation**. In the Classical Greek example, the voicelessness of the nominative suffix moves in the opposite direction. We call this **regressive assimilation**.

Another example of regressive assimilation can be found in Spanish. Word-final nasal consonants assimilate in place of articulation to a following consonant in many different contexts. For example, the preposition *con* 'with' can be described as having at least three phonetic realizations: [kom], [kon], and [koŋ]. (In fact, there are five phonetic realizations of *con*, but we are simplifying for clarity.) Their distribution is predictable, just like that of the English past tense suffixes. We find [kom] before labial consonants, [kon] before alveolars and vowels, and [koŋ] before velars. Again, we can identify a basic form, in this case /kon/. We know it is basic because it occurs in two unlike environments: before certain consonants and before all vowels.

(4) Castilian Spanish *con*
   a. [kom]
       conmigo   'with me'
       con María   'with Maria'
       con Pedro   'with Pedro'
       con Beatríz   'with Beatrice'
   b. [kon]
       contigo   'with you (sg)'
       con Diego   'with Diego'
       con nadie   'with no one'
       con él   'with him'
   c. [koŋ]
       con Gabriela   'with Gabriela'
       con Carlos   'with Carlos'

Assimilation like that seen with Spanish *con* is rampant in the world's languages and thus a frequent source of allomorphy.

Epenthesis is another common source of allomorphy. Frequently, for example, languages epenthesize consonants in contexts where a final vowel in one word would otherwise come up against an initial vowel in the following word, particularly when the two have a strong syntactic bond. We call this unwanted vowel–vowel contact **hiatus**. French is a language that doesn't like hiatus, and it has all sorts of ways of eliminating it in certain syntactic contexts. The plural article *les* [le] 'the' is pronounced [lez] when it is followed by a vowel-initial word (5a); the masculine demonstrative *ce* [sə] becomes *cet* [sɛt], which happens to be homophonous with the feminine demonstrative *cette* (5b); and the feminine genitive adjectives *ma* [ma], *ta* [ta], and *sa* [sa] are replaced by the masculine forms *mon* [mon], *ton* [ton], and *son* [son] (5c). Regarding the last three forms, it is important to note, however, that when they

function as masculine genitive adjectives, the vowel is nasalized and the
final /n/ is not pronounced before a consonant. It is only pronounced
before vowel-initial words – another hiatus context (6).

(5) a. les maisons   [lemezõ]   'the houses'
        les ami(e)s   [lezami]   'the friends'
    b. ce médecin   [səmedsɛ̃]   'this doctor'
        cet âne (m)   [sɛtɑn]   'this donkey'
    c. ma tante   [matɑ̃t]   'my aunt'
        mon analyse (f)   [monanaliz]   'my analysis'

(6) a. mon chien   [mõʃjɛ̃]   'my dog'
    b. mon oncle   [monõkl]   'my uncle'

Similarly, in the Vallader dialect of Rumantsch, the pronouns *da* 'from'
and *a* 'to' become *dad* and *ad* respectively before words beginning with a
vowel:

(7) a. da Zernez   'from Zernez'
        dad Ardez   'from Ardez'
    b. a Cuoira   'to Chur'
        ad Arosa   'to Arosa'

An instructive case is that of Spanish, as shown by the following set of
data. We have put stressed syllables in boldface type:

(8) a. el **a**gua   'the water'
    b. el **al**ma   'the soul'
    c. el **á**guila   'the eagle'
    d. el **au**la   'the classroom'
    e. el **a**ve   'the bird'
    f. el **ha**cha   'the axe'
    g. el **ham**bre   'hunger'
    h   la a**be**ja, *el a**be**ja   'the bee'
    i. la ha**ri**na, *el ha**ri**na 'the flour'
    j. la **is**la, *el **is**la   'the island'
    k. la **ho**ra, *el **ho**ra   'the hour'

All of the Spanish nouns above are feminine, which may surprise you if
you know already that *el* is the masculine definite article, and *la* is the
feminine. In Spanish, *la* must be replaced by *el* before a feminine noun
that begins with a stressed [a] (8a–g). This does not occur before any other
vowel sound, as shown by the last two examples (8j, k). We include (8h)
and (8i) because both *abeja* and *harina* begin with [a] but are stressed on

the penultimate (second-to-last) syllable. This exempts them from the *la* → *el* rule.

We see that the Spanish anti-hiatus rule has a limited application. It applies only at the juncture between the feminine definite article and a stressed [a]. What's more, it has at least two lexical exceptions: it does not apply in the case of *la a* 'the a' or *la hache* 'the h' (letters of the alphabet).[1] As morphologists, we are used to dealing with cases like this. Unlike syntax, which tends to be very regular, morphology is full of irregularities and exceptions. **[Exercises 3–6]**

■ 3.2 Prosodic Morphology

Prosodic morphology deals with the interaction of morphology and prosodic structure. Prosodic structure, in turn, is particularly concerned with the timing units of languages, e.g., the word and syllable, and vowel length. From this general category we are going to present three phenomena: phonotactic constraints, root-and-pattern morphology, and reduplication.

■ 3.2.1 Phonotactic constraints

Phonotactic constraints are constraints on the phonological shape of stems and words. Phonotactic constraints are often, but not always, connected with syllable structure.

At their most basic, phonotactic constraints determine the minimum length of content words in particular languages. For example, in Mohawk, each content word contains at least two syllables (Michelson 1988, cited by Hayes 1995: 47). Other languages require that content words consist of at least a heavy syllable, where heavy means that the syllable contains a long vowel, diphthong, or a vowel and a weight-bearing (moraic) consonant.[2] Many languages do not have minimal word constraints. Romanian, Hungarian, and Icelandic are all examples (Hayes 1995: 88–9).

Does English have a minimal word constraint? An analysis of nicknames suggests that it does (see McCarthy and Prince 1998: 287–8). Let's make a list of some English first names and their corresponding short forms, or nicknames:

(9) English nicknames
  a. Alexander → Alex
     Caroline → Carrie
     Katherine → Cathy, Kitty

 b. Josephine → Jo
     Louisa, Louis → Lou
     Susan, Suzanne → Sue
     Tyler → Ty
 c. Beverly → Bev
     Christopher → Chris
     Robert → Rob, Bob
     Stephanie → Steph

Even if we were to keep going, we would find that any nickname we can think of falls into one of these three sets. They are either polysyllabic (9a) (in this case, bisyllabic) names or monosyllabic names (9b–c) that have either a diphthong, a coda, or both. No native English nicknames consist of a single, light syllable. From this data, it seems that English falls in with the set of languages that have a minimal word constraint. Even the shortest of names, nicknames, must consist minimally of a heavy syllable or two light syllables. And it is difficult, if not impossible, to find an English content word that contradicts this conclusion.

We also find that languages have restrictions on the possible shapes of roots. Nida (1965: 66) reports that in the Mayan languages, roots are predominantly of the shape CVC and in Bantu they are generally CVCV. In Hebrew, Arabic, and other Semitic languages, roots generally consist of three consonants: CCC.

■ 3.2.2 Root-and-pattern morphology

We ended the last section by saying that in Semitic languages such as Hebrew and Arabic, roots generally consist of three consonants. To form words, vowels are superimposed on this consonantal pattern. We call this type of morphology **root-and-pattern**.

Biblical Hebrew root with sample forms (Seow 1995: 23)

M–L–X: malax   'he reigned'
        yimlox   'he reigns, he will reign'
        molex   'reigning, one who reigns'
        melex   'king'
        malxut   'kingship, reign'
        mamlaxah   'kingdom, sovereignty'

In root-and-pattern morphology, the root consonants in a given inflectional or derivational paradigm combine with vowels and sometimes
consonants in a fixed pattern. It is possible to think of the consonantal root
being superimposed on a template. Thus, in the box opposite, *malax* 'he
reigned' consists of a root M-L-X and a template _*a*_*a*_. The consonants
fit into the empty slots of the template. *Yimlox* 'he reigns' can be thought
of as the root M-L-X and a template *yi*_ _*o*_. (We use *y* here to represent
IPA [j] in adherence with the traditional system of Hebrew transliteration.)

Words of a given class typically share a single pattern. The box opposite contains the word *melex* 'king'. In Hebrew grammar, *melex* is called a
segolate noun (if you do not already know this term, you do not need to
learn it for this course). Segolate nouns consist of two syllables, and they
are stressed on the penultimate (second-to-last) syllable.[3] The group of
segolate nouns can be subdivided into three different classes. All of the
nouns in *melex*'s class share its vocalic pattern. Thus we find *berex* 'knee',
regel 'foot, leg', *nefeʃ* 'soul', and *ʃeved* 'servant'. The triconsonantal roots
of these forms are, in order: B-R-X, R-G-L, N-F-ʃ, and ʃ-B-D ([b] and [v]
are variants of the same underlying phoneme).

As an aside, the root-and-pattern morphology of Hebrew and Arabic
is reflected in their writing systems, which use the primary symbols to
represent consonants and diacritics to represent vowels.

While by definition there are no exceptions to the minimal word
constraints presented in the previous section, we do sometimes find
exceptions to generalizations about possible root shapes. In the Semitic
languages, for example, we find roots consisting of two consonants (CC)
and four (CCCC). But these are rare compared to triconsonantal roots.

■ 3.2.3 Reduplication

In **reduplication**, a continuous substring from either the beginning or the
end of a word is copied. Languages may use reduplication for inflection
or derivation. Plural reduplication in Ilokano, an Austronesian language
of the Philippines, is illustrated below (McCarthy and Prince 1998: 285).
The reduplicated portion of the word is in italics:

(10) kaldíŋ   'goat'   *kal*-kaldíŋ   'goats'
      púsa   'cat'   *pus*-púsa   'cats'
      kláse   'class'   *klas*-kláse   'classes'
      jyánitor   'janitor'   *jyan*-jyánitor   'janitors'
      róʔot   'litter'   *ro:*-róʔot   'litter (pl)'
      trák   'truck'   *tra:*-trák   'trucks'

The inclusion of borrowings in the data set above shows that reduplication is a productive means of forming plurals in Ilokano.

Reduplication bears an important similarity to root-and-pattern morphology. The reduplicant typically must follow a certain pattern or adhere to some other prosodic requirement. In Ilokano plurals, as you can see, the reduplicant is always of the shape C(C)VC or C(C)VV. **[Exercise 7]**

■ 3.3 Primary and Secondary Affixes

Over the years, our knowledge of morphological structure has been enhanced by work in phonology. We can learn a lot by observing the phonological processes that take place or do not take place within particular sets of morphologically complex words.

One distinction that has come out of work that pairs morphology and phonology is between **primary** and **secondary affixes**, also known as **level 1** and **level 2 affixes** or **class 1** and **class 2 affixes**. In English, this distinction is intimately connected with language history. Primary affixes in English are often of Latin-Romance origin, while secondary affixes are often of native Germanic origin. (English is a Germanic language.) However, we de-emphasize this fact in the following discussion because etymology can only take us so far in morphological analysis. The primary–secondary distinction is a living process, regardless of its history, and in English, as in other languages of the world, it cannot be explained away as etymological residue.

Below are some examples, from Kiparsky (1983), of words bearing *-(i)an*, a primary affix (11), and ones bearing *-ism*, a secondary affix (12):

(11) a. Mendel   → Mendelian
      b. Mongol   → Mongolian
      c. Parkinson   → Parkinsonian
      d. Shakespeare → Shakespearian
      e. grammar   → grammarian

(12) a. Mendel   → Mendelism
      b. Mongol   → Mongolism
      c. Parkinson   → Parkinsonism
      d. national   → nationalism
      e. capital   → capitalism

If you read the words in (11) and (12) to yourself, you will hear an important difference. Words with *-(i)an* have a stress shift. The stress in

Mendel is on the first syllable, while in *Mendelian*, it is on the second. Likewise, *Parkinson* is stressed on the first syllable, but *Parkinsonian* is stressed on the third. We can generalize by saying that in all words with *-(i)an*, stress is on the syllable that immediately precedes the suffix. Stems suffixed with *-ism*, on the other hand, are stressed on the same syllable as their unaffixed counterparts. *Nationalism* is stressed on the first syllable, just like *national*. This is the first and most famous difference between primary and secondary affixes. Primary affixes cause a stress shift, while secondary affixes do not.

If primary and secondary affixes both occur in the same word, we can make a second prediction. The primary affix will occur closer to the stem than the secondary affix. Therefore, *Parkinsonianism* is a possible word, but **Parkinsonismian* is not.

Now consider the words *reparable* and *repairable*. Both have *repair* as their stem, but it is slightly disguised in the first. Semantically, both mean 'capable of being repaired', but only the second would be used to describe a broken appliance. *Reparable* has the additional sense of 'liable to be paid back or recovered' as with *reparable damages*. These words show that the suffix *-able* in English is actually two suffixes. One is primary, as in *reparable*, and the other is secondary, as in *repairable*. Traditional usage among morphologists is to use the symbol '+' to mark the juncture between a stem and a primary affix and to use '#' to mark the juncture between a stem and a secondary affix. We will use these symbols to differentiate between the two types of *-able* here.

Other word pairs that show the opposition between +able and #able are *prefer+able* [préf(ə)rəbḷ] vs. *prefer#able* [prəférəbḷ] and *compar+able* [kámp(ə)rəbḷ] vs. *compar#able* [kampǽrəbḷ]. Phonologically, the stem in the first is stressed differently in combination with +able than it is in isolation: compare the pronunciation of *prefer+able* and *prefer*. This is typical of primary affixes. In addition, the semantics of the forms containing the primary affix +able are less direct, or less compositional, than the semantics of the forms containing the secondary affix #able. If we say two models are not *cómparable* (contains the primary affix +able), we mean that they are unlike. If we say that they are not *compárable* (contains the secondary affix #able), we mean that it is not possible, in a literal sense, to compare them. The semantics of forms containing the secondary affix #able are so predictable that they are often not even listed in dictionaries.

Looking at other +able vs. #able pairs, we discover other phonological characteristics of primary affixation. Consider the following words:

(13)   +able   #able
  a.   defensible   defendable
  b.   perceptible perceivable
  c.   divisible   dividable

Forms with +able in (13) exhibit allomorphy in the stem. They use a form that is recognizable from nouns, namely *defense, perception,* and *division,* instead of the citation form of the lexeme: *defend, perceive,* and *divide.* The fact that +able can be spelled *+ible* is unimportant here. Further examples of stem allomorphs occurring with the primary affix +able are given in the leftmost column of (14):

(14)   +able   base   #able   base
  a.   cultivable   cultiv   cultivatable   cultivate
  b.   educable   educ   educatable   educate
  c.   irrigable   irrig   irrigatable   irrigate
  d.   navigable   navig   navigatable   navigate
  e.   demonstrable demonstr   demonstratable   demonstrate

The second pair of columns in (14) show that the secondary affix #able differs from +able in attaching to the citation form of the lexeme: CULTIV-ATE, EDUCATE, IRRIGATE, NAVIGATE, and DEMONSTRATE.

Another difference between primary +able and secondary #able is that in words of the form X#*able*, X must be a transitive verb. In (14), *cultivate, educate, irrigate, navigate,* and *demonstrate* are all transitive. +able, on the other hand, is sometimes found on stems that are not transitive verbs, such as *poss-* (from Latin *posse* 'to be able'), as in *possible,* or *ris-* (from Latin *ride:re* 'to laugh'), as in *risible.*

We have said that we would de-emphasize etymology in our discussion of primary and secondary affixes, but here it becomes important. Many words with primary affixes – including *possible* and *risible* – were borrowed directly into English from French or Latin. They are fossilized; speakers have learned to use them, not created them on their own. However, even such fossilized examples as *possible* and *risible* are significant, because they illustrate another point: speakers are able to isolate both primary and secondary affixes when presented with words that contain them. *Possible* may be stored in the lexicon as a whole, but that does not mean that it is unanalyzable. A person, such as a child or a second-language learner, encountering *possible* for the first time will recognize it as an adjective because it ends in *-ible.*

In talking about the distinction between primary and secondary affixes, we have focused on suffixes. Prefixes can be primary or secondary as well. An example of a primary prefix is in+, and an example of a second-ary one is un#. Both mean 'not'. Phonologically, in+ has allomorphs. It surfaces as *ir-*, *im-*, *in-*, and *il-* in words like *irreplacable, immortal, inoperable*, and *illegal*. Un# does not have any allomorphs. *Un-* is of Germanic origin, with cognates in earlier stages of English, in contrast to *in-*, which came to English from Latin, through French.

in+, like +able, attaches to allomorphic stems:

(15)   in+   un#
    a. irregulable   unregulatable
    b. inviolable   unviolatable
    c. imperceptible   unperceivable
    d. indivisible   undividable

The stems it attaches to are stressed differently than the lexical stem of the corresponding lexeme:

(16)   in+   un#
    a. irréparable   unrepáirable   (cf. repáir)
    b. irrévocable   unrevókable   (cf. revóke)

And in+ may attach to non-lexical stems, while un# does not. (In+ attaches to lexical stems as well, for example, *impalpable, impossible*.)

(17) a. inept   *unept
      d. inert   *unert

Compare well-formed words prefixed with un# such as *ungodly, unhinge, unlike, unsteady*. *Godly, hinge, like,* and *steady* are all lexical stems. An exception to this general observation is *unkempt*. There is no lexical stem *kempt*. But as usual, this morphological fact about English finds an explanation when we look to the history of the word. Indeed, *kempt* used to exist. It was the past participle of the Old English word *cemban* 'to comb'.

Un# is also more productive than *in+*. You can test this claim yourself by thinking of some adjectives that do not usually have an in+ or un# prefixed form. Which sounds better, *inferocious* or *unferocious*? *inwet* or *unwet*? *indead* or *undead*?

If you are observant, you have noticed a final and very important difference between in+ and un#. The former has a special relationship with +able, and the latter with #able. Words with +able are prefixed with in+ and not un#, while words with #able are prefixed with un#.

We have included our discussion of primary and secondary affixes in a chapter that deals with the interaction between phonology and morphology because that is the context in which this distinction has most often been treated and because it led to important work in phonology. Our objective was not to give a comprehensive account of the topic, but rather to give an overview, and thus we have left many issues untouched. Under the heading "lexical phonology," phonologists have used the distinction between the two types of affixes to explore the possibility that different phonological rules apply at different levels of a morphological derivation (for a detailed overview, see Kenstowicz 1994). But as we have seen, primary and secondary affixes have semantic consequences as well. In particular, the semantics of primary affixes is less likely to be fully compositional. [Exercises 8 and 9]

■ 3.4   Linguistic Exaptation, Leveling, and Analogy

Rudes (1980) and Lass (1990) have both raised the question of what to do with "linguistic left-overs" (Rudes's term) or "linguistic junk" (Lass's term). In both cases, it has to do with morphemes that lose their semantic content or morphosyntactic function as a result of language change, and are left as contentless, functionless strings of phonemes floating around in the system. Rudes's and Lass's investigations on this question cover a variety of cases. They show that languages are in general intolerant of useless elements, and speakers reanalyze them as having a new role. Lass calls this process linguistic **exaptation**, extending a term originally coined by Stephen Jay Gould and Elizabeth Vrba in the context of evolutionary biology to the study of language change. In evolutionary biology, exaptation occurs when a structure or feature takes on a function different from that which it developed for through natural selection.[4]

Carstairs-McCarthy (1994) and Cameron-Faulkner and Carstairs-McCarthy (2000), in their work on inflectional classes and gender, and stem alternation, respectively, suggest that linguistic exaptation is pervasive. Carstairs-McCarthy considers the ingenuity that speakers show in assigning new roles to inflectional contrasts whose original purpose has been lost as being related to Clark's (1987: 2) Principle of Contrast, "Every two forms contrast in meaning." Linguistic exaptation is therefore a natural consequence of a core psycholinguistic mechanism that makes it easier for speakers to master complex inflectional systems or to learn the meanings of new vocabulary items, and we expect to find it playing an important role in the evolution of inflectional systems cross-linguistically.

One place that linguistic exaptation has occurred is Germanic (Lass 1990: 83–7). There, Indo-European vowel alternations within verbal paradigms came to encode the present/past distinction (e.g., English *write*, *wrote*). They had originally been used to encode aspectual distinctions. The case that we are going to focus on here, however, is the one discussed by Rudes: the development of the verbal suffix *-esc* in Romance. Our story begins with Latin, where the suffix *-sc* attached to sequences of verb stem plus theme vowel to form the inchoative aspect (which has the general meaning 'to begin to'). Compare the Latin verb form *paleo* 'I am pale', with its inchoative counterpart *palesco* 'I begin to pale'. Similarly, *amo* in Latin means 'I love', while *amasco* means 'I am beginning to love', and *florere* is 'to flower' while *florescere* is 'to begin to flower' (examples from Rudes 1980). English doesn't have a productive inchoative aspect, but we do have pairs like *white* and *whiten* 'become pale; begin to be pale' that illustrate the phenomenon.

Another term needs definition. A theme vowel, in the morphology of Latin, was a vowel that attached to the verb stem and can be seen as determining its inflection class. For example, one Latin verb class was identified by the theme vowel /a/. As Latin developed into the modern Romance languages, the inchoative suffix declined in productivity and eventually ceased to be productive at all. But while the semantic function of the affix eroded, the phonological material survived into various Romance languages, including Italian, Romanian, and dialects of Rhaeto-Romance. It was altered in one significant way: the theme vowel that originally fell between the verb stem and the inchoative suffix (which had varied among /a/, /i/, and /e/, depending on the verb) ceased to be identifiable as a theme vowel, and came to be segmented along with the suffix in one invariable form. In both Romanian and Rhaeto-Romance, the suffix was reanalyzed as *-esc*. In Italian, it was reanalyzed as *-isc*. At this stage, we had what Lass calls "linguistic junk," phonemes without a function. Within Lass's model, there were three possibilities regarding the future development of the suffix *-esc/-isc*:

i.   It could disappear entirely.
ii.   It could be kept as "marginal garbage," i.e., meaningless idiosyncrasies of the verbs already bearing it.
iii. It could be kept, but instead of being relegated to the marginal role of (b), it could be used for something new, taking on a new meaning or function.

What happened was (iii). It became productive once again, and is a distinctive feature of the verbal morphology of certain Romance languages. The question is, why?

Although the classical conception of morpheme is a pairing between sound and meaning, we have defined it as the smallest grammatically significant unit in a word. What makes the development of -esc in the Romance languages distinctive is that its function was phonological, rather than syntactic or semantic. It is meaningless. We can exemplify this by looking at the paradigm of a verb that contains this morpheme. As seen below, the suffix occurs in the first, second, and third person singular and third person plural of the present indicative of the verbs that have it (so-called fourth **conjugation** verbs) in Romanian, illustrated here by *a citi* 'to read' (Rudes 1980: 333). (It also occurs in these persons in the present subjunctive and imperative.) But the core meaning of verbs obviously does not change depending on what the subject is:

(18) 1sg citésc   1pl citím
      2sg citéşti   2pl citíţi
      3sg citéşte   3pl citésc

We can describe the new-found role of the -esc suffix in (18) as that of a stem-extender. The addition of -esc in the singular persons and in the third person plural had an effect on word stress. If not for the presence of the suffix, verbs like *a citi*, above, would be stressed on the root in the 1–3sg and 3pl forms, and on the suffix in the 1–2pl forms. Since the diachronic, or historic, development of vowels in Romanian and other languages varies depending on stress, this would have had the effect of creating two stems for many verbs. In other words, the renewed productivity of the suffix -esc long after its original meaning of inchoative aspect was lost is due to its regularizing effect on the stress of non-past verb forms. This is reflective of a larger tendency cross-linguistically. As languages evolve over time, they often show a preference for regularity within paradigms.

The story of the evolution of the Latin inchoative affix has another twist. Recall from above that one of the languages where it is productive and phonologically conditioned (appearing where stress would otherwise fall on the stem) is Italian. There, it is realized as [isk] or [iʃʃ], depending on the following vowel. From Italian, it was borrowed into Maltese.

Maltese is a Semitic language. Semitic is known for root-and-pattern morphology, as we saw in section 3.2.2 above. Over the course of time, however, the productive verbal morphology of Maltese has become affixal, with only relics of the original root-and-pattern type remaining (Hoberman and Aronoff 2003). One consequence of this change is that Maltese easily borrows verbs intact from other languages – especially

Romance. This is not so straightforward in other Semitic languages like Hebrew and Arabic. For example, as noted by Hoberman and Aronoff, Hebrew borrows nouns intact (e.g., *telefon*), but "verbs must follow the patterns dictated by the morphological patterns of the language's verbal morphology." Thus, one form of the verb 'to telephone' is *tilfen*.

When Maltese borrows Italian verbs containing the <-isc-> augment, it borrows the augment as well, which always takes the shape [iʃʃ], written <ixx>. This augment appears under the same conditions as in Italian: when stress would otherwise fall on the stem. But since the stress patterns of Maltese verbs differ from those of Italian verbs, these conditions are met in different tense, person, and number forms. This is shown in the box on this page. Following Hoberman and Aronoff, we have indicated stress, though the orthographies of neither language do so.

Italian and Maltese verb paradigms (Hoberman and Aronoff 2003)

	Italian	Maltese
	suggerisco	*issuġġeri*
Perfect		
sg 1	*suggeríi*	*issuġġeréjt*
sg 2	*suggerísti*	*issuġġeréjt*
sg 3m	*suggerí*	*issuġġeríxxa*
sg 3f	–	*issuġġeríet*
pl 1	*suggerímmo*	*issuġġeréjna*
pl 2	*suggeríste*	*issuġġeréjtu*
pl 3	*suggerírono*	*issuġġeréw [-éww]*
Imperfect		
sg 1	*suggerísco*	*nissuġġeríxxi*
sg 2	*suggerísci*	*tissuġġeríxxi*
sg 3m	*suggerísce*	*jissuġġeríxxi*
sg 3f	–	*tissuġġeríxxi*
pl 1	*suggeriámo*	*nissuġġeríxxu*
pl 2	*suggerite*	*tissuġġeríxxu*
pl 3	*suggeríscono*	*jissuġġeríxxu*
Imperative		
sg	*suggerísci*	*suggeríxxi*
pl	*suggerite*	*suggeríxxu*

In some cases, the augment appears in parallel forms in both languages, but in other cases, it doesn't. Maltese has borrowed a morpheme and the rule that governs its distribution, but not the verb forms themselves.

The tendency for languages to prefer regular paradigms over irregular ones explored above leads to what we call **leveling**. In other words, sound alternations that do not signal important differences in meaning are often eliminated. A classic example of leveling comes from Latin. In Prehistoric Latin, the stems of words like *colo:s* 'color' and *hono:s* 'worth' ended in -*s* throughout the nominal paradigm:[5]

(19) Prehistoric Latin
      Nominative   colo:s
      Genitive   *colo:s-es
      Dative   *colo:s-ei
      Accusative   *colo:s-em
      Ablative   *colo:s-i

Through regular sound change, intervocalic /s/ became /r/, a process called rhotacism:

(20) Old Latin
      Nominative   colo:s
      Genitive   colo:r-is
      Dative   colo:r-ei/-e:
      Accusative   colo:r-em
      Ablative   colo:r-e

At this point, the paradigm was characterized by two stems, one ending in /s/ (the nominative form) and one ending in /r/ (the oblique forms). Eventually, the final /s/ of the nominative form was replaced by /r/ in order to conform with the stem of the oblique forms. Note also that the /o/ preceding the /r/ of the nominative form shortened:[6]

(21) Classical Latin
      Nominative   color
      Genitive   colo:r-is
      Dative   colo:r-i:
      Accusative   colo:r-em
      Ablative   colo:r-e

A second example of leveling comes from the history of Spanish. Latin, from which Spanish developed, had a class of verbs that was characterized by a nasal infix in the present stem. The nasal infix was present in many forms of the verb, but was absent from others (notably the past tense):

(22) a.   rumpō   'I break'   *but* rūpī   'I broke'
      b.   vincō   'I defeat'   *but* vīcī   'I defeated'

In the history of Spanish, the /n/ infix has been generalized to all forms
of the verbs that once had it only in a limited number of forms of the
paradigm. Hence we have the Modern Spanish forms *romper* 'to break',
rompo 'I break', *rompí* 'I broke', and *vencer* 'to defeat', *venzo* 'I defeat',
vencí 'I defeated'.

When talking about leveling, we often use the term **analogy** (A is to
B as C is to D). The nasal infix of verbs that had it was generalized
throughout the paradigm by analogy with verbs that did not have such
an alternation at all and instead had a single form of the stem throughout
the paradigm. Analogy is usually expressed as two equations, with the
missing form represented by a **variable** X (A: B as C : X; solve for X).
Using Modern Spanish forms for simplicity, the equation would be as
follows, where *conocer* 'to know' is chosen randomly as a representative
of verbs that did not have the nasal infix, and X represents the form that
needs to be supplied by analogy to *conocí*:

(23) conocer : conocí
      vencer : X = vencí
      Informally, *conocer* is to *conocí* as *vencer* is to X, solved as *vencí*.

More broadly, four-part analogy is used to describe the generalization
or extension of a morphological pattern across (as opposed to within)
paradigms (Hock 1991: 168). Through it, whole classes of words come to
behave more similarly. Hock gives the example of English plurals. It is
because of four-part analogy that the plural of *cow* is *cows*, replacing the
earlier form *kine*. The new plural *cows* generalizes the plural formation
familiar from other words, such as *stone*, *stones*, as in (24). Here, as in
most instances of analogy, the pattern that serves as the basis of the
analogy (in this case the regular plural suffix -s) is more productive.

(24) stone : stone-s
      cow   : X = cow-s

Sometimes the older form that existed before analogical leveling re-
mains as a relic, used for special meanings. The old plural of *brother* is
brethren. These days, it is used only to refer to fellow-members of a church
or social organization, not to brothers in the literal sense of the term. The
title of a book about the United States Supreme Court, *The Brethren*, uses
this form to emphasize the special nature of the relationship among the
members of this most elite of groups.

Leveling and analogy are powerful forces in the development of languages over time. They are driven by a seemingly innate preference in speakers for regularity in the form of phonological and morphological similarity between members of a paradigm or a class of words. [Exercise 10]

■ 3.5 Morphophonology and Secret Languages

We now turn to a couple of secret languages, both of which are permutations of existing languages. They are only two examples of a phenomenon that is found around the world. Secret languages have been attested in English, French, Spanish, Dutch, Thai, Cuna (Sherzer 1970), and Haitian Creole, to name a few. They can be seen as examples of creative language use, and thus they should be considered external to the mental grammar. What, then, is the place of these languages in a book on morphology? In the examples that we present, speakers go from the existing language to the secret language through the regular application of phonological rules in what might be considered a morphological derivation. Secret languages thus can be seen as external evidence that nonetheless provides insight into morphology. They also exploit notions that are independently motivated in phonology and morphology, notably the syllable and onset.

One secret language you may already be familiar with is Pig Latin. In one variation, words that start with vowels are suffixed with *way* [wej]. Words that begin with a consonant or consonant cluster shift the entire onset sequence to the end, and then are suffixed with *ay* [ej]:

(25) igpay atinlay   'Pig Latin'
      eefray ormfay   'free form'
      inflectionway   'inflection'

When speakers manipulate words in this fashion, they make use of their subconscious knowledge of linguistic entities such as onset and nucleus. Language games are therefore an instructive union of phonology and morphology.

Another secret language is verlan [vɛʁlɑ̃], which is based on French. The word *verlan* is derived by reversing the syllables of *l'envers* [lɑ̃vɛʁ] 'the other way around'. Verlan works best with words of two syllables, because in these the two syllables can simply be reversed:

(26) Standard French   Verlan
    a. pourri [puʁi]   ripou [ʁipu]   'rotten' (gen. refers to cor-
                                                             rupt police)
    b. branché [bʁɑ̃ʃe]   chébran [ʃebʁɑ̃]   'plugged in, informed'
    c. pétard [petaʁ]   tarpé [taʁpe]   'cannabis joint'
    d. bagnole [baɲol]   gnolba [ɲolba]   'car'

Monosyllables are verlanized differently depending on whether they are open or closed. In open monosyllables, such as *pue* [py] 'stinks', the order of consonant and vowel is reversed, yielding forms like [yp]. Closed monosyllables, such as *femme* [fam] 'woman', are treated as if they end in a schwa (Bullock 1996: 185), and therefore as if they are underlyingly bisyllabic. The syllables are reversed, and the final vowel is dropped: [famə] → [fa.mə] → [mə.fa] → [mœf]. Note that the schwa is realized as [œ]; this is because schwa cannot be in stressed position in French. Trisyllabic words are put into verlan by changing the order of the syllables, but there are no fixed rules on how. For simplicity's sake, we are not going to deal with these forms here.

For Bullock (1996), the interesting question is how the phonology of secret languages like verlan compares to the phonology of the language they are based on. We see with verlan that it respects the basic syllable structure of French. Speakers of verlan, as with speakers of Pig Latin, know on some level prosodic entities such as onset, nucleus, coda, and syllable. On the other hand, Bullock and her predecessors who have looked at French secret languages note that the phonology of verlan is not the same as that of the standard language. We see in (26d) that [ɲ] is a licit onset in verlan. It is not in standard French. Furthermore, in verlan, only the liquids [l] and [ʁ] are permitted in the codas of polysyllabic words. Bullock presents the example of *bifton*, syllabified in standard French as *bif.ton*. In verlan, it would become *fton.bi* [ftõ.bi], because [f] cannot form the coda of a polysyllabic word. This example deviates from standard French phonology in another way: [ft] is not a possible onset in French. Finally, it is significant that we formulated the constraint on codas by referring to "polysyllabic words." In verlan monosyllables, consonants other than [l] and [ʁ] are welcome in word codas:

(27)   Standard French   Verlan
    a. disque [disk]   skeud [skød]   'CD, record'
    b. mec   [mɛk]   keum [kœm]   'man'

In natural languages we would not expect to find a coda constraint that holds in polysyllabic words but not monosyllables. It is intimately related to the fact that no verlan form is native, and no verlan speaker is mono-lingual. All of verlan is based on standard French, and speakers of verlan invariably speak French, if not natively, then under more natural condi-tions. According to Bullock, the 'rules' of verlan are artificial compared to those of the standard – and natural – language.

Returning to Pig Latin, in the version presented here, words that start with a consonant cluster postpose the entire cluster, then add the suffix -*ay*. But another version of the secret language postposes only the first letter (e.g., *losetcay* for *closet*). Any rule that operates on letters rather than on phonological entities such as onsets is unnatural. Languages are first and foremost oral, and orthographies are simply systems imposed on them by people. Because of characteristics like these, secret languages must be looked upon as somewhat artificial, and should not on their own be used to make conclusions about the workings of natural languages. **[Exercise 11]**

■ 3.6 Summary

This chapter has taken the reader on a brief tour of morphophonology. We began by investigating allomorphs, which were introduced in chap-ter 1, in greater detail. We then turned to the field of prosodic morpho-logy, selecting a few topics – minimal word constraints, root-and-pattern morphology, and reduplication – for discussion. This was followed by a descriptive, non-theoretical look at primary and secondary affixes and the differences between them. The section on linguistic exaptation, leveling, and analogy dealt with a completely different type of morphophonological phenomenon. It differs from other portions of this book in taking a historical perspective; for the most part we have been concerned with synchronic phenomena. Lastly we looked at some secret languages. In one sense, they are artificial, and thus should not be used on their own to draw conclusions about natural language. On the other hand, they reflect the regular application of rules that we often find in morphological derivation and provide external evidence for prosodic notions such as syllables and onsets.

In the Kujamaat Jóola portion of this chapter, we continue our focus on the interaction of morphology and phonology. We begin by investigating vowel harmony, a process that leads to the creation of allomorphs. We then take a look at the derivational affix in Kujamaat Jóola that expresses the notion 'from'. It differs from most derivational affixes in the language in that it is secondary, while most are primary.

■ Kujamaat Jóola Morphophonology

■ Vowel harmony

The most salient feature of Kujamaat Jóola's phonology happens to be something that is profoundly related to its morphology – **vowel harmony**. Vowel harmony is the agreement among vowels in a word with respect to a given feature, such as height, rounding, or backness. In Finnish, for example, vowels harmonize for backness. All the vowels in a given word must be either front or back. The vowel of a suffix therefore changes, depending on whether the vowels of the unsuffixed word are front or back, as shown by the partial nominal declension paradigms in (1):

(1)	'house'	'forest'
Nominative	talo	metsä
Partitive	talo-a	metsä-ä
Ablative	talo-lta	metsä-ltä
Inessive	talo-ssa	metsä-ssä
Elative	talo-sta	metsä-stä

The /a/ vowel of the case-endings may be realized as back [ɑ] or front |æ| (orthographic <ä>) depending on the backness of the preceding vowel.

In Kujamaat Jóola, there are two sets of vowels, tense and lax:

(2)   Tense   Lax

   i   u   i   u

      e   o   ɛ   ɔ

         ə   a

It may seem strange that schwa is classified as a tense vowel, but as explained by Sapir (1975: 3), the tense–lax distinction in West African languages is typically different from that of European languages. In West African languages, like Kujamaat Jóola, tense vowels are relatively higher and closer to center than lax vowels. This explains why schwa, which is higher and more central than /a/, is considered its tense counterpart. The difference between high tense and lax vowels is hard to perceive for foreigners, but the same is not true for the lower vowels, where distinctions are readily apparent.

All vowels in a word must be either tense or lax. Since tense vowels are dominant, whenever any tense vowel is found in a morphologically complex word, vowels that are otherwise lax become tense.[7] Harmony spreads out both ways from a tense vowel:

(3) Lax stem   Tense stem
     baj   'have!'   jitum   'lead away!'
     bajɛn   'cause to have!'   jitumen   'cause to lead away!'
     nibajɛnu   'I caused you   nijitumenu   'I caused you to be
                 to have'   led away'
     bəjul   'have from!'   jitumul   'bring!'
     nibəjulu   'I have for you'   nijitumulu   'I brought you'

As we see in (3), the process of vowel harmony leads to the existence of two allomorphs, or variants, for all morphemes with lax vowels that can occur together in a word with morphemes containing tense vowels. The stem /baj-/ 'have', for instance, may be realized as [baj-] or [bəj-]. The causative marker /-ɛn/ also occurs as [-en], and the subject prefixes /ni-/ 'I' and /u-/ 'you (sg)' as [ni-] and [u-]. Morphemes containing tense vowels, by contrast, never alternate, because tense vowels always win. The stem /jitum/ 'bring' always appears with the same shape, because its vowels are underlyingly tense. Likewise, the directional marker /-ul/ has an underlyingly tense vowel. Both /jitum/ and /-ul/ trigger vowel harmony, but are never affected by it. We can tell whether a morpheme's vowels are basically tense or lax by whether it alternates; alternating morphemes whose vowels are sometimes lax and sometimes tense are basically lax, while non-alternating morphemes whose vowels are always tense are basically tense.

The importance of the tense–lax distinction in Kujamaat Jóola goes well beyond phonology and morphology. In a 1975 article, Sapir explores the social role played by tense and lax vowel harmony. It turns out that vowel harmony is not absolute. Some speakers make relatively more use of it, and their speech is considered to be *kələ* 'big' by other Kujamaat Jóola speakers. Those who make relatively less use of it have speech that is called *mis* 'thin'. Big and thin are always relative terms. There are no speakers who have only tense vowels or only lax vowels. It is a *"quantitative tendency . . .* to favor lax or tense pronunciation" (Sapir 1975: 5; emphasis his) that determines whether someone's speech is 'big' or 'thin'.

As Sapir relates, he first became aware of the big–thin distinction while working with three Kujamaat Jóola speakers, AB (thin), KB (intermediate), and AK (big), on a dictionary project. The big–thin distinction came across in three general areas. Of highest importance was variation in the application of vowel harmony. While vowel harmony is obligatory in the language, the extent and degree of vowel harmony are not fixed. A tense morpheme might affect all of the vowels of a base, or only an adjacent vowel (Sapir 1975: 6):

(4)   pan + a + kan + do   'he will put it within'
    Full harmony: pənəkəndo
    Partial harmony: panakəndo

Likewise, vowels affected by vowel harmony "may only partially tense, that is, they may become tainted with tenseness, not completely tense." This fact is particularly interesting, because it shows that the phonological feature [tense] is not an all-or-nothing matter.

A second area in which the big–thin distinction is apparent is suffixes. Three Kujamaat Jóola suffixes have regional variants that differ in part in containing tense versus lax vowels. AB, Sapir's 'thin' consultant, used the lax variants of the three suffixes. KB, the intermediate consultant, used the lax variants of two, but the tense variant of the third. AK, Sapir's 'big' consultant, used the tense variants of two suffixes. The tense and lax variants of the third suffix were in free variation (Sapir 1975: 5):

(5) AB, thin   KB, intermediate   AK, big
     -ati   -əti   -əti   negative infinitive
     -ɛrit   -ɛrit   -urit   'never'
     -uli   -uli   -oli~-ɔli '1pl exclusive'

The final area in which the big–thin distinction showed up was vocabulary. There is quite a bit of lexical variation between the Kujamaat Jóola speakers of different villages. Sometimes lexical items are completely distinct. Sometimes, however, dialectal forms are only slightly different and are due in part or in full to the tense–lax distinction. Here are a few examples (Sapir 1975: 5):

(6) AB, thin   KB, intermediate   AK, big
     -kuuk   -kook   -kook   'take big handfuls of food'
     -kuntajɛn   -kuntejen   -kuntejen 'to kneel'
     bagɔri   bəgori   bəgori   'money'
     -map   -map   -məp   'shinny up a tree'

As seen in (6), the intermediate speaker shares the lax variant of 'shinny up a tree' with the thin speaker, but shares the tense variants of the other three forms with the 'big' speaker. For more detail on this and the other two areas that contribute to the big–thin distinction (harmony, variation in the form of suffixes), we refer the reader to Sapir (1975).

The big–thin distinction, as mentioned above, is not absolute, but instead must be seen as falling out along a continuum. A Kujamaat Jóola speaker will be able to place another's speech as being bigger or thinner than his or her own. Regional dialects differ in terms of their relative bigness or thinness, and Kujamaat Jóola speakers even refer to other languages as being various degrees of big. The fundamental role of the big–thin distinction in Kujamaat Jóola society is identification of someone else as being similar or different. The closer in speech a person is to another, the more likely that that person is "reliable and trustworthy, or at least predictable" (Sapir 1975: 10).

Below is part of Sapir's description of a conversation that he had with a Kujamaat Jóola woman, who characterized the speech of Sindian, the village of KB, Sapir's intermediate consultant, as being "heavy" and "hard to understand" (1975: 10). Sapir explains that to his knowledge, speakers of the woman's dialect didn't have any difficulty at all in understanding Sindian speech. It was more that Sindian speech was simply different:

> Although Sindian speech was heavy it was not nearly so heavy as Kasa, a different dialect where there are some real difficulties. In turn Kasa was not as heavy as Wolof, the dominant language of Sénégal, nor was Wolof as heavy as French. English, my speech and the official language of the neighboring ex-colony of Gambia, was to this woman unquestionably the heaviest speech imaginable, just kəkəkəkəkə like so many pied crows.

One of the most interesting aspects of the big–thin distinction is how speakers are placed in one category or another. Recall that Sapir had three consultants. One talked 'big' (AK) and one 'thin' (AB), and the third fell between them. As Sapir notes, there was nothing in the speech of the third individual that placed it closer to the 'thin' or the 'big' speaker. But this individual, KB, called his speech 'big', and the other two agreed. The reason for this had nothing to do with the tense–lax distinction. It was social. KB and AK, the 'big' speaker, were both Muslims, younger, and from outlying villages. Furthermore, they had worked with Sapir previously. AB, the 'thin' speaker, was Catholic, older, and from the administrative center. He was also fairly new to the project. Thus, KB's decision to call himself 'big' had more to do with his perceived similarities to AK than with the tenseness of his speech.

Because the decision to classify someone as 'big' or 'thin' is based in part on social factors, Kujamaat Jóola people can disagree about whether someone talks 'big' or 'thin'. Sapir gives another example, where two of his consultants disagreed over whether the speech of Kagnaru, a village, was 'big' or 'thin'. KB, who considered his speech 'big', classified Kagnaru's dialect as 'thin'. It was true that the people of Kagnaru spoke 'thinner' than KB. But they did not speak as 'thin' as AB. KB's labeling of their speech as 'thin' came more from the difficult relationship between his village and theirs. AB disagreed with KB. For him, the speech of Kagnaru was 'big':

> Although he admitted that Kagnaru might speak 'thinner' than [KB's village] they were both 'bigger' speakers than himself and he saw no reason why he should be grouped with them. And socially, didn't the Kagnaru people intermarry with [KB's village] and quarrel with villages connected to his own family? And weren't they for the most part Muslims? (Sapir 1975: 13)

This passage highlights sociolinguistics of the big–thin distinction.

This short excursion into vowel harmony and the metalinguistic role of the tense–lax distinction should convince the reader that a morphologist must also be a bit of a phonologist. An understanding of Kujamaat Jóola vowel harmony is essential if we are to identify the morphological building blocks of the language – the smallest grammatically significant pieces. We need to recognize, for example, that although the first singular subject prefix may be realized as [ni-] or [nɪ-], in both cases we are dealing with the same underlying form, /ni-/. What's more, if we were out in the field working with Kujamaat Jóola consultants, it would be essential to realize that variation in vowel harmony plays not a morphological role, but a social one. What we started off considering as a phenomenon at the intersection of Kujamaat Jóola phonology and morphology turned out to be a tripartite issue that brings together phonology, morphology, and sociolinguistics.

▓ A secondary affix

In section 3.3 we explored the distinction between primary and secondary affixes in detail. In Kujamaat Jóola, most deriviational affixes are primary. However, one is not: -ulɔ, -ul; -u. This affix, which is secondary, implies that an action begins away from the speaker; it can sometimes be translated 'from' or 'over'. Note that it has a tense vowel in two of its variants.

(7) a. pən- ə-   rin̦   dakar
FUT- 3AGR- arrive Dakar
'He will arrive at Dakar'   (speaker not at Dakar)

b. pən- ə-   rin̦   -u̱   dakar
FUT- 3AGR- arrive -OVER Dakar
'He will arrive at Dakar'   (speaker at Dakar)

(8) ni-   wɔnk- ul-   ɔ-   wɔnk
1AGR- call-   OVER- 3OBJ- REDUP
'I called him over'

We will introduce other verbal derivational affixes in chapter 5. We treat -u̱ 'from' separately from them because, as discussed by Sapir, its morphophonology sets it apart.

First, -u̱ 'from' can follow inflectional markers. This makes it exceptional not only among Kujamaat Jóola derivational affixes, but among derivational affixes cross-linguistically (see section 6.2.1).

(9) nə-   rin̦-   e   -u̱   -rin̦
3AGR- arrive- HAB- FROM- REDUP
'He habitually arrives from . . .'

-u̱ is also exceptional because it does not act as an added syllable on the verb stem for purposes of calculating the allomorphs of the infinitive. Recall from chapter 2 that infinitives, like nouns, are assigned to noun classes, and that monosyllabic stems take the class 3 prefix ε-, while stems of more than one syllable take the class 7 prefix ka-. As seen in (10), other derivational suffixes, represented here by the causative -εn, result in the infinitive being assigned to class 7, while -u̱ 'from' does not. (The causative suffix will be discussed in chapter 5.)

(10) εbaj   'to have' (class 3)
ebaju̱   'to have from . . .' (class 3)
kabajεn   'to cause to have' (class 7)

Finally, the derivational suffix -u̱ 'from' differs from other derivational affixes in that it does not reduplicate when the verb stem is reduplicated for verb emphasis (11b). Other derivational suffixes, again represented by the causative, do participate in reduplication:

(11) a. ni̱-   pu̱r- em-   pu̱rem
1AGR- leave- CAUSE -REDUP
'I caused to leave'

b. nị-   pụr-   ụlo-   pụr
   1AGR- leave- FROM-   REDUP
   'I left from'

All of these properties suggest that -ụ 'from' in Kujamaat Jóola is a secondary affix. In short:

- It can follow inflectional markers.
- It does not count as an extra syllable of the verb stem when determining which noun class the infinitive should be assigned to.
- It does not reduplicate along with the verb stem for verb emphasis.

These properties look almost nothing like the diagnostics we applied to English in section 3.3. There, secondary affixes differed from primary affixes in the following ways:

- Secondary affixes occur farther from the stem than primary affixes.
- Secondary affixes do not cause a stress shift, while primary affixes do.
- Secondary affixes are more likely than primary affixes to require their stem to be the citation form of the lexeme.
- Secondary affixes are likely to be more productive than primary affixes.

The only parallel between the two bulleted lists is between their first members. In both English and Kujamaat Jóola, secondary affixes appear farther from the stem than primary affixes.

This section has made two important points. The first is that the primary–secondary affix distinction is just as important in Kujamaat Jóola as in English. To rephrase this in broader terms, while much of this book focuses on English morphology, the facts you learn are readily transferable to the study of the morphology of other languages. The second important point is that the properties of the secondary affix -ụ 'from' in Kujamaat Jóola are different from those of secondary affixes in English. While the same phenomena appear in the morphology of language after language, the way we come to understand or describe those phenomena must often be different.

Exercises

1. Classical Greek (adapted from Nida 1965: 27)
   We introduced the formation of the Classical Greek nominative and
   genitive forms early in the chapter using two forms. More data are
   given below. For each pair, determine the basic form of the stem.
   What problems do the data raise?

Nominative		Genitive		Basic stem
a. aitʰiops	'Ethiopian'	aitʰiopos	'of an Ethiopian'	aitʰiop-
b. pʰleps	'vein'	pʰlebos	'of a vein'	pʰleb-
c. pʰulaks	'watchman'	pʰulakos	'of a watchman'	
d. aiks	'goat'	aigos	'of a goat'	
e. tʰɛs	'serf'	tʰɛtos	'of a serf'	
f. elpis	'hope'	elpidos	'of hope'	
g. ornis	'bird'	ornitʰos	'of a bird'	
h. gigas	'giant'	gigantos	'of a giant'	
i. hris	'nose'	hrinos	'of a nose'	

2. English (adapted from Nida 1965: 30)
   First, rewrite the following forms phonetically. Next, break the
   morphologically complex forms in column two into their constituent parts. Finally, determine the best underlying representation of
   the stems.
   a. hymn   hymnal
   b. solemn   solemnize
   c. condemn   condemnation
   d. damn   damnation
   e. autumn   autumnal

3. Huave, Mexico (Nida 1965: 17)
   Identify the morpheme that has allomorphs and describe their
   phonologically defined distribution.
   a. nahimb   'broom'
   b. nahndot   'dust'
   c. naʃei   'man'
   d. ahimb   'to sweep'
   e. -hta   'female'
   f. -ʃei   'male'
   g. nahta   'woman'
   h. ahndot   'to dust'

4. Zoque (Nida 1965: 21)

   Describe the phonological environment of all allomorphs in the following set of data. What accounts for their appearance?

   a. ʔəs mpama 'my clothes'   pama 'clothes'
   b. ʔəs ŋkayu 'my horse'   kayu 'horse'
   c. ʔəs ntuwi 'my dog'   tuwi 'dog'
   d. ʔəs mpoco 'my younger sibling'   poco 'younger sibling'
   e. ʔəs ŋkose 'my older sister'   kose 'older sister'
   f. ʔəs ncin   'my pine'   cin   'pine'

5. Tarahumara, Mexico (Nida 1965: 22)

   Describe the phonological environment of all allomorphs and then describe the type of assimilation that determines their distribution.

   a. mitʃiru   'to make shavings'
   b. mitʃiruku   'shavings'
   c. sikwitʃi   'anthill'
   d. sikwiki   'ant'
   e. ritu   'to be icy'
   f. rituku   'ice'
   g. reme   'to make tortillas'
   h. remeke   'tortillas'
   i. patʃi   'to grow ears of corn'
   j. patʃiki   'an ear of corn'
   k. opatʃa   'to be dressed'
   l. opatʃ'aka   'garment'

6. Tsotsil, Mexico (Nida 1965: 23)

   A. Identify all morphemes.
   B. List the morphemes that have allomorphs.
   C. Describe the phonological distribution of these allomorphs.

   Supplementary information: For this problem, it is preferable to consider that there are two different verbalizing suffixes, one consisting of the structure −V and the other of −VC.

   a. -k'uʃi   'to put a wedge in'   -k'uʃ 'wedge'
   b. -ʃik'u   'to put a prop under'   -ʃik' 'prop used beneath an object'
   c. -ʃoni   'to put a prop against' -ʃon   'prop used against an object'
   d. -vovi   'to go crazy'   vov   'crazy'
   e. -t'uʃi   'to become wet'   t'uʃ   'wet'
   f. -sakub   'to become white'   sak   'white'

g. -lekub   'to become good'   lek   'good'
h. -ʔik'ub   'to become black'   ʔik'   'black'
i. -tuib   'to become smelly' tu   'smelly'

7. Hausa, a language of Sudan, employs reduplication as a derivational process. If you examine the following data, however, you will see that reduplication in Hausa does not always follow the same pattern. Sort the following data out into sets based on reduplication type, then write Input > Output rules that express the reduplication processes in general terms (data from Hodge 1947: 39–40, presented in Nida 1965: 70–1).

a. ʔayàà   'tiger nut'   ʔayààʔayàà   'a similar but inedible nut'
b. sʔawrii   'retarded growth'   sʔàsʔawraa   'one of retarded growth'
c. mòòriyaa 'usefulness'   mammooraa   'usefulness'
d. gawčʔii   'brittleness'   gàggawsʔa   'a brittle one'
e. tawrii   'toughness'   tàttawraa   'a tough person'
f. muunìì   'ugliness'   mùmmuunaa   'an ugly person'
g. kʔumčii   'dense brush'   kʔunkʔumčii   'a narrow one or place'
h. gaašii   'hair'   gàlgaasàà   'hairy person'
i. mààtaa   'woman'   màlmaatàà   'eunuch'
j. kʔibàà   'fat'   kʔibààkʔibàà 'a fat person'

8. The following words are all suffixed with a primary affix (in bold). What are the changes to the stem triggered by the affix? Be as thorough as possible. Refer to the basic form of the stem in formulating your answer.
    a. diploma**cy**
    b. public**ize**
    c. different**ial**
    d. san**ity**
    e. electric**ity**
    f. pollut**ion**

9. Determine whether the following English suffixes are primary or secondary. Give arguments for your decision and support them with several examples.
    a. -ness   (e.g., loneliness)
    b. -ive   (e.g., permissive)
    c. -ous   (e.g., glorious)
    d. -ship   (e.g., partisanship)

10. A. Examine the following two paradigms. The one on the left is from early Old French and the one on the right is from later Old French. What difference among the stems of the various forms (in bold) in each paradigm has been leveled out? What differences still remain? Ignore cross-paradigmatic changes in the representation of vowels.

1sg **truef**   **treuve**
2sg **trueves**   **treuves**
3sg **trueve**   **treuve**
1pl **trovóns**   **trouvons**
2pl **trovéz**   **trouvez**
3pl **truevent**   **truevent**

B. Now compare the forms in the right column above with the Modern French paradigm given below. How has the stem (in bold) of the modern-day paradigm become even more regular?

1sg **trouve**   1pl **trouvons**
2sg **trouves**   2pl **trouvez**
3sg **trouve**   3pl **trouvent**

11. The forms in column B are drawn from a secret language based on French. The basic French forms are given in column A. Identify the morphological process that leads from the forms in column A to those in column B. Next, determine what inconsistency, if any, there is in the application of the rule (data from Bullock 1996: 186, citing Plénat 1983: 98–101).

	A	B	
a.	fois [fwa]	favwa	'time'
b.	poignet [pwaɲɛ]	pwavaɲavɛ	'fist'
c.	atelier [atəlje]	avatavəlavje	'studio'
d.	choir [ʃwaʁ]	ʃavwaʁ	'fall' (v)
e.	vieux [vjø]	vavjø	'old'
f.	derrière [dɛʁjɛʁ]	davɛʁjavə [sic]	'behind'
g.	poursuivait [puʁswivɛ]	pavuʁsɥavivavɛ	'was pursuing'
h.	pointe [pwɛ̃tə]	pavwɛ̃tavə	'point'
i.	bien [bjɛ̃]	bavjɛ̃	'well'
j.	ses yeux [sezjø]	savɛzavjø	'his/her eyes'
k.	point [pwɛ̃]	pavwɛ̃	'point'
l.	variable [vaʁiablə]	vavaʁjavaβlavə [sic]	'variable'
m.	client [klijã]	klavijavã	'client'

NOTES

1 A reader has pointed out that the exceptions of *la a* 'the a' and *la hache* 'the h' are reduced from *la letra a* 'the letter a' and *la letra hache* 'the letter h'. Additionally, names of letters are often linguistically exceptional. In Ancient Greek, for example, although letter names are nouns, they do not take any inflectional endings.

2 If you are not already familiar with the terms "weight-bearing consonant" and "mora," you do not need to learn them for this course. We mention them in this context only to be complete.

3 One of the first lessons a student learns in solving problems having to do with accent or stress is to count not from the beginning of a word, but from the end. Most stress systems work that way, though a few, such as that of Hungarian, count from the beginning.

4 Some of the discussion in this section is adapted from Fudeman (2004).

5 We thank Alan Nussbaum for help with the Latin data presented in this section.

6 In the case of both *color* and *honor*, the older nominative forms *colo:s* and *hono:s* hung around for a long time. We use *color* here because it has the advantage of attesting the old nominative *colo:s* while still showing the new nominative *color* at a relatively early date. Relic forms are relatively common when it comes to analogical change. Unlike regular sound changes, which can be accounted for in purely phonetic terms (cf. Latin rhotacism), analogy is sensitive to morphologic, syntactic, and semantic factors.

7 The picture is complicated by sociolinguistic factors, as we will see later in this section.

4 Derivation and the Lexicon

■ 4.1 The Saussurean Sign

Ferdinand de Saussure (1857–1913), one of the first modern linguists, believed that language was a system of signs. He defined a linguistic sign as an arbitrary pairing between what he called the *signifiant* 'signifier', a particular sequence of sounds, and the *signifié* 'signified', the concept that is denoted by the sound sequence. These three terms, **sign**, **signifier**, and **signified**, are still standard in linguistics.

Saussure distinguished between **motivated** and **unmotivated** signs. A sign is motivated to the extent that by inspection you can get clues as to what it means. A walk signal at a crosswalk is an example of a motivated sign, because the stylized image of a person walking indicates whether you should or should not cross the street. A stop sign is partially motivated. The fact that it has eight sides is arbitrary, but its red color is not – red is often associated in our culture with danger and a call to alertness. Red is also the color lit up on a traffic light when drivers are required to stop. The numeral 8 is an unmotivated sign. Nothing about its form represents the number eight.

Signs can lose their motivation: consider the name of the basketball team, the *Los Angeles Lakers*. The team started out in Minneapolis, Minnesota – the land of a thousand lakes; so it made perfect sense to call themselves the Lakers. Once the team moved to LA, then *Lakers* made no sense at all, though they kept the name and some have tried to make something of it by reinterpreting the first two letters of *Lakers* as having something to do with Los Angeles.

Motivation is not all-or-none and signs can be partially motivated. The name of the Ithaca Lakers of central New York, a local *baseball* team, is not a fully motivated sign. After all, when we hear the name the *Lakers*, we think first of basketball. But we don't want to say that the name *Ithaca Lakers* is completely unmotivated, either, because it is obvious that this particular name was chosen because Ithaca, like Minneapolis, is set in a region of lakes. Since people can still see the *lake-* in *Lakers*, and even see it from the field where they play, on a good day, we say that *Ithaca Lakers* is a partially motivated sign.

■ 4.2   Motivation and Compositionality

We can relate motivation to the logical notion of **composition** or **compositionality**. We say that something is logically compositional if it is defined entirely in terms of its parts. For example, the word *doghouse* is compositional, at least in its original sense, because its meaning is derivable from its two components, *dog* and *house*. Because it is purely compositional, we could also call *doghouse* a motivated sign (although if we break it down, the sound shapes of *dog* and *house* are purely arbitrary and unmotivated). But in the expression *in the doghouse* 'in a state of disfavor or repudiation', the word is not compositional, since there is nothing in particular about doghouses to suggest that an occupant of one should be in disfavor. **[Exercises 1–2]**

Another example of a compositional form is the Kujamaat Jóola dubitive-incompletive, which expresses an action that was never completed or whose existence is in doubt. For emphasis, the dubitive-incompletive suffix (INC) is doubled (1b). It can even be repeated several times (Thomas and Sapir 1967: 350, note 2):

(1) a. ni-   ŋar- ɛːn
       1SG.SUB-take- INC
       'I was taking'
    b. ni-   ŋar- ɛːn- ɛːn
       1SG.SUB-take- INC- INC
       'I was taking (emphasis on incompletive aspect of action)'

Expressing emphasis through doubling should be considered compositional.

The following set of English words is particularly significant in light of partial motivation and compositionality:

(2)   behead   'to remove someone's head'
      befriend 'to make yourself a friend to someone'
      besiege   'to lay siege to'
      bewitch   'to place under one's power as if by magic'

Our first response to this list is to say that these are all morphologically complex words formed with the prefix *be-*. But are they motivated signs? In each case, the prefix *be-* has a different effect on the meaning of the stem (*-head, -friend, -siege, -witch*). In the word *behead*, it indicates 'deprive of' (as in the obsolete verbs *beland* and *belimb*), but it means nothing of the sort in the other forms. This suggests that these forms are not completely motivated. However, the meanings of the stems in (2) are never completely lost, simply transformed. The forms are therefore partially motivated.

The question of whether or not the forms in (2) are compositional is more difficult and depends in large part on our approach to linguistic analysis. It is undoubtedly the case that formation of words with the prefix *be-* is no longer productive in English. Some linguists will nevertheless want to analyze forms like *behead* and *bewitch* as having two parts. Our approach, however, will be to say that these forms are stored whole in the lexicon – they are memorized. We would say the same for forms like *crayfish, raspberry, boysenberry,* and *cranberry.*[1] While the isolatability of the stems *fish* and *berry* make it possible to isolate *cray-, rasp-, boysen-,* and *cran-* as affixes, doing so is largely an academic exercise; we will assume so, at least, until the opposite can be shown by experimental means.

The preceding data lead into a major issue to be addressed in this chapter: the relationship between derivation and the lexicon. Recall that although some linguists consider the lexicon to be equivalent to the morphology, our definition of lexicon is a list of forms that speakers of a language know or memorize. One question we need to ask is whether lexemes formed by productive derivational processes are ever stored in the lexicon. We will address this question explicitly in sections 4.2.1 on compounding and 4.2.2 on zero-derivation. In the remaining sections of 4.2 we will present various types of derivational processes, so that students can become familiar with them.

■ 4.2.1   Compounding

One type of derivational process that we have already seen is compounding. Here are some basic examples:

(3)   English compounds
      tool + bar
      amusement + park
      puppy + love
      coffee + house

To give a more extreme example, if someone asks us what Violet does for a living, we might respond:

(4)   She's a high voltage electricity grid systems supervisor.

There is evidence that *high voltage electricity grid systems supervisor* is a single noun. First, its distribution matches that of any other noun, so we can insert it into phrases like [a good N] or [N for hire]. Second, *high voltage electricity grid systems supervisor* behaves as a single unit for the purposes of ***wh*-movement**. Question–answer pairs that break it up are at the very least awkward. In chapter 2 we related this characteristic of words to the notion of lexical integrity:

(5)   a.   Q: Which electricity grid systems supervisor did you see?
           A: ?The high voltage one.
      b.   Q: Which systems supervisor did you see?
           A: *The high voltage electricity grid one.
      c.   Q: Which supervisor did you see?
           A: *The high voltage electricity grid systems one.

Contrast these with syntactic strings of modifier plus noun which are easily broken up, as shown in (6):

(6) Q: Which supervisor did you talk to?
     A: The tall one.

Continuing with the notion of lexical integrity, we can ask whether it is possible to describe part of the string *high voltage electricity grid systems supervisor* with a modifier. When we try, the result is very awkward (7):

(7) ?A very high voltage electricity grid systems supervisor

The most natural interpretation of (7) is the figurative one whereby *very high voltage* is used as an adjectival phrase modifying a smaller compound [electricity grid] giving the intermediate form *very high voltage electricity grid*, which in turn modifies [systems supervisor], giving the entire form in (7).

Finally, we can point to the structure of *high voltage electricity grid systems supervisor* as evidence that it is a single noun formed by compounding. Words in English are generally head-final, meaning that the lexical category of the form as a whole matches that of its final constituent. A *dogsled* is a kind of sled, not a kind of dog; the *Red River Valley* is a valley, not a color or a body of water; and affixed words like *pollution* take on the lexical category of the suffix (in this case, noun) rather than that of the stem (*pollute*, a verb).[2] As speakers of English we know this, and without ever having heard *high voltage electricity grid systems supervisor* before, we know it designates a type of supervisor. Phrases, in contrast to words, are less likely to be head-final. The head of [NP John's walking into work without a tie] is *walking*, not *tie*, and the head of [NP the house on the hill] is *house*, not *hill*.

Having established that *high voltage electricity grid systems supervisor* is a single word of the category N, we can ask ourselves, "Does this noun live in my lexicon?" Probably not. This compound is formed by a very productive process and there is nothing irregular involved in it. It is absolutely compositional and fully motivated. **[Exercise 3]**

Words like this that are used but not stored are called **nonce forms** or **hapax legomena** (*hapax legomenon* in the singular). Nonce means 'a particular occasion', and hapax legomena is a Greek term meaning 'said once' that is used to refer to words that occur only once in the recorded corpus of a given language. These are words that somebody made up, used, and then threw away. The existence of nonce forms is one type of evidence that speakers create words on the fly as they speak.

In discussing compounds, linguists sometimes use the terms **endocentric** and **exocentric**. These terms are related to the notions of motivation and compositionality presented earlier. An endocentric compound is one that has a head. The head expresses the core meaning of the compound, and it belongs to the same lexical category as the compound as a whole. For example, *goldfish* is an endocentric compound. It has a head, *fish*, which determines both the meaning and the lexical category – noun – of the compound as a whole. Compounds whose lexical category or meaning are not determinable from the head are exocentric. *Figurehead* is just such a compound, because it is not a type of head. Whether a compound is endocentric or exocentric is sometimes a matter of opinion. Fabb (1998: 67) gives the example of *greenhouse*, which is endocentric if you think of it as a type of house, but exocentric if you do not.

(8) Endocentric compounds
     jackknife
     board game
     bluebird
     high chair
     sailboat

(9) Exocentric compounds
     funny farm
     lazybones
     loony bin
     scarecrow
     pickpocket

Identify each of the following compounds as either endocentric or exocentric. For answers, turn the page.

a. lawmaker
b. make-up (i.e., cosmetics)
c. no-hitter
d. mainstream
e. waxwing
f. playpen
g. aftertaste
h. graveyard

◼ 4.2.2   Zero-derivation

Further evidence that derived words are not necessarily found in the lexicon comes from first language acquisition. While English-speaking adults typically have production vocabularies of 20,000 to 50,000 words, children's vocabularies are much smaller, ranging from about 50–600 words at age 2 to about 14,000 at age 6. To make up for this, children frequently coin new words (Clark 1995: 393, 399–401). One way in which children do this is to use **zero-derivation**, or **conversion**, a productive derivational process in English. Zero-derivation changes the lexical category of a word without changing its phonological shape. The following are all examples of novel verbs formed by 2- to 5-year-olds by zero-derivation (examples taken from Clark 1995: 402):

(10) a. SC (2;4, as his mother prepared to brush his hair): *Don't hair me.*
     b. JA (2;6, seated in a rocking chair): *Rocker me, mommy.*
     c. SC (2;7, hitting baby sister with toy broom): *I broomed her.*
     d. SC (2;9, playing with toy lawnmower): *I'm lawning.*
     e. DM (3;0, pretending to be Superman): *I'm supermanning.*
     f. FR (3;3, of a doll that disappeared): *I guess she magicked.*
     g. KA (4;0, pretending to be a doctor fixing a broken arm): *We're gonna cast that.*
     h. RT (4;0): *Is Anna going to babysitter me?*
     i. CE (4;11): *We already decorationed our tree.*
     j. KA (5;0): *Will you chocolate my milk?*

The fact that children, as well as adults, spontaneously create verbs like *to lawn* or *to broom* that they have never heard before tells us that there is more to morphology than the lexicon – there is also a generative component. Furthermore, the fact that the verbs in (10) were uttered once does not imply that they were automatically inserted into the speaker's lexicon, as we would be able to show if later on we asked the same children to describe similar situations and it turned out that they did not use the nonce forms in (10).

We must mention directionality of derivation here. How do we know that a verb is derived from a noun or vice versa? If it is not obvious, we must research the answer in a good dictionary, one that contains etymologies.

Answers to endocentric–exocentric exercise:

a. lawmaker: endocentric
b. make-up: exocentric
c. no-hitter: exocentric
d. mainstream: exocentric
e. waxwing: exocentric
f. playpen: endocentric
g. aftertaste: endocentric
h. graveyard: endocentric

It may happen that over time, a word formed by zero-derivation or any other productive derivational process becomes lexicalized. So it is with the English verbs *chair*, *leaf*, *ship*, *table*, and *weather*. Another example of a verb that was originally derived via zero-derivation but is now listed in the lexicon is *mail*. In this case, we know that the noun came first because it was borrowed from the French *male* (Modern French *malle*) 'bag, trunk', referring to the receptacle in which letters were carried. Evidence that the verb is now stored in the lexicon comes from its frequency, as well as from the fact that its existence blocks the coining of potential but non-occurring derived forms, such as **mailbox* 'to put in a mailbox in order to send to someone' (e.g., **I'm going to mailbox this parcel*). (We say more about blocking in section 8.3.5.)

■ 4.2.3   Affixation

The next type of derivational process we consider here is affixation. We have already looked at a number of affixes, so in this section we will focus on a few particular affixes, the types of stems they attach to, and the words they produce. We will also build on the discussion of chapter 3 on primary and secondary affixes by exploring other restrictions we find on combinations of affixes.

Recall first from section 1.2 that affixation may involve prefixes, suffixes, infixes, and perhaps circumfixes. Since our primary focus in this section will be on English, we will be dealing only with the first two types, although as you can see in the box, English does have a productive infixing process that incorporates swearwords.

Prefixes:	*un* + do
	cyber + dieter[3]
	hemi + sphere
Suffixes:	rough + *age*
	arachno + *phobia*
	cut + *ie*
Infixes:	fan + *fuckin* + tastic
	abso + *effing* + lutely
Circumfix:	Kujamaat Jóola *u-* . . . *-al* (first person plural inclusive subject):
	u-bɔɲ-ɛːn-ɛːn-ɔrut-*al*-ɔ 'We had not yet sent him'

We can characterize the stem an affix attaches to as bound or free and as belonging to a particular lexical category. Take the following words formed via prefixation with *re-*:

(11) a. reignite   d. reanalyze
      b. reboot   e. recertify
      c. reread   f. rebuild

Re- attaches to stems belonging to the lexical category Verb. It produces words that are also verbs. All of the stems to which it attaches in the preceding examples are free. *Ignite, boot, read, analyze, certify,* and *build* may all stand alone; they do not need to bear a prefix or suffix. The same cannot be said for all stems that seem to bear the prefix *re-*, based on their meaning. The following words are all formed with *re-*, which imparts a sense of repetition or doing again. Yet the stems are unable to stand on their own. They are bound.

(12) a. repeat
      b. resuscitate
      c. relegate

What is the lexical stem of each the following words? Is the lexical stem bound or free? For answers, turn the page.

a. bookish   e. comfy
b. notable   f. generalization
c. unfathomable   g. inky
d. monstrous   h. archaism

Answers to the bound–free exercise:

a. book; free
b. not(e); free (here let pronunciation be your guide; don't be misled by the fact that *not-* is not spelled with an *e* in *notable*)
c. fathomable; free (it is also possible to consider the root *fathom* to be the lexical stem, if you are considering suffixation of *-able* as well as prefixation of *un-*)
d. monstr-; bound (unless we interpret *monstr-* as a variant of *monster*)
e. comf-; bound
f. generalize; free (*general* is the stem – free – of *generalize*)
g. ink; free
h. archa-; bound

While some of these forms, including *monstrous* and *archaism*, are best considered as being stored whole in speakers' lexicons, speakers recognize that they are made up of more than one morph. Without having seen *monstrous* before, you know that it is an adjective, on the basis of its similarity with forms like *glorious*, and you know that *archaism* is a noun, on the basis of words like *fetishism*.

Sometimes an affix may attach to stems of more than one category. One such affix is *-ish*. It may attach to nouns, as in *prudish, bookish, girlish,* or *childish,* adjectives, as in *oldish* or *smallish,* or verbs, as in *ticklish.* In each case, the resulting form is an adjective. **[Exercise 4]**

So far we have mentioned stem type (bound vs. free) and lexical category as two factors that can constrain affixation. Another type of restriction we find is on the combination of affixes. Aronoff and Fuhrhop (2002) observe that many English speakers cannot say **dressingless,* though both *-ing* and *-less* are secondary suffixes, and the word has a logical meaning: **a dressingless* salad. The perceived ungrammaticality of *dressingless* by those speakers can be related to the fact that the combination **-ingless* in English is vanishingly rare (a notable exception is *meaningless*).

In German, Aronoff and Fuhrhop observe another type of restriction on affixation. The following examples show how affixation can be recursive. In (13a) we have a verbal stem 'teach', which can be made into a noun with the addition of *-er*. This noun, in turn, can be made into an adjective, which can then be turned into a complex noun, *Lehrerhaftigkeit* 'teacherlikeness'.

(13)   a.   lehr(en) 'teach' (verb) →
     b.   Lehrer 'teacher' (person term) →
     c.   lehrerhaft 'like a teacher' (adjective) →
     d.   Lehrerhaftigkeit 'teacherlikeness'

Significant here is the fact that *Lehrerhaftigkeit* cannot now undergo further derivational affixation. In fact, no noun in *-igkeit* can. It is what Aronoff and Fuhrhop call a **closing suffix**. The existence of closing suffixes in German means that affixation in that language can never be as recursive as German compounding, which can go on and on, just like in English. (Recall the word *high voltage electricity grid systems supervisor* from earlier in this chapter.)[4]

■ **4.2.4   Other derivational processes**

So far we have looked at compounding, zero-derivation, and affixation. What are other examples of derivational processes?

4.2.4.1   Blending

One type of derivational process that is common in English is **blending**. Blends, also called **portmanteau** words, are formed by combining parts of more than one word.[5] Speakers may be aware that a word has been formed via blending, as with *spork* (< *spoon* + *fork*), or the history of the word may be obscured, as with *motel* (< *motor* + *hotel*). Further examples of blends are given below:

(14)   a.   smog   <   smoke + fog
     b.   chunnel   <   channel + tunnel
     c.   chortle   <   chuckle + snort
     d.   bit   <   binary + digit

Neither blending nor any of the other derivational processes we have been talking about are limited to English, of course. While blends are rare or absent in many Indo-European languages, they are common in Hebrew, examples of which are given below (Bat-El 1996), and Japanese:

(15)   a.   prígurt   'fruit yogurt'   <   prí 'fruit' + yógurt 'yogurt'
     b.   kadurégel   'football'   <   kadúr 'ball' + régel 'foot'
     c.   maškár   'cold drink'   <   mašké 'drink' + kár 'cold'

d.	kalcéfet	'easy-to-make ice cream'	< kál 'easy, light' + kacéfet 'whipped cream'
e.	ramzór	'traffic light'	< ramáz 'to hint' + ʔor 'light'
f.	pomelít	'hybrid of pomelo and grapefruit'	< poméla 'pomelo' + ʔeškolít 'grapefruit'
g.	šmanmúx	'dumpy'	< šmanmán 'plump' + namúx 'short'

Blending is an example of creative language use. It generally does not adhere to strict constraints, as does affixation. For example, we note in (14d) that *bit* comes from 'binary digit'. Nothing in the grammar would have prevented speakers from coining the word **binit* from the same parts. The word-formation processes discussed below, including acronym formation, clipping, folk etymology, and backformation, are treated by linguists separately from *productive* derivational (lexeme formation) phenomena.

4.2.4.2 Acronyms

Acronyms are formed by taking the initial letters of a string of words and combining them to form a new one. In the study of human language, speech must always be considered primary, and writing secondary, and the fact that acronym formation depends on orthography and not pronunciation means that it is, in a sense, an artificial process, external to the general phenomenon of lexeme formation. If you question our statement that acronym formation is orthographically based, just say (16c) *NATO* aloud, followed by *North Atlantic Treaty Organization*. The pronunciation of the *A* and *O* reflects the name of the letters, not the initial sounds of the words.

Speakers may be aware or unaware that a particular form originated as an acronym. How many acronyms on the left would you have been able to break down into their parts on the right?

(16) a. scuba   self-contained underwater breathing apparatus
      b. radar   radio detecting and ranging
      c. NATO   North Atlantic Treaty Organization
      d. AIDS   Acquired Immune-Deficiency Syndrome
      e. FBI   Federal Bureau of Investigation

FBI differs from the other acronyms in (16) in being pronounced letter by letter, rather than as a word *[fbi], *[fbaj]. While in practice, people still refer to it as an acronym, some linguists prefer to call it an initialism.

The following French words are derived from acronyms, as well:

(17) a. DEUG   Diplôme d'études universitaires générales
          [dœg] or [døg] (type of diploma)
      b. ONU   Organisation des Nations Unies
          [ony]   (United Nations)
      c. sida   Syndrome d'Immunodéficience Acquise
          [sida]   (AIDS)
      d. ovni   Objet volant non identifié
          [ɔvni]   (Unidentified flying object)
      e. PDG   Président directeur général
          [pedeʒe]   (head of a company)

Like *FBI*, *PDG* is pronounced letter by letter.

A characteristic of acronyms in some languages is that they can serve as the base for further morphological operations, particularly affixation. The following are examples from French:

(18) a. cégétiste someone from the *CGT* (*Confédération générale du travail*)
      b. énarque   former student at the *ENA* (*École nationale d'administration*)
      c. onusien   bureaucrat of the United Nations (French *ONU*)
      d. sidologue doctor or biologist specializing in AIDS (French *sida*)
      e. antisida   AIDS prevention

4.2.4.3 Clipping

Clipping is the creation of a new word by **truncation** of an existing one. Many nicknames are formed via this process:

(19) Rob (< Robert)
      Trish (< Patricia)
      Sue (< Susan)

Words may also be formed via clipping, as with *bra* (< *brassiere*), *ad* (< *advertisement*), *co-ed* (< *co-educational*), *typo* (< *typographical error*), or *fan* (< *fanatic*).

4.2.4.4 Folk etymology

Some words are formed via **folk etymology**. This happens when speakers of a language reinterpret a form – typically a borrowing from another language – on the basis of words or morphemes that already exist in the language. Examples of folk etymologies are given in (20):

(20)   cockroach   <   Spanish *cucaracha*
        woodchuck   <   a pre-existing Algonquian form (e.g., Cree *wuchak*)
        witch hazel <   *wych* [= weak] *hazel*

Folk etymology is a historical process of reanalysis. We include it here because it is a source of words, but it is not a true derivational process.

4.2.4.5   Backformation

Backformation is the creation of a word by removing what appears to be an affix. Like folk etymology, it is an example of historical reanalysis and is not a productive derivational process. It is responsible for the occurrence of words such as *surveil*, from *surveillance*, or *liposuct*, from *liposuction*. Some very familiar words were originally derived by backformation. *Peddle* and *edit* postdate *peddler* and *editor*, although the uninitiated might guess that it was the other way around. Historically, *cherry* comes from Old Norman French *cherise*, minus the [s], which English speakers mistook for the plural affix. Similarly, *pea* comes from *pease*, which speakers also reanalyzed as a plural.

In order to recognize whether a form has resulted from backformation or clipping, it is often necessary to know its history.

The words in column B were derived from the forms in column A. Identify the word-formation processes responsible for each.

	A	B
a.	garage, sale	garage sale
b.	refuse + nik	refusenik
c.	promenade	prom
d.	baby-sitter	baby-sit
e.	blanket (n)	blanket (v)
f.	cheese, hot dog	cheese dog
g.	asparagus	sparrow grass
h.	under + estimate	underestimate
i.	photo opportunity	photo op
j.	chocolate, alcoholic	chocoholic
k.	mothers against drunk driving	MADD

Answers: a. compounding, b. affixation (suffixation), c. clipping, d. backformation, e. zero-derivation or conversion, f. blending, g. folk etymology, h. affixation (prefixation), i. clipping, j. blending, k. acronym formation

■ 4.3   Derivation and Structure

Having considered the issue of lexical storage of derived forms, let's go back to the notion of derivation and structure. We can schematize derivation as follows:

(21) Input   → Output
      Lexeme X   Lexeme Y

If we can have lexeme X as an input and lexeme Y as an output, then it should also be possible to take lexeme Y as an input to a second function:

(22) Input   → Output
      Lexeme Y   Lexeme Z

This is precisely what we do when we form words like *unfriendly*:

(23) Function 1: add *-ly*
      friend   → friendly
      Function 2: add *un-*
      friendly   → unfriendly

We can even go on to form *unfriendliness* from *unfriendly* via a function that adds *-ness*. In each case, the output of one derivation serves as the input to the next.

To determine the order of functions leading to a form, it helps to consider other words that contain the same parts. Consider the example of *unfriendly*. *Un-* attaches to nouns only in exceptional cases (e.g., *uncola*). However, it regularly attaches to adjectives. We use this fact in determining that the function 'Add *-ly*', which forms adjectives, must come before the function 'Add *un-*'. In the case of *unfriendly* you can determine the order of functions even more easily because you already know that *friendly* is a possible word, but *unfriend* is not.

Let's go back to the compound we came across earlier: *high voltage electricity grid systems supervisor*. This compound clearly has an internal structure. [High voltage] is a compound, as are [electricity grid] and [systems supervisor]. [[High voltage] [electricity grid]] is also a compound, and in turn, [[[high voltage] [electricity grid]] [systems supervisor]]. What we have done is take English words, make compounds of them, and then use those compound words again to yield further compound words. The output of the first compounding function serves as the input to the second and third compounding functions.

The same occurs with any kind of affix, and this is what gives derivational morphology its power. In some sense we can think of derivation as always being binary. We take a form and apply a function to it. We then take the output of that function and perform another function on it. We can keep on going, getting bigger and bigger things, simply by adding one thing at a time. (When we get to inflection, we will see that this is not always the case.)

The fact that speakers of many languages can add phonological material to either end of a word sometimes leads to complex structures. Take the two English words in (24):

(24) a. reinterpretation
      b. poststructuralist

These words have the following structures:

(25) a. [[re- [interpret]$_V$]$_V$ -ation]$_N$
      b. [post- [[[structur]$_N$ -al]$_A$ -ist]$_A$]$_A$

(25a) tells us that *reinterpretation* is the act of reinterpreting, not *re-* the act of interpreting. We start out with a verb, *interpret*, form a new verb via the prefix *re-*, and finally form a noun by adding the suffix *-ation*. In the case of *poststructuralist*, we start out with the noun *structure*, make an adjective via the adjectival suffix *-al*, create a new adjective by adding the suffix *-ist*, and a further one by adding the prefix *post-*. *Poststructuralist* (*structuralist*, too) can in turn be made into a noun by what we saw earlier, zero-derivation.

The bracketing structures in (25) are convenient, in part because they are so compact. But the structure of morphologically complex words is made most clear when we use tree diagrams, like the following:

(26)

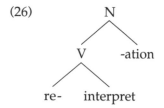

This diagram clearly shows that *re-* and the verb *interpret* form a unit, a verb, which attaches to the noun-forming suffix *-ation*. In order to draw a tree diagram, it is first necessary to break a word down into its components and to fully understand how they fit together.

> Draw tree diagrams of the following words. For answers, turn the page.
>
> a. lawnmower
> b. biodefenses
> c. insightful

The following argument demonstrates that even identical strings may have distinct structures. Consider the structure of the two words *pseudonaturalistic* and *supernaturalistic*:

(27) a.   b.

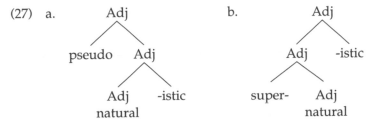

In both cases we start out with the adjective *natural*, which we purposely have not broken down into *nature* and *-al*, although we could have. In (27a) we first make a new adjective, *naturalistic*, which we then modify with the prefix *pseudo-*, yielding a word with the meaning 'falsely naturalistic'. In (27b), however, we take the adjective *natural* and add the prefix *super-* to it, giving *supernatural* 'pertaining to an existence outside the natural world'. It is to this form that we add the suffix *-istic*. English morphology is such that we could form a different *supernaturalistic*, this time with the same structure as *pseudonaturalistic* in (27a). This *supernaturalistic* would mean 'really naturalistic'.[6]

Combining prefixation and suffixation leads to other potentially ambiguous forms in English. Three famous examples are given in (28):

(28) a. undressed
     b. unpacked
     c. unzipped

The ambiguity of the forms in (28) is due to the fact that the prefix *un-* has at least two distinct roles in English, depending on what it attaches to. When prefixed to a verb, *un-* is a so-called **reversative** with the basic meaning 'undo the action of the verb'. If you *unpack* a suitcase, you return the suitcase to the state it was in before the packing action took place. If you *untie* a package, you return it to the state it was in prior to being tied. When attached to adjectives, including participial

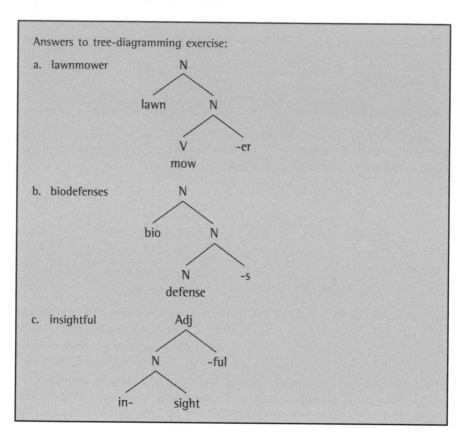

Answers to tree-diagramming exercise:

a. lawnmower

b. biodefenses

c. insightful

adjectives like *wounded* or *stressed*, *un-* means 'not'. If a soldier leaves the battlefield *unwounded*, it is not the case that he was first wounded and then unwounded, because it is impossible to *unwound* a person (we say instead that we *cure* them). The soldier in question is 'not wounded'. This second *un-* is the one we see in forms like *unafraid*, *uncertain*, and *un-American*.

Our analysis of an example like *unzipped* (28c) depends on our interpretation of its prefix *un-*. One possibility is that its structure is as follows:

(29) [[un-zip(p)] ed]

Here the prefixation of the reversative *un-* yields the meaning 'cause to be zipped no longer'. The suffix *-ed* is then added to create the past tense or the past participle. The second possibility is that *unzipped* has the structure in (30):

(30) [un- [zipped]]

This form has the meaning 'not zipped', or, in the case of a computer file, 'having never been stored on a zip disk'. The crucial semantic distinction between (29) and (30) is that only (29) requires that a zipping action have taken place at some past point. Structurally, (29) and (30) differ in the ordering of the affixation processes. In short, morphological structure depends not only on the elements you use, but on the order in which the elements have been applied.

Let's look at some other words. Is *unwashed* ambiguous? It is not; we cannot *unwash* something. *Unwashed* can only mean 'not washed'. Similarly, *undisturbed* can only mean 'not disturbed'. The only word we know of that works the other way is *unraveled*. Although English speakers do not use it very often, there is a verb *ravel*. But it means the same thing as *unravel*: 'separate or undo the threads or fibers of something'. As a result, if something is unraveled, it cannot mean 'not raveled'. It can only mean that it has come undone. **[Exercises 5–7]**

Bloomfield (1933) provides us with some more complicated examples of this sort from Tagalog. Tagalog is like English in that you can add things to the front and to the end of a word or stem. But unlike in English, in Tagalog you can also put things in the middle. As a result, the order of operations and the linear order are not reflective of one another at all.

The following set of examples involves reduplication of the first syllable (31b) and infixation of -*um*- (31c) (Bloomfield 1933: 221). The failure of the infix to participate in reduplication tells us that the infix is not inserted until after the first syllable has been reduplicated. Otherwise, we would expect *tutuma:wa*, which we don't find:

(31) a. 'ta:wa   'a laugh'
      b. ta:'ta:wa   'one who will laugh'
      c. tuma:'ta:wa   'one who is laughing'

As Bloomfield shows us (p. 222), Tagalog also has forms like those in (32) which involve the same operations, reduplication and infixation, but in the opposite order:

(32) a. 'pi:lit   'effort'
      b. pu'mi:lit   'one who is compelled'
      c. -pupu:'mi:lit   in [nag-pu:pu'mi:lit], 'one who makes an extreme
                           effort'

We see in (32c) that the reduplicated syllable *pu-* includes the vowel of the infix -*um*-. This tells us that in this construction, infixation precedes reduplication. If reduplication had preceded infixation, we would have expected the non-occurring form *pumi:pi:lit*.

The next set of examples raises still another issue (p. 222):

(33) a. 'puːtul   'a cut'
      b. /paŋpuːtul/ → pa'muː-tul   'that used for cutting'
      c. pamu'muːtul   'a cutting in quantity'

We begin with *puːtul* 'cut' (33a). If we add the prefix *paŋ-* to it, the final nasal /ŋ/ coalesces with the following stop, yielding [m] (33b). We then reduplicate the first syllable of the internal stem, giving (33c). The reduplication doesn't take place at the beginning of the word: it takes place inside. Ordering reduplication before prefixation yields the wrong form:

(34) a. puːtul
      b. puːpuːtul (reduplication)
      c. paŋpuːpuːtul → *pamuːpuːtul (prefixation, coalescence)

With this example, Bloomfield shows that the linear order and the structural order of a set of elements can be very different.

Once Tagalog speakers form the word *pamuːtul* (33b), they retain its internal structure, and this is what enables them to reduplicate the initial syllable of a stem, even when it is buried within the layer of an intermediate derivation. Some linguists claim that this isn't possible, but their view is contradicted by evidence across languages that speakers can reach inside morphologically complex forms and pull out an internal piece. In the morphological literature this goes by the unfortunate name of **head operation**, because such an operation generally involves the **head** or stem of a word. Consider the following English examples:

(35) flower child → flower children
      frogman → frogmen

The fact that the plural of *flower child* is *flower children* instead of **flower childs* means that speakers apply the pluralization operation to the head of the compound, *child*, which has an unproductive, irregular plural ending, instead of on the compound as a whole. Similarly, to pluralize *frogman*, you pluralize its head, not the word itself. Head operations are possible because word-level morphology is a two-way street where creation of word forms is just as much a part of the human language faculty as is their analysis. Again, we can cite evidence for this from child language acquisition. Clark (1993: 404) uses the examples below to illustrate that, at an early age, children are able to analyze the complex word forms that they hear:

(36) a. D (2;9,10): *You know why this is a HIGH-chair? Because it is high.*

 b. D (2;9,24): *Eve, you know what you do on runways? You run on them because they start with "run."*

 c. Mo: *We're going to a place called Sundance.*
   D (2;11,0): *And you dance there. If there is music, we will dance there.*

 d. D (3;2,20), as he climbed into the car, holding both index fingers up to his head): *D'you know what headlights are?*
   Mo: *No.*
   D: *They're lights that go on in your head!*

■ 4.4 Summary

Derivation forms complex lexemes, which may or may not be stored in the speaker's mental lexicon. These complex lexemes, unlike simple signs like *dog*, have internal morphological structure. They may also serve as the basis of further derivation, leading to yet more complex lexemes. Derived lexemes that are not perfectly compositional must be retained in the mental lexicon. The result is that the lexicon does not consist solely of simple signs. Many of its members may be partially motivated complex words.

■ Derivation in Kujamaat Jóola

We conclude this chapter by taking a look at a few nominal derivational suffixes in Kujamaat Jóola. We will present verbal derivational suffixes in the next chapter.

To our knowledge, all derivational morphology in Kujamaat Jóola is suffixal. Sapir (1965: 49) mentions that there are some compounds in the language but that compounding is unproductive.

Illustrated below are -a (1), which takes a stem and forms agentive or instrumental nouns, -ay (2), which is used to build abstract nouns, and -um (3), which creates nouns that are a result of the stem's action. The vowel in -um is invariably tense, meaning that it has the effect of tensing any lax vowel in the stem. [Exercise 8] Note particularly, in reviewing the forms below, how they vary in noun class (as shown by the different prefixes), largely on the basis of semantics.

(1) ɛ-lib-a   'knife'
     a-tɛb-a   'builder'
     a-lɔb-a   'gossip (person)'
     ɛ-raːf-a   'baby's bottle (lit. suckler)'
     a-pal-a   'friend'

(2) mu-lɔb-ay   'scandal'
     ba-pal-ay   'friendship'
     ba-ti-ay   'brotherhood'

(3) bulib-um   'cut (n.)'
     bə-ti-um   'group of same-sex siblings'
     mu-lob-um   'bad feelings, i.e. result of scandal'
     bu-pəl-um   'association, i.e. result of friendship'

The instrumental suffix -a can be suffixed to a noun ending in -um, to form a noun meaning 'instrument of result'. This suffix is unusual in that its /u/ may be tense or lax:

(4) a. ɛ-   ɲitɔ-   um-a > eɲitoːmə 'ladder'
         3CL-   climb

     b. bu-   pal-um-a   > bupəlumə 'association of friends'
         9CL-   friend

Exercises

1. We said in the chapter that *doghouse*, at least in its original sense, is compositional. Now compare it to the following forms:
   a. whorehouse
   b. storehouse
   c. teahouse
   d. town house
   e. nuthouse
   All of these could also be called compositional, as well. Still, looking at them as a group, alongside *doghouse*, what problems do they raise?

2. Imagine what a *bug house* would be. Jot down your definition(s). Now do an online search for *bug house*. Comment on your findings, discussing them in light of the notion of compositionality. How predictable was the meaning of *bug house a priori*?

3. Think of a compound noun that has at least three parts. Now, using the diagnostics presented in this section or in chapter 2, establish that it is indeed a compound.

4. Examine the following data from English and sort them into groups depending on the possible stem types that the adjective-forming suffix *-ish* may attach to (bound vs. free; lexical category) (Nida 1965: 120).
   a. reddish
   b. oldish
   c. childish
   d. boyish
   e. Spanish
   f. old-maidish
   g. prudish
   h. selfish
   i. doggish
   j. bookish
   k. Turkish
   l. English
   m. foolish
   n. purplish
   o. uppish

    p.   Irish
    q.   British
    r.   thievish
    s.   flattish
    t.   ticklish

5. Divide the following words fully into morphemes and draw tree diagrams or bracketing structures for them.
    a. unbelievable
    b. stickiness
    c. sticky buns
    d. unpretentiousness
    e. know-it-all
    f. ungentlemanliness

6. In chapter 2, we said that speakers typically modify a compound as a whole with adjectives rather than one member of a compound. A *brown deer tick* is a brown tick, not a tick that lives on brown deer. However, morphological generalizations are often not absolute, and in chapter 2, exercise 1, we presented the following two compounds that we have come across in the media:
    a. German car dealership
    b. rich country club
    In isolation, both of these are ambiguous between a compound reading and a phrasal meaning. First, write out the two possible interpretations of each. Then draw tree diagrams or bracketing structures that clearly differentiate each interpretation.

7. Two possible analyses of the complex word *uncomfortably* are given below. Which one is correct? Give arguments for your position.
    a. [un- [[[comfort] -abl] -ly]]
    b. [[un- [[comfort] -abl]] -ly]

8. Draw tree structures for the following two Kujamaat Jóola nouns. Refer to the Kujamaat Jóola section of the chapter for more information on the affixes, if necessary.
    a. ɛ-   ɲitɔ-um-a > eɲitomə   'ladder'
        3CL- climb
    b. bu- pal-um-a > bupələmə 'association of friends'
        9CL- friend

NOTES

1   *Cran-* occurs in the names of some juice products, such as *cranapple* juice, but this form is best seen as a blend. *Cran-*, *rasp-*, and to a lesser extent *boysen-* and *cray-* are often brought up as examples by linguists, but where do they come from? *Cranberry* comes from German *kranbeere*, etymologically 'crane berry'. *Rasp-* in *raspberry* is of unknown origin, but it has an archaic cognate *raspis*, a kind of wine. *Boysenberry* (a hybrid of the loganberry and various blackberries) is named for the man who developed it, Rudolf Boysen. Finally, *crayfish* arose through a folk etymology: the original form was *crevice* 'crab', borrowed from Old French. (Etymologies courtesy of the *American Heritage Dictionary*, second college edition, and the *Oxford Dictionary of English Etymology*.)

2   There are exceptions to this generalization, e.g., *entomb*.

3   We came across the word *cyberdieter* in the December 19, 2002, edition of *The Economist*. It was used to refer to the customers of an online dieting firm.

4   Most speakers of English believe that German has more complex compounds than English does, but this is an illusion, rooted in the typographical fact that the component words of German compounds are run together, while English compounds are usually separated by spaces. Structurally, compounds in the two languages are almost identical.

5   We will say more about portmanteau words in section 6.1.1.

6   For expository purposes, we left *-istic* as it is, although it is of course made up of two suffixes, *-ist* and *-ic*.

5 Derivation and Semantics

The *Utne Reader* quoted the following Bucharest sign in its March–April 1996 issue:

> The lift is being fixed for the next day.
> During that time we regret that you will be unbearable.

Unbearable is a perfectly good English word derived from the verb *bear* 'carry', or is it? Why is this sign so funny? It's funny, first of all, because *unbearable* already exists in English with the meaning 'difficult to tolerate', and this is the meaning we first think of when we read the sign. But this isn't the whole story. If we replace *unbearable* with a similar but unambiguous word, like *untransportable*, the sentence is no longer humorous, but it still sounds less than native. It's because words like *unbearable*, *untransportable*, and *uneatable* describe inherent qualities of people or things, qualities that don't change simply because an elevator is out of order. To take another example, the fact that I'm nauseous doesn't make the delicious chocolate cupcakes in the window *uneatable*.

In this simple sign, there is a complex interaction between affixation and semantics going on, and that is the sort of thing that we will be exploring in this chapter. We are going to begin by introducing a fundamental problem in lexical semantics, or the study of word meaning. This is the observation that the meanings of individual lexemes can be highly diverse. We will then examine in some detail the semantics of derived lexemes to see what generalizations we can draw.

■ 5.1   The Polysemy Problem

The most fundamental aspect of a word's meaning is that it refers to some entity or relation (real or imaginary) in the world. We can refer to this entity or relation as the word's **semantic type**. The word *reptile* refers to all individuals in the world that are reptiles. Verbs like *respect* or *love* refer to relationships between individuals. Formal approaches to grammar have provided us with terminology that allows us to make even more fine-tuned distinctions between words. We can differentiate *bear* from *teddy bear* by saying that the first is animate but the second is not, or *foliage* from *leaf* and *literature* from *book* on the basis of the mass/count distinction. Verbs are given labels such as *ergative*, *unaccusative*, *transitive*, or *intransitive*. (For a more detailed discussion, see Pustejovsky 1995: 8 ff.)

The main problem of lexical semantics, or word meaning, is that the meanings of individual lexemes are highly diverse. We call this the problem of **polysemy**. As an example, take the verb *lose*. Consulting the *American Heritage Dictionary* we find the following definitions, among others: (i) 'To be unable to find; mislay . . . To incur the deprivation of, as by negligence or accident'; (ii) 'To be unable to maintain, sustain, or keep: *lost his financial backers*', (iii) 'To be deprived of: *lost everything when*

the business failed ... To be deprived of through death: *lost her husband'*; (iv) 'To rid oneself of: *lose ten pounds'*. All of these meanings of *lose* are related – they are all instances of the same lexeme. Because *lose* has more than one meaning, we say that it is polysemous.

A single form can have two or more related meanings, in which case we are dealing with polysemy. Polysemy can be contrasted with homophony, where two or more words have different and unrelated meanings. Determine which of these relations is exemplified by the forms below. For answers, turn the page.

a.   check: to verify; a piece of paper used in place of cash
b.   snake: a long, slender reptile without legs; a despicable person
c.   head: the part of the human body that sits upon the neck and shoulders; the leader of a group or organization
d.   tree: a plant with a woody stem and branches; a diagram showing relationships between members of a group, such as a family
e.   bat: a wooden club; a flying rodent
f.   itch: an uncomfortable tingling sensation on the skin; a desire

---

There are many types of polysemy. In the next several examples, we present some general types of polysemy, focusing on nouns. While some nouns are inherently mass or count nouns, others can be either, as with *watermelon*:

(1)   a.   I don't like watermelon. (mass)
      b.   I sold three watermelons. (count)

Besides the mass/count alternation, there are several other well-known alternations we find in noun meaning. A few are illustrated below:

(2)   Figure–ground reversal
      a.   Hugh broke the *window*.
      b.   The kids climbed through the *window*.

(3)   Container–contained alternation
      a.   A hot *glass* put under cold water will shatter.
      b.   Franny downed the *glass* in two seconds flat.

(4)   Place–people alternation
      a.   The president and his family live in the *White House*.
      b.   The *White House* announced yesterday that the peace talks will continue.

(5) Characteristic–person alternation
   a.   Sarah would have gotten the part if it weren't for her scratchy *voice*.
   b.   It was well known that The *Voice* didn't drink . . . he was sharp, he wanted to stay sharp. (Irving 1989: 262)

The sentences in (2–5) contain pairs of words with very different – even contradictory – interpretations. Yet they represent single lexemes. In (2a) window refers to a solid barrier, but in (2b) an aperture; *glass* (3a–b) can refer to the container or to the liquid inside. Examples like these show that the same phonetic string can convey different, but related meanings depending on the linguistic and pragmatic context. (As seen in 2.3.3 a given phonetic string may also convey unrelated meanings, in which case we are dealing with homophones.) **[Exercises 1–3]**

This introduction to polysemy leads into the discussion in the following section, which focuses on the semantics of derived lexemes.

■ 5.2   The Semantics of Derived Lexemes

When somebody makes up a word, they are inventing it for use under a particular circumstance. Sometimes the circumstance can be very peculiar. Take the sentence in (6):

(6)   Joe was Houdini'd and died.

In order to understand this sentence, you have to know something about the event that the speaker is describing. You also have to know who Houdini was – a famous escape artist – and how he died. He died following a series of punches to his stomach (a fan was testing the strength of his abdominal muscles, which Houdini prided himself on). So when we say "Joe was Houdini'd and died," what we mean is that he was punched in the stomach and died in the way that Houdini did. This is a dramatic example of how you might need to know pragmatic factors about the type of situation in order to understand a particular lexeme. We'll say more about examples like (6) below.

The second factor that can affect a word's meaning is its history. We might think of every lexeme not just as a word and its meaning, but as the word and every time it has ever been used: every time we hear the word, we revise its lexical entry in some way. That this indeed goes on is particularly evident from first language acquisition research. Children in earlier stages of language acquisition may **underextend** a word by using

Answers to polysemy–homophony exercise:

a. homophony
b. polysemy
c. polysemy
d. polysemy
e. homophony
f. polysemy

it to refer to only a subset of its actual referents, or **overextend** a word by using it to refer to objects or individuals that are typically covered by the word, as well as to others that are "perceptually similar" (Clark 1993: 33). For example, a child might underextend the word *dog* by using it to refer to more typical examples of the species, but not to varieties like Chihuahua or Pekingese (Kay and Anglin 1982), or overextend *tree* by using it to refer to potted plants, trees, and even balsam fir wreaths.[1] Such under- and overextensions are generally very short-lived, which indicates that children revise lexical entries as they are exposed to more and more tokens of a word.

It is not unreasonable to think that the meaning of a word is a compilation of every single use of that word that you have ever heard or said. Every word has a history. It has your own personal history – how you have heard the word. And it has the history of the word as it has been used by other people. Over time, the meanings of words become more and more complex and diverse in various ways. This makes the task of the morphologist looking for semantic patterns of word formation more complicated than it would be if the semantics of word formation were purely compositional (as the semantics of syntactic constructions are often considered to be). A syntactic construction may have pragmatics to deal with, but it doesn't have history.

One question you might want to ask is what kinds of meanings arise via lexeme-formation rules. Are derived forms like lexemes, with potentially very complicated meanings? Or are they like syntactic collocations, with simple meanings? **[Exercise 4]**

■ **5.2.1   The semantics of affixation**

Let's take the English suffix *-ism*. This affix has some very highly lexicalized meanings, one of which is 'doctrinal system of principles'. This is the meaning that we find in words like the following, and many others having to do with religion, philosophy, science, politics, or the arts:

(7) Catholicism Platonism romanticism McCarthyism
     Judaism   Marxism   realism   socialism
     Buddhism   idealism   surrealism   fascism

The suffix *-ism* has another meaning which is even more specific and lexicalized: 'a peculiarity of speech'. We talk about *colloquialisms*, *spoonerisms*, *Reaganisms*, or *Bushisms*. (*Reaganism* can either be a system of beliefs, or a peculiarity of speech. *Bushism* seems to be only a peculiarity of speech.) So *-ism* is an example of a suffix with two very highly lexicalized meanings, both of which might be considered to be more characteristic of words than of affixes.

The German suffix *-ei* is like *-ism* in that it also has at least two very highly lexicalized meanings. The first, illustrated by the words in (8), takes a noun and makes another noun meaning 'the place in which X works'. The second, seen in (9), takes a verb stem and creates a noun referring to the 'act of doing X':

(8) a. Bäcker 'baker'   → Bäckerei 'bakery'
     b. Drucker 'printer'   → Druckerei 'printing office, print shop'
     c. Sattler 'saddler'   → Sattlerei 'saddlery, saddler's workshop'
     d. Tischler 'joiner'   → Tischlerei 'joinery'

(9) a. plaudern 'chat (v)'   → Plauderei 'chat (n)'
     b. zittern 'tremble'   → Zitterei 'trembling'
     c. prügeln 'clobber'   → Prügelei 'brawl, fight'
     d. quengeln 'whine'   → Quengelei 'whining'

Note that English has a cognate suffix *-ery*, *-ry*, cf. *bakery*, *tannery*, *winery*; *bribery*, *flattery*, *foolery*. This suffix is of French origin. **[Exercises 5 and 6]**

■ 5.2.2 The semantics of zero–derivation

We now address a type of word formation which is much more abstract: zero-derivation.[2] We will see that zero-derivation results in lexemes whose interpretation is context-dependent in much the same way as the words we looked at in section 5.1 above.[3] All of the data on zero-derived verbs that we discuss here come from Clark and Clark (1979), but the analysis we present is that of Aronoff (1980).

The peculiarity of zero-derived verbs is that they often have a wide range of meanings. To give you just one example, the verb *to sand* denotes two very different actions. The most common meaning is 'to rub with sandpaper'. The second meaning is 'to spread or cover with sand', as is done in winter to make roads less slippery.

While *sand* is well established as a verb, zero-derivation is a product-ive derivational process in English (cf. 4.2.2), as shown by the following nonce forms presented by Clark and Clark. All of these sentences are actual quotations:

(10) a. Ruth Buzzi *houseguested* with Bill Dodge (Herb Caen, *SF Chronicle*)
      b. He *wristed* the ball over the net (tennis commentator)
      c. When you're starting to *Sunday School* members, then I think you're going too far (a Californian legislator)
      d. Will you *cigarette* me? (Mae West)
      e. We all *Wayned* and *Cagneyed* (*NY Times magazine*)

Clark and Clark classify noun-to-verb derivations into various categor-ies. For each category, they give numerous examples, of which we have given only a few:

(11) Location   (N is at a place)   blanket, saddle, roof
                    (put something at N)   kennel, ground, cellar
      Duration   (spend the duration of N)   summer, holiday,
                                                 vacation, weekend
      Agent   (N acts)   jockey, referee, umpire,
                                                 pilot
      Goal   (make into N)   fool, orphan, baby,
                                                 cripple, pile, loop,
                                                 powder
      Instrument   (use N)   ship, nail, glue,
                                                 shampoo, fork
      Miscellaneous   lunch, hay, whale, dog

The descriptions given in (11) for each of the categories are slightly vague. One of the meanings given for the Location category is 'put something at N'. To be more precise, verbs like *kennel*, *ground* (e.g., a teenager), or *cellar* involve keeping, not simply putting. Likewise, the true description of the Instrument category is much trickier than 'use N' because often you don't use the noun – you use something else. For example, while shipping originally took place via ship, today we ship things by truck or air. We might redefine this category as 'do what you do with N'. Even this, however, needs to be interpreted fairly broadly. Clark and Clark describe a fictional Max, who has a strange fetish – he likes to sneak up to people and stroke the backs of their legs with a teapot. When one of Max's friends says to another, "Well, this time Max has gone too far. He tried to *teapot* a policeman," we need to interpret *teapot* as 'rub the back of the leg with a teapot'. By no stretch of the imagination is this what we would normally think of upon reading the definition 'do what you do with N'.

The miscellaneous category includes some interesting words. We use the verb *whale* to mean 'catch whales' or *fish* to mean 'catch fish', but are hard pressed to come up with many other verbs of this type. We don't use a verb *deer* to mean 'hunt deer' or *butterfly* for 'catch butterflies'. The verb *dog* patterns with words like *clown* in having the meaning 'act like a dog'. *Cub*, *foal*, and *pup* all mean to 'give birth to' these animals.

The zero-derived verbs with the most extensive semantic possibilities are probably those that are derived from personal names. To understand them, you need to know the history of the person, and often of a particular event. To understand the sentence in (6), repeated in (12), you have to know the circumstances of Houdini's death:

(12)   Joe was Houdini'd and died.

But to understand the sentences in (13) (from Clark and Clark 1979: 784), you have to know other things about Houdini, namely that he was famous for sensational and seemingly impossible escapes (13a) and that his lifetime crusade was to show up phony mediums and spiritualists for the frauds that they were:

(13)   a.   My sister Houdini'd her way out of the locked closet.
       b.   I would love to Houdini those ESP experiments.

The semantic obscurity of verbs derived from personal names results in speakers forgetting very rapidly that there even was a zero-derivation. While any English speaker can see the connection between *nurse* (noun) and *nurse* (verb) or *bottle* (noun) and *bottle* (verb), most aren't aware that *boycott* and *lynch* are of the same ilk.[4]

Robert Lees, in his classic book on English nominals (1960), derived the meanings of denominal verbs from sentences containing them. So the verb *summer* would be derived from the phrase *spend the summer* and the verb *kennel* from *keep in a kennel*. Marchand (1969) had a similar strategy: he associated a denominal verb with a sentence containing the noun from which it is derived. More recently, Hale and Keyser (1993) also relate the lexical semantics of verbs to a syntactic structure.

The question is, given the sometimes idiosyncratic array of meanings that zero-derived verbs may have, what kind of semantics can we write for the noun-to-verb rule? We can potentially go two ways. We can either be very inclusive, or specific, and formulate rules that will give all of the cases. Or we can do the opposite and write a very general – what we call a sparse – rule. A sparse rule basically says very little but will, as you will see, yield the right answer.

Let's review all of the examples of zero-derived verbs that we have given here and ask ourselves what is going on, in general. The general answer is that each verb has something to do with the noun. Because it is a verb, it has the meaning of some action or activity, and on basic Gricean principles of cooperation (Grice 1975), we know that that action or activity will be connected to the noun. Grice tells us that when people speak to one another, they have to assume that they are being cooperative. We will give a more specific answer below, but first we need to examine a fact about evaluative adjectives like *good*, *bad*, or *wonderful*.

In one sense, the meanings of evaluative adjectives are apparently infinite. *Wonderful* means something very different in the sentences *Moby-Dick is a wonderful book* and *George is a wonderful nurse*. For one thing, the first sentence is true only if *Moby-Dick* is both a book and wonderful. But the second sentence can be true even if George is not a nurse but a stockbroker. This is because *wonderful* can be construed as describing either the noun *nurse* or the activity associated with it. George is a *wonderful nurse* as long as he takes care of sick people (such as his kids) quite wonderfully. However, we do not need to say that evaluative adjectives are polysemous. Instead, following Katz (1964), we can say that evaluative adjectives modify "that component of the meaning of a noun which has to do with the particular respect in which evaluations are made, within the language, of things in the extension of the noun" (p. 751).[5] We can refer to this as the **evaluative domain** of the word.

What is significant is that the evaluative domain of simple lexemes like *nurse*, *knife*, or *dog* is the same as the evaluative domain of zero-derived verbs like *pilot* or *shampoo*. If Mary is good at piloting, it means that she is a good pilot. If this is good shampoo, it is good for what you do with shampoo. What this tells us is that the mechanisms by which speakers assign meanings to evaluative adjectives and to zero-derived verbs on the basis of context are likely the same.

To summarize the analysis that we have just presented, the wide array of meanings of zero-derived verbs results from two properties. The first is that the rule by which they are formed is very simple, specifying only that we take a noun and form a verb. The second is that conversational convention dictates only that the verb have something to do with the noun. We can reasonably pare this analysis down even further and say that the proper analysis of zero-derived verbs is that they are simply verbs. The fact that they denote an activity connected with the noun is derivable on purely conversational grounds. **[Exercises 7 and 8]**

While other derivational formations don't have as dramatic an array of potential meanings as do zero-derived verbs, we still find variety. Aronoff (1976: 38) points out that new English nouns of the form *X-ousness* have three possible meanings, depending on context:

(14) a. 'the fact that Y is X-ous'
          His callousness surprised me 'The fact that he was callous surprised me'
      b. 'the extent to which Y is X-ous'
          His callousness surprised me 'The extent to which he was callous surprised me'
      c. 'the quality or state of being X-ous'
          Callousness is not a virtue 'The quality or state of being callous is not a virtue'

The difference between lexemes of the form *X-ousness* and zero-derived verbs lies in the rules that produce them. While the meaning of words like *callousness* is constrained by the semantics of the suffixes *-ous* and *-ness*, as well as by the meaning of the stem itself, the meaning of zero-derived verbs is constrained only by the meaning of the base noun.

■ 5.2.3 More on the semantics of affixation: English agent nouns in *-er*

We next give you an example of another derivation that works in the same way as zero-derived verbs, but is a little simpler. Marchand gives examples of English agent nouns in *-er*. He points out that they fall into four basic categories, which can then be broken down even further into two separate sets. The four basic categories are listed below:

(15) Persons: baker, dancer, gambler, driver
      Animals: pointer, retriever, warbler, trotter
      Material objects: blotter, eraser, fertilizer, shutter
      Immaterial objects: reminder, clincher, thriller, eye-opener

These nouns can be further divided into their habitual and non-habitual uses. So if we say:

(16) He is a *gambler*

we usually mean that he gambles all the time. You can also use agent nouns non-habitually:

(17)   All *ticket-holders* may enter

If you are trying to get the meaning of agent nouns in English, you have to say that they fall into the four categories listed in (15), multiplied by the two categories habitual vs. non-habitual. We need to do this because even a word that is normally understood to be habitual, like *blotter*, can be used in a non-habitual sense. If you use something that's not a blotter as a blotter, then it must be a non-habitual blotter, because it is only being used as such on this particular occasion.

There are two possible analyses of agent nouns, both of which are reasonable. We won't try to choose between them here. One is the strategy that we used above with zero-derived verbs, to assign the derivation a sparse semantic rule. We can follow Marchand in saying that an agent noun is 'someone or something connected with what the base denotes', or alternatively, 'somebody or something whose function or characteristic is to perform a particular act'. For now we will assume the latter. It permits the categories person, animal, material object, and immaterial object, as well as a habitual or non-habitual interpretation.

The other method which linguists might use to account for possible meanings of *X-er* agent nouns involves **prototypes**, also called **archetypes**. The idea is that not all members of a given category are equal. You can have prototypical, or typical, members of a category, and then you can have more marginal members. In this case, it is probably reasonable to say that the prototypical agentive is a person who habitually performs a particular type of action. So the prototypical agentive is a word like *baker*, *dancer*, *gambler*, or *driver*, in the habitual sense. These somehow reflect the core of the meaning of this particular formation. Other forms, like *retriever*, *blotter*, or *clincher*, involve relaxation of the core meaning. We use them to distinguish one specimen from other members of its class. So a pointer is a kind of dog that has the characteristic of pointing; specifically, it has been bred to stand still and point out the prey to the hunter. And a retriever is a kind of dog that goes and gets the prey – retrieves it – once it has been killed.

Even within a specific class like that of retrievers, you can get central and marginal exemplars. Most people don't know that poodles (the big ones, anyway) are retrievers. The fact that we can make a sentence like, "You can use a poodle as a retriever," tells you that retrieving is not a salient, central characteristic of poodles – they are best known for being fuzzy. **[Exercises 9 and 10]**

When we claim that persons are the prototypical members of the category of agentive nouns, we can also argue that some other members of the category – material objects like screwdrivers, for example – aren't agents at all. Instead, they are instruments, because they don't have will. Of course, if there were a special profession for people who drive in screws, then one might say that such a person was a screwdriver, and then screwdrivers could be agents. In short, the second method of analyzing agentives is to establish a central case, the prototype, and to work out from that to get the others. Note that when it comes to denominal verbs, we do not have the option of applying this analysis because there is no central case, no prototype.

■ 5.3 Summary

In this chapter we have explored the semantics of derivation, looking at a group of derivational operations in English, some of which are semantically very particular, such as -ism, and others of which are very abstract. Our point has been to show that the meanings of morphologically complex words are partially predictable from the meanings of their parts. It is only through use in context that they acquire particular meanings. Over time, a single word may acquire a number of distinct lexicalized meanings and, as a result, a complex lexical entry.

In the Kujamaat Jóola portion of this chapter, we continue the theme of derivation and semantics by examining some verbal derivational suffixes. These express causative, reflexive, and reciprocal meaning, as well as the fact that an action begins away from the speaker. We begin with a necessary overview of verbal inflection and derivation in Kujamaat Jóola, but the former will be treated in fuller detail in the next chapter.

■ Derivation and Verbs in Kujamaat Jóola

Kujamaat Jóola, like many languages, exploits derivation and inflection to express a wide range of syntactic and semantic categories. What we would express in English as a sentence is often encompassed by a single Kujamaat Jóola verb, as in (1):

(1)   u-bɔɲ-ɛːn-ɛːn-ɔrut-al-ɔ
      1PL.INCL -send-INC-INC-NEG-1PL.INCL-3SG.OBJ
      'We had not yet sent him'

The core of (1) is a lexical root – *bɔɲ* 'send' – which provides the basic meaning of the verb. The rest of the meaning is conveyed by affixes on either side of the root. The first person plural inclusive subject is expressed by the circumfix *u- . . . -al*; the emphatic dubitive-incompletive by repetition of the dubitive-incompletive suffix *-ɛːn*; the meaning 'not yet' by *-ɔrut*; and the third person singular object by *-ɔ*. With the exception of the circumfixal subject marker, the relationship between meaning and form is one to one: the meaning of the word as a whole is the sum of its parts. Linguists refer to this type of morphology as agglutinative.

One characteristic of agglutinative morphology, identified by Horne (1966), is that affixation is not obligatory. We see this in Kujamaat Jóola in that a bare root is used for the positive imperative:

(2)   ri   'eat!'
      jɔl   'come!'
      tɛk   'hit!'

The order of morphemes in any language is typically fairly rigid, and Kujamaat Jóola is no exception. The following diagram schematizes the basic structure of the verb. At its core is the lexical stem, which may be simple or derived. The stem is followed by what Sapir refers to as position 1 suffixes, including aspectual and negative markers, as well as a derivational directional suffix and the second members of the past subordinate and first person plural inclusive circumfixes. Position 1 suffixes are followed by the position 2 suffixes: the passive marker, object pronominals (direct, indirect, or both), and noun emphasis marker. Finally, the third position is filled by verb reduplication and the simple subordinate marker. Immediately preceding the verb stem are the subject markers and relative pronouns (position 1 prefixes); the leftmost position (position 2) is filled by the resultative, the resultative negative, the negative imperative, and the past subordinate markers. Many of these terms are probably new to you. They will become more familiar over the course of this and the next chapter. **[Exercise 11]**

The Kujamaat Jóola verb

2-	1-		-1	-2	-3
res	subject	STEM	aspect	object	subord
res neg	rel pronoun		mood	passive	redup
neg imper			past subord	noun	
past subord			negation	emphasis	
			directional		

■ The stem

Some examples of Kujamaat Jóola roots are given below:

(3) -tɛy-   'run'
     -juk-   'see'
     -manj-   'know'
     -cɛŋ-   'ask'

Inflectional affixes may attach to a root, or the root can be extended by the addition of derivational affixes. The root plus derivational affixes is called a stem. You have already encountered one verbal derivation suffix in chapter 3, -*u* 'from'. Five more are listed below, with examples:

(4) Productive verbal derivational suffixes
     a. -ɛn   causative
         -lint-   'make a rumbling noise'
         -linten-   'cause something to make a rumbling noise'
     b. -ɔ   reflexive-descriptive
         -buŋ-   'braid someone's hair'
         -buŋɔ-   'braid one's own hair'
     c. -ɔrɔ   strong reflexive
         -buj-   'kill'
         -bujɔrɔ-   'kill one's self'
     d. -ɔr   reciprocal
         -jim-   'forget'
         -jimɔr-   'forget each other'
     e. -um   directive
         -ribɛn-   'follow'
         -ribenum-   'follow by means of'

We see in (4c) that the root -*buj*- 'kill' can be suffixed with the strong reflexive to form -*bujɔrɔ*- 'kill one's self'. If a speaker were to add the reflexive-descriptive suffix (cf. (4b)) instead, the result is a verb with more idiosyncratic semantics, -*bujɔ*- 'be wounded'. The difference between affixation of the reflexive and strong reflexive is not always so striking, however, as we see in (5):

(5)   a.   ni-   pɔs-   ɔ-   pɔsɔ   i-   ban
           1AGR- wash- REFL- REDUP 1AGR- finish
           'I have finished washing myself'
      b.   ni-   pɔs-   ɔrɔ- pɔsɔrɔ i-   ban
           1AGR- wash- REFL- REDUP 1AGR- finish
           'I have finished washing *myself*'

The sometimes-idiosyncratic meaning of verbs bearing the reflexive suffix reflects a major point of this chapter, that the meanings of morphologically complex words are not always fully predictable from those of their parts. Through use in context, morphologically complex words may acquire lexicalized meanings and, as a result, become listed in the lexicon. This must be true of -*bujɔ*- 'be wounded'. **[Exercise 12]**

Evidence that both roots and the roots plus derivational affixes count as stems in Kujamaat Jóola verb morphology comes from the following observations:

(6)   Both can be used as the positive imperative
          pur bɔ   'go out from there!'
          purum bɔ   'go out via that way!'

(7)   Both participate in full reduplication, which is productive and serves as the marker of verb emphasis or verb focus.
      a.   na-   bɔ-   bɔl   e-   lïw-   ey
           3SG.SUB-roast- REDUP3CL- meat- DEF3
           'He roasted the meat'
      b.   na-   bɔl-   ɔ-   bɔlɔ
           3SG.SUB-roast- REFL- REDUP
           'he burned himself'

(8)   Both may serve as nominal stems
      a.   ɛ-jɔj   ka-jɔj-ɛn
           3CL-assemble, gather   7CL-assemble-CAUS
           'to assemble, gather'   'to cause (people) to assemble'
      b.   fu-jɔj   ka-jɔj -ɛn-a
           5CL-assemble   7CL-assemble-CAUS-AGENT
           'assembly, gathering'   'gatherer of people, leader who brings
                                      people together by force of charisma'

The stem in Bantu languages (also in the Niger-Congo family) may also consist of a root plus derivational suffixes (Hyman 1993; Mchombo 1993). For example, Mchombo shows that the Chichewa verb stem plus derivational affixes functions as a unit in that it may be nominalized (but units larger than the verb stem may not), undergo reduplication, and be used as the bare imperative. Chichewa is similar to Kujamaat Jóola in these respects. In addition, the Chichewa verb stem serves as the domain for a phonological process, tense-lax vowel harmony. **[Exercises 13–15]**

Exercises

1. Look up the word *run* in the dictionary and read over its many possible meanings. List at least five meanings of *run* that exemplify polysemy. Next, determine whether there are any homophonous forms of *run*, forms with different and unrelated meanings.

2. Write sentence pairs that illustrate the following semantic alternations:
   a. figure–ground reversal
   b. container–contained alternation
   c. place–people alternation
   d. person–characteristic alternation

3. The following words do not have plurals or, if they do, their plurals have a special meaning. Describe the meaning of the plural form of each word, if it exists. Then try to come up with an account of the behavior of these nouns as a group.
   a. water
   b. rice
   c. fish
   d. air
   e. laughter
   f. courage
   g. heat (i.e., hot temperature)
   h. humidity

4. Hebrew, as we have already seen, is a language with root-and-pattern morphology. Rewrite each of the following adjectives, replacing the consonants with C. Reproduce the vowels as they are. Example (a) has been done for you. Does a semantically based pattern emerge, and if so, what is it? If you find any exceptions, make a hypothesis to explain it/them.
   a. kaʃeh   'hard'   CaCeC
   b. kaxol   'blue'
   c. rax   'soft'
   d. ʔadom   'red'
   e. nakiy   'clean'
   f. maluax   'salty'
   g. gaʃum   'rainy'

h. varod   'pink'
i. yarok   'green'
j. texelet 'light blue'

5. Sort the following words into two groups based on the semantics of
    the suffix -*ful*. How is it used in each set? Is either -*ful* productive?
    a. careful
    b. deceitful
    c. prayerful
    d. handful
    e. sorrowful
    f. earful
    g. mouthful
    h. playful
    i. bagful

6. Determine whether the italicized forms in the following pairs are
    related in meaning. If they are, describe the relationship.
    a. all-night*er*   danc*er*
    b. danc*er*   badg*er*
    c. milk*y*   ink*y*
    d. He*'s* done it   He*'s* here
    e. funn*y*   Bobb*y*
    f. gold*en*   wood*en*
    g. merri*ment*   ce*ment*
    h. friend*ly*   quick*ly*
    i. advis*er*   govern*or*
    j. duch*ess*   sorcer*ess*

7. The following was spotted on a sign outside a campus movie
    theater:

    The cinema will not be screening films Dec. 13–Jan. 19

    The dates correspond to the winter break, and from the context we
    can deduce that the sign means that the cinema won't be *showing*
    films. What does *screening* mean more often? (Note that the mean-
    ing 'to show a motion picture on a screen' is indeed attested in
    dictionaries, but not as a primary definition.) Why is the meaning
    intended here equally acceptable?

8. Create a new word using zero-derivation and a proper name. For example, one student came up with the sentence, "He pulled a Clinton." (We'll leave you to come up with a meaning of *Clinton* that fits this context.)

9. For each of the following pairs, determine which word denotes a more prototypical member of the group for you.
   a. cheese: gorgonzola or cheddar?
   b. dwelling: house or apartment?
   c. bird: robin or chickadee?
   d. bread: sliced American loaf or baguette?
   e. bear: koala or grizzly?

10. How might cultural, geographic, and socio-economic factors affect what one considers a prototype of a tree? a skyscraper? a cat?

11. Consider the diagram of the verb in the section on Kujamaat Jóola. How similar are the morphemes within a given position class with respect to the type of information they convey?

12. We saw that the Kujamaat Jóola reflexive can have a fairly idiosyncratic meaning when compared to the stem. Can you think of any examples from another language where a reflexive verb has acquired a particular meaning that does not immediately reflect the meaning of its parts?[6]

13. How does the Kujamaat Jóola expression of the causative, reflexive, and reciprocal differ from their expression in English and any other languages you know?

14. We have identified the Kujamaat Jóola causative, reflexive, strong reflexive, and reciprocal as derivational (rather than inflectional) affixes. On the basis of the discussion of inflection and derivation in section 2.4 and in this chapter, justify this decision.

15. In chapter 2 we wrote:

   > noun class systems can be powerful inflectional and derivational mechanisms. We have seen that by changing a noun's class marker, not only can Kujamaat Jóola speakers make important number distinctions – singular, plural, mass, or collective – but they can also create diminutives or augmentatives, personify non-humans, or dehumanize humans.

While this is true, and noun class systems can indeed be seen as both inflectional and derivational mechanisms, it is still the case that the noun class prefixes themselves are best considered inflectional morphemes. Keeping this in mind, and referring to the treatment of derivation and semantics in this chapter, outline a possible analysis of the Kujamaat Jóola paradigm below. It shows that the stem -sɛk 'woman' is associated with a variety of different meanings depending on the noun class prefix that it bears. You may find it helpful to refer to the discussion of Kujamaat Jóola noun classes in chapter 2.

a.   -sɛk   'woman'
b.   a-sɛk   'woman'   (class 1)
c.   ku-sɛk   'women'   (class 2)
d.   ji-sɛk   'small woman'   (class 10)
e.   mu-sɛk   'small women'   (class 11)
f.   ba-sɛk   'many small women' (class 13)
g.   fu-sɛk   'big woman'   (class 5)
h.   ɲi-sɛk   'big women'   (class 12)

NOTES

1   We know a child who did precisely this.

2   Another good example is noun–noun compounding; see Downing (1977).

3   In what follows, we will be focusing on zero-derivation of verbs from nouns. English also allows the other possibility, zero-derivation of nouns from verbs. Nouns derived from verbs generally signify an instance or result of the activity denoted by the verb. So the noun *hit* denotes an 'instance of hitting', while the noun *run* can denote either an instance (*She went for a run*) or a result (*She scored two runs*). It is possible to form a verb from the noun *run* in this second baseball sense of the term: *we outrunned them* (meaning that we scored more runs than they did). The fact that the past tense of *outrun* in this sense is not **outran* shows that the verb is derived from the noun in this case. This whole sequence (verb to noun to verb) indicates that these rules are directional, contrary to what some people have claimed.

4   *Lynch* 'the punishment of persons suspected of crime without due process of law' appeared in 1811 and comes from Captain William Lynch of Pittsylvania County, Virginia. Lynch and his neighbors were plagued by criminals, but couldn't appeal to the courts because they were too far away. The men drew up a contract on September 22, 1780, in which they agreed to deal with the criminals themselves, even inflicting corporal punishment if necessary. Charles C. Boycott was an English land agent in County Mayo, Ireland. He was ostracized in 1880 for preferring to evict his tenants than to reduce rents,

and found himself and his family without servants, farm help, or even mail delivery. His name came to be synonymous with this kind of cold-shoulder treatment, whether it be abstention from buying a product or dealing with a person, as a means of protest (definitions and etymologies from *American Heritage Dictionary of the English Language*).

5   The term **extension** is defined in the glossary.
6   This would be a good question for discussion, since not all students will be able to do this.

6   Inflection

What is the plural of *euro*, the name of the European currency? The answer seems obvious: *euros* – one euro, two euros, voilà! After all, -*s* is the productive plural marker in English and is normally used with new **coinages**, which is just what we do with words like *modem* or *byte* (*modems, bytes*). But spend a little time in Ireland, the only largely English-speaking country in the euro zone, and you will soon discover that a pint of Guinness in the local pub will set you back four euro and not four euros. Why?

The answer lies in the multilingual nature of the euro zone. The name of the currency itself bespeaks such multilingualism: its devisers had to come up with a name that could be both written and pronounced in all of the languages in the zone. And indeed, though it is pronounced differently in each of the languages ([ojro] in German, [œʁo] in French, and [ɛvro] in Greek, for example), it is pronounceable in all of them. But the plural also must be not only pronounced but also written in each of the languages. Look at a 10-euro bill and you will see the clever solution to this multilingual problem that was found. First, unlike the US 10-dollar bill, where *ten dollars* is written out in full, or the bilingual Canadian bill, which say *dix·ten dollars*, the word for 'ten' is written in numerals: *10*. The reason is simple: *10* can be written identically while still being pronounced differently in each of the languages of the zone, and still mean exactly the same thing. But the second problem is that the plural form of *euro*, which follows the numeral, must also be written uniformly on the bill and, though several major European languages besides English use the plural marker -*s* (French, German, and Spanish do), not all would tolerate it (Italian, for example, never uses an -*s* plural). A mathematician might have solved this problem of uniformity by extending the use of symbols to the notation >*1*, which technically means 'plural', but the expression *10 euro >1* is not only silly-looking, but also redundant. The solution, therefore, was to avoid the redundancy and not use any plural marker on *euro* in writing. The bill reads simply *10 EURO/EYPΩ* and the spoken languages have all followed the same practice of not using any plural marker either, making the plural of euro *euro* in Ireland.

The linguistic point of this story is that even when several languages share the same word, as they do with *euro*, the inflectional systems of the languages differ, and this difference normally affects the forms of the words. When blue jeans became the rage in the Soviet Union years ago, they were called [dʒinzɨ], with the plural marker [ɨ] added despite the presence of the [s], because the -*s* was not recognized as anything but part of the basic stem. Conversely, when the old-fashioned English term for 'headlight', *sealed beam*, was borrowed into Israeli Hebrew as [silbim], the final [im] sequence was interpreted as a Hebrew plural marker, making [silbim] a plural, with the corresponding singular therefore being [silb]. So [silb], the Israeli Hebrew word for 'headlight', is borrowed directly from English, in the minds of Hebrew speakers who know, to the great surprise of English speakers.

Inflection varies from one language to another more than any other systematic aspect of language. This chapter will deal with inflectional systems, showing how they vary across languages so widely but still remain quite relentlessly systematic within themselves.

■ 6.1   What is Inflection?

We already encountered inflection in section 2.4, but here we explore it in more detail. The word itself comes from traditional Latin grammar. Its root *flect-*, which we see in the English word *flex*, means 'bend'.[1] We give this etymology to evoke the image of a speaker "bending," or, perhaps more clearly, altering the shape of a word so it will fit in a particular position within a sentence. Every sentence is a syntactic frame with positions for a series of words. In order to fill one of those positions, you take a lexeme from the lexicon and bend it to fit. In this way, inflectional morphology is determined by syntax.

What kinds of things do lexemes express through inflection? In general we speak of inflection expressing **morphosyntactic** information, syntactic information that is expressed morphologically. This includes the abstract syntactic categories of tense, aspect, number, and case. Specific values for these categories, such as past, imperfective, plural, or genitive, are generally referred to as **morphosyntactic features** or **morphosyntactic properties**, the latter a term from Matthews (1991).

Examples of words + *inflectional morphemes*

Nouns: book + *s*
            fox + *es*
Verbs: read + *s*
            load + *ed*
            see + *n*
            drink + *ing*

So inflection is the realization of morphosyntactic features through morphological means. What those means are will be addressed later in this chapter.

In order to fully understand inflection, we must situate it in the grammar. Since we are claiming that the syntax provides the morphology with morphosyntactic features, the job of the morphology must be to get from there to the actual phonological realization:

(1)

This diagram portrays the relationship between the syntax, morphology, and phonology as derivational, but it is equally possible to model a non-derivational, parallel relationship. Either way, a diagram like (1) is bound to be deceptively simple. We are still left asking precisely how words become inflected. We now turn to an exploration of the answers to that question.

■ 6.1.1 Exponence

Exponence, a term coined by Peter Matthews, refers to the realization of morphosyntactic features via inflection. In the word *seas*, the morpheme [z] is the **exponent** of the morphosyntactic feature plural, and in *sailed*, [d] is the exponent of past tense or past participle (Matthews 1991: 175). In both cases there is a one-to-one relationship between form and meaning, since one morpheme realizes one morphosyntactic feature, a situation that Matthews calls **simple exponence**.

When we go beyond simple exponence, we get into data that have been central to modern theories of morphology. One type is what Matthews first called **cumulative exponence**. These are cases where more than one morphosyntactic feature maps onto a single form. We find this in Latin verbal inflections. In the Latin first person singular present indicative active form, five features (person, number, tense, mood, voice) are spelled out with a single morpheme, *-ō*:

(2) cant-ō
     sing-1SG.PRES.IND.ACT
     'I sing'

Another example of cumulative exponence is subject–object agreement in Cherokee, an Iroquoian language. Verbs in Cherokee bear prefixes that agree with their subject and object in person, number, and animacy. What is most important in the present context is that some single prefixes, including those listed in (3), indicate both subject and object simultaneously (Scancarelli 1987: 71):

(3)   ski-, skw-   2SG.SUB/1SG.OBJ
      sti: 2DU.SUB/3SG.INAN.OBJ
      kaci:y   1SG.SUB/3PL.AN.OBJ
      ci:y   1SG.SUB/3SG.AN.OBJ

Examples of subject/object prefixes in context are given below (tones are not marked; /v/ is a nasalized central vowel). Following Scancarelli, verbs are given in both their surface and phonemic forms, with the phonemic forms aligned with the glosses:

(4) a. sv:kthv kaci:ne:lv:?i   (Scancarelli 1987: 68)
         /kaci:y-   ?ne:lv:?i/
         apple 1SG.SUB/3PL.AN.OBJ-give.PERF
         'I gave them an apple'
     b. ci:ko:wthiha   (Scancarelli 1987: 74)
         /ci:y-   ko:?wthiha/
         1SG.SUB/3SG.AN.OBJ-see.PRES
         'I see him'

Lastly, inflection for case, number, and gender in many Indo-European languages involves cumulative exponence. The *-os* ending of the Modern Greek adjective *kalós* 'good' indicates that it is masculine, nominative, and singular. The *-á* of Russian *stolá* 'table' denotes both genitive and singular.

Related to cumulative exponence is the notion of a portmanteau, a term coined by Lewis Carroll for words of his own invention that were combinations of other words. For example, *slithy* is his combination of *slimy* and *lithe*.[2] In a portmanteau word, what were historically two or more distinct words (and what may still be, in some contexts) are fused together. The French definite determiner occurs in two forms, *le* (masculine) and *la* (feminine). The feminine form can be preceded by the prepositions *à* 'in, to' or *de* 'of, from', as shown below:

(5)   à la plage   'to/at the beach'
      de la plage   'from/of the beach'

The masculine form, however, may not follow either of these prepositions. Instead, we get a portmanteau word:

(6) au [o] marché   'to/at the market' (*à le marché)
     du [dy] marché   'from/of the market' (*de le marché)

The existence of cumulative exponence is very important to a proper characterization of the morphology–syntax interface. We see that fairly complex syntactic structures may get reduced morphologically. [Exercise 1]

We also find the opposite of cumulative exponence. In **extended exponence**, a single morphological feature is realized simultaneously on more than one form. One example presented by Matthews (1991) is the Ancient Greek perfective. The verb *elelýkete* 'you had unfastened' (stem *-ly-*) is marked as perfective by reduplication (*le-*), *-k-* infixation, and the presence of a special stem (*-ly-* versus *-ly:-*). We cannot single out any one of them – they mark the perfect together. Likewise, in Kujamaat Jóola, deverbal nouns can be formed from some infinitives by changing the noun class and tensing the vowels (7). One or the other isn't sufficient. This is another example of extended exponence:

(7) a.   ɛ-ka:y   'to divorce' (a man by a woman)
          bu̱-kə:y   'a divorce' (man by woman)
     b.   ka-kɔɲɛn   'to send a message'
          ku̱-koɲen   'a message'
     c.   ɛ-lɔk   'to cry (of an animal), bark'
          bu̱-lok   'an animal cry, bark'

The most complicated cases are those where we get a combination of cumulative and extended exponence. In Latin, the notion perfect is realized by having a special verb stem in addition to a special set of suffixes that encode person, number, and mood (we might also want to list voice, although the perfect is realized periphrastically in the passive):

(8) a.   re:x   -isti:
          rule.PERF-2SG.ACT. PERF
          'you ruled'
     b.   re:x   -e:runt
          rule.PERF-3PL.ACT.PERF
          'they ruled'

Here the mapping from the syntax to the phonology is both many to one and one to many. First, the stem *re:x-* is a perfective stem (compare the present stem *reg-*), and the ending is a perfective ending. This exemplifies extended exponence. Second, the endings *-isti:* and *-e:runt* simultaneously express second person singular, active voice, and perfective and third person plural, active voice, and perfective, respectively. This is cumulative exponence. **[Exercise 2]**

We now turn to the distinction between **context-free** and **context-sensitive inflection**. We refer to context-free inflection when there is a simple directional mapping between a morphosyntactic feature and a particular phonological string. Imagine that English has a feature [PRESENT PARTICIPLE] or [PROGRESSIVE]. Because this feature is always realized as /-ɪŋ/, we refer to context-free inflection: all present participles in English bear the same suffix.[3] In context-sensitive inflection, the realization of a morphosyntactic feature varies. For example, the feature [PAST] in English corresponds to several possible phonological realizations, as seen in the following table.

Phonological realizations of the feature [PAST] in English	
a.	Ablaut	ran, sat, won, drank, shone . . .
b.	Suppletion	was, went . . .
c.	Ø	hit, cut, put . . .
d.	/-t/	sent, lent . . .
e.	/-d/	helped [-t], shrugged [-d], wanted [-əd] . . .

We also find partial suppletion, as with *thought* and *brought*, both of which also bear the /-t/ suffix seen in the box above. They therefore exemplify extended exponence. Inflection for past tense in English is context-sensitive in the sense that the feature [PAST] is realized as many things depending on the lexeme it attaches to, with /-d/ suffixation being the default case.[4] As you continue to look at morphological data from a variety of languages, you will discover that context-sensitive inflection is much more common than context-free inflection.

■ 6.1.2 Inherent vs. assigned inflection

We must distinguish between **inherent** and **assigned** inflection. Nouns and pronouns are marked as having a particular gender in the speaker's mental lexicon, and thus for them, gender is inherent. For any other lexical category that reflects the gender of nouns and pronouns, such as adjective and verb, gender cannot be inherent. It must be assigned.

Number is generally not inherent, hence it is not marked in the lexicon. There are exceptions. Some words, like *pants*, have inherent number that is marked in the lexicon – in this case, plural. In some languages, there are even verbs that occur only in the singular or in the plural. They can also be said to have inherent number.

An example of assigned inflection is case. Nouns and pronouns in the lexicon do not have case. They obtain case by virtue of their position in the sentence. For example, nouns in object position will surface with an objective case in many languages.

◼ 6.1.3   Government vs. concord

Once we talk about the difference between inherent and assigned, we can address the question of how inflection may be assigned, which is generally in one of two ways: **government** or **concord**. Another word for concord is **agreement**.

Concord or agreement occurs when one element in a sentence takes on the morphosyntactic features of another element. One familiar example of concord is noun–adjective agreement in the Romance languages or German. Adjectives take on the number and gender of the noun that they modify.

Kujamaat Jóola nouns also trigger concord. The adjectives that modify them must be like them in gender or noun class. Similarly, verbs in Kujamaat Jóola reflect the noun class of their subject. We explore Kujamaat Jóola agreement in detail in the second half of this chapter.

The other way in which a word can acquire a category is government. Government is more or less what it sounds like: one word dictates the form of another.[5] Case assignment by verbs is usually thought of in this way. When a noun is required to appear in objective case, for example, it cannot be said that it agrees with – reflects the case of – the verb. This is because verbs don't have case. The same holds for prepositions. Prepositions do not have case-marked forms, either, but in many languages they require that their object surface with a particular case, such as dative or accusative. This is attributed to government of the prepositional object by the preposition itself.

We cannot talk about morphosyntactic features themselves as being "government features" or "concord features." It might seem, for instance, that case should be described as a "government feature" because nouns receive case under government by a verb or preposition. In (9), the noun object of the verb is in the accusative case because the verb *sehen* demands that its direct object be accusative:

(9)   Wir haben [_{NP}den   jungen   Piloten]   gesehen (German)
      we   have   [_{NP}the.M.ACC young.ACC pilot.ACC] seen

                                     Accusative

      'We saw the young pilot'

The problem is that the definite article *den* and the adjective *jungen* are usually thought to then acquire this same case via concord with the noun. If this is true, then the mechanism of inflection is independent of inflectional features.[6]

6.1.4 Inflectional categories

While most languages have morphological inflection of some sort, the actual inflectional categories can differ quite widely across languages. In this section, we will survey briefly both the most common categories and some of the ways in which languages may differ. It is convenient to make a first broad cut into nominal and verbal categories, though the nominal categories often appear on adjectives and verbs through concord. The most common nominal categories are **number** (Corbett 2000), **gender** (Corbett 1991), and **case** (Blake 2001).

Though some languages do not inflect for number, many languages make an obligatory inflectional distinction between **singular** and **plural** number of nouns and pronouns, which spills over to verbs and adjectives through concord. Less common, but not very unusual, is **dual** number, which distinguishes nouns referring to two items from those referring either to one or to more than two. Dual inflection is never found in the absence of singular and plural, and when a language has the category dual, it changes the meaning of the plural from 'more than one' to 'more than two'. We see a similar effect in English, where the dual quantifier *both* causes the plural quantifier *all* to mean 'more than two': a person who has two children must say *both my children*, not *all my children*. There are even a few languages with **trial** number, marking nouns that refer to sets of three, or **paucal** number (from Latin *pauca* 'few').

Gender is less common than number and more varied. Because of the connection of the English word *gender* to biological sex and because genders in European languages are sex-based, we tend to think that linguistic genders are always sex-based. For example, the Romance languages (e.g., French, Portuguese, and Spanish) have two genders, masculine and feminine, corresponding very roughly to male and female, at least in so far as nouns that refer to male persons are almost invariably masculine and those referring to females feminine. But just as common among the world's languages are genders based on animacy, shape, or other natural properties. Languages of North America, when they exhibit gender, most commonly have the two genders animate and inanimate, while the large Niger-Congo family of Africa has genders based on shape as well. Languages also vary greatly in the number of genders they have, ranging from the minimal two up to more than a dozen in some languages of Papua New Guinea. And though genders are always semantic in their origin, most languages with obligatory gender have nouns whose gender assignment is arbitrary, a well-worn example being the German word for 'girl', *Mädchen*, which is neuter in gender. In languages like French or Spanish, with only masculine and feminine genders, objects must also have genders, which results in the French word *fourchette* 'fork' being feminine, but *couteau* 'knife' masculine. In this particular case, it is possible to predict these gender assignments on purely morphological grounds, but certainly not on semantics, unless one has a very good imagination.

The case of a nominal expression is determined by its syntactic function. The simplest cases are **nominative** and **accusative**, usually reserved for syntactic subjects and objects respectively (the peculiar names of these and other cases are Latin translations of terms from the Greek grammarians).[7] Some languages have a case used only for the subjects of transitive sentences, the **ergative**, with an **absolutive** case reserved for both objects of **transitives** and subjects of **intransitives**. The **genitive** and **dative** (also Latin terms) are used for possessors and indirect objects. Other cases are more directly semantic in nature and might include such notions as **instrumental** or **locative** (denoting a place). Just as with gender, languages differ widely in the number of cases they encode in their morphology. Most languages do not show case inflection at all, by which we mean that nominals do not differ in their form depending on their syntactic function (some languages – Japanese is an example – have case markers, but they are independent words and not inflectional affixes). Languages that have only a small number of cases tend to stick to the central syntactic categories of nominative and accusative (or ergative and absolutive), along with genitive and perhaps dative. The ancient Semitic languages, for example, had only the basic three of nominative, accusative, and genitive.

The last nominal inflectional category that we will discuss is **person**. Universally, there are only three persons, and all spoken languages have all three. Nouns are always third person, and first and second person forms are always pronouns. The major differences among languages are in the plural, especially the first person plural. Here a language may distinguish between a form meaning 'me and others, but not you', which we call an **exclusive** form, and an **inclusive** form, meaning 'me and others, including you'. As an inflectional category, person, like gender, is often most prominently displayed through agreement, specifically agreement of verbs with their subject or object, and some languages have quite elaborate systems of person marking on the verb.

Verbal inflection expresses a number of types of morphosyntactic categories related to events, which vary quite widely across languages. These include **tense** (Comrie 1985), **aspect** (Comrie 1976), **mood** (Palmer 2001), and **voice**. A language may express some of these categories other than by verb inflection. English, for example, has an elaborate system for expressing aspect, mood, and voice, but the only category marked directly on the verb is tense, which can be either present or past: *departs* vs. *departed*. (In truth, the so-called English present tense is better thought of as non-past, as seen in expressions like *the train departs tomorrow at nine*.) The others are expressed by a fairly elaborate system of auxiliary or helping verbs, resulting in such long expressions as *should have been being considered*. Tense is directly connected to time and languages often express three tenses morphologically: past, present, and future. Other tenses are sometimes found, such as remote past. Aspect has more to do with the way in which we view the unfolding of an event than with its simple position in time. For example, many languages distinguish **imperfective** from **perfective** aspect, where the first denotes an action in progress while the second denotes a completed action. For example, the Russian imperfect verb *lechit* 'treat' is imperfective, while its perfective counterpart is *vylechit* 'cure'. Mood reflects a speaker's commitment to a proposition. English **modal** auxiliary verbs, for example, include *may* and *must*, which express different degrees of commitment to obligation or truth, as in the following two series, the first having to do with obligation, the second truth: *you may leave* vs. *you must leave*; or *she may have seen him* vs. *she must have seen him*. Voice has to do with the role of the subject as either agent or patient. The most common distinction is between the **active** and **passive** voices, where the subject of the latter is the patient, rather than the (unmarked) active. Again, English has a distinction between active and passive that is expressed through auxiliary verbs. In Latin, the same distinction is expressed

through inflection directly on the verb: *amo* 'I love' vs. *amor* 'I am loved'.
[Exercise 3]

■ 6.2   Inflection vs. Derivation

Within a lexeme-based theory of morphology, the difference between
derivation and inflection boils down to this: derivation gives you new
lexemes, and inflection gives you the forms of a lexeme that are determined by syntactic environment. But what exactly does this mean, and
is there really a need for such a distinction? This section explores the
answers to these questions, and in the process, goes deeper into the
relation between morphology and syntax.

■ 6.2.1   Differences between inflection and derivation

The first question we can ask about the distinction between inflection
and derivation is whether there is any formal basis for distinguishing
the two types of morphology. Can we tell them apart because they do
different things to words?

One generalization is that inflectional morphology does not change
the core lexical meaning or the lexical category of the word to which it
applies. A noun with a plural suffix attached to it is still a noun; *slurp*
means 'eat or drink noisily' whether it is past or present; and so on.
Derivational morphology may or may not affect the lexical category of a
word it applies to, and it typically changes its meaning. *Glory* is a noun,
and *glorious* is an adjective. While their meanings are related, they cannot
be said to mean the same thing in the way that *slurp* and *slurps* do.

A second generalization is that inflection, but not derivation, is determined by syntax. We already discussed this characteristic above. Which
form of a lexeme surfaces in a given position depends on its relationship
with the words around it. Perhaps when you were younger, you tried
mad-libs like the following:

Four score and seven _____ ago our _____ brought forth,

                      Noun   Noun

upon this _____ , a new nation, conceived in _____ . . .

           Noun   Noun

The person eliciting the words for the blanks in the Gettysburg address above automatically knows to put the first noun provided by his or her partner in the plural because "four score and seven" implies more than one (eighty-seven, to be exact). There is no need for the mad-lib instructions to specify "plural noun." Similarly, if a person eliciting words for a mad-lib says, "Verb," the reply will probably come in the citation form of the lexeme: *read*, *slurp*, *love*, or *kiss*, for example. But he or she will know whether it is necessary to add an -*s*, -*ed*, or -*ing* when inserting it into the blank, because it will be determined by context. The mad-lib instructions do not need to specify "third person singular" or "present participle."

A third generalization we can make is that inflectional morphology tends to be more productive than derivational morphology. Inflectional morphology can apply to words of a given category with relative freedom. Virtually any noun in English can be made plural with the addition of [z] or one of its two phonologically conditioned allomorphs. The only exceptions are those that have irregular plurals, such as *children* or *phenomena*, and those that logically do not allow a plural form: mass nouns like *rice* and abstract nouns like *intelligence* generally fall into this category. On the other hand, not every adjective can take the derivational affix -*ly* that forms adverbs. We can say *quickly*, but not ?*friendlily*.

Another generalization that has been made is that derivational affixes tend to occur closer to the root or stem than inflectional affixes. For example, (10) shows that the English third person singular present inflectional suffix -*s* occurs outside of derivational suffixes like the deadjectival -*ize*, and the plural ending -*s* follows derivational affixes including the deverbal -*al*:

(10) a. popular-ize-s
          commercial-ize-s
      b. upheav-al-s
          arriv-al-s

Similarly, Japanese derivational suffixes like passive -*rare* or causative -*sase* precede inflectional suffixes marking tense and aspect:[8]

(11) a. tabe-ru   tabe-ta
          eat- IMP   eat- PERF
          'eats'   'ate'
      b. tabe-rare- ru   tabe-rare- ta
          eat- PASS-IMP   eat- PASS-PERF
          'is eaten'   'was eaten'

c.   tabe-sase- ru   tabe-sase- ta
     eat- CAUS-IMP   eat- CAUS-PERF
     'makes eat'   'made eat'

This generalization is largely true, but there are many exceptions in the world's languages, so it is not a reliable diagnostic for distinguishing between inflection and derivation. (In chapter 3, we saw that the Kujamaat Jóola derivational suffix -*u* 'from' may follow inflectional suffixes.)

Should the relationship between the words in the left and right columns of each example be characterized as inflection or derivation? For answers, turn the page.

a.	take	took
b.	atom	atomize
c.	scribe	scribes
d.	megabyte	meg
e.	jostle	jostling
f.	go	went
g.	logic	logical
h.	shake	shaken
i.	ice	de-ice
j.	child	children

Finally, note that some linguists consider derived lexemes, but not inflected forms, to be present in the lexicon. This generalization is not absolute, since psycholinguistic studies have shown that speakers store at least some inflected words in their lexicons. Likewise, many derived forms are created on the fly, without ever being recorded in the lexicon. **[Exercises 4 and 5]**

Inflection vs. derivation

- Inflection does not change the core lexical meaning or the lexical category of the word to which it applies; derivation does the former and may do the latter.
- Inflection is the realization of morphosyntactic features, i.e., those that are relevant to the syntax, such as case and number. Derivation is not.
- Inflectional morphology is more productive than derivational morphology.
- Derivational morphology tends to occur closer to the root or stem than inflectional morphology.
- Derived lexemes are more likely to be stored in the lexicon than inflected forms.

6.2.2 The formal similarity between inflection and derivation

Despite the generalizations made above, the morphological form that inflection and derivation may take is very similar. Cross-linguistically, both can be expressed through prefixal, suffixal, or non-segmental means. The difference between inflection and derivation is therefore not so much a difference in form as a difference in function – what they do and what they tell us.

6.3   Inventory of Inflectional Morphology Types

What are the ways in which speakers can inflect, or "bend," lexemes to make them fit into a certain syntactic slot? We present a list of inflectional morphology types here. Although it is not comprehensive, it will give you a broad understanding of how inflection may be expressed.

6.3.1 Affixation and stem alternations

Since our focus in the non-Kujamaat-Jóola portions of this book has been English, we have had ample opportunity to look at the expression of inflection through affixation. In English, this is the most common means by which inflectional categories are expressed. For that reason we do not address affixation on its own here. Instead we present it with stem alternations, another means of expressing inflection in the world's languages. We wish to emphasize that just as affixation does not necessarily occur with stem alternations, stem alternations do not necessarily occur with affixation. We present them together merely for organizational purposes.

Latin, discussed briefly in section 6.1.1, is one language where in many cases, affixation interacts obligatorily with stem alternations in the expression of inflectional categories. Above we gave the example of *re:xisti:* 'you ruled'. The perfective stem *re:x-* can be contrasted with the present stem *reg-*. It supplements affixation in the expression of the perfect. Below we give further examples of Latin present stems alongside perfective stems. The expression of the perfect would involve not only the perfective stem, but also a series of suffixes:

(12)   Present stem   Perfective stem
   a. am-   ama:v-   'love'
   b. po:t-   po:ta:v-   'drink'

> Answers to inflection vs. derivation exercise:
>
> a. inflection
> b. derivation
> c. inflection
> d. derivation
> e. inflection (as long as both are verbs)
> f. inflection
> g. derivation
> h. inflection
> i. derivation
> j. inflection

c.	crep-	crepu-	'rattle'
d.	horr-	horru-	'bristle'
e.	juv-	ju:v-	'help'
f.	aug-	aux-	'increase'
g.	fi:g-	fi:x-	'fasten'
h.	ri:d-	ri:s-	'laugh'
i.	mord-	momord-	'bite'
j.	spond-	spopond-	'promise'
k.	prand-	prand-	'lunch'
l.	ascend-	ascend-	'climb'

In (12) we have tried to show a variety of alternation types that present–perfective stems fall into in Latin, but we do not attempt to be fully comprehensive. (12a–b) show the regular way of forming perfective stems from present stems in the so-called first conjugation of Latin (verbs ending in -a:re). (12c–d) are examples of verbs that have a perfective stem in -u. In (12e) we see an example of a verb whose stem vowel lengthens in the perfective. Examples (12f–h) have a perfective stem in -s. (What is written x was pronounced [ks].) (12i–j) display reduplication in the perfective stem. Finally, in (12k–l) we see that for some verbs, the present and perfective stems are identical.

Stem alternations are also a major exponent of inflection in the Apachean languages, a subset of Athapaskan which includes both Navajo and Apache. Active verbs in the Apachean languages are those that describe processes (e.g., 'become white') or movements and actions (e.g., 'walk', 'jump', 'throw'). They contrast with neuter verbs, which generally express a state of being or position (e.g., 'be white', 'be sitting'). Active verbs are regularly conjugated in several paradigms: imperfective, perfective, progressive, future, customary, iterative, and optative. The expression of these inflectional categories can generally be described as extended exponence, since it involves both prefixes and, sometimes, a special stem. Some active verbs have two conjugation patterns. The two patterns express aspectual contrasts such as momentaneous vs. continuative, which are distinguished principally through stem alternations. In (13) we provide the stems of the Navajo verb meaning 'handle a round object'. The first set of stems are those that occur in the momentaneous; the second set are those found in the continuative. (The discussion in this paragraph is paraphrased from Hoijer 1971: 130, and the examples come from there, as well.) In the following examples, vowels with hooks under them are nasalized, and acute accents mark high tone. This is in accordance with Navajo orthography.

(13)   Navajo stem alternations: 'handle a round object'
       Momentaneous:
       -ʔaah   imperfective
       -ʔą́   perfective
       -ʔáál̷   future, progressive, optative
       -ʔááh   customary and iterative
       Continuative:
       -ʔá   imperfective
       -ʔą́   perfective
       -ʔaal̷   future and progressive
       -ʔaah   customary and iterative
       -ʔaʔ   optative

We see in (13) that there are four momentaneous stems for the verb 'handle a round object' and five for the continuative. The perfective stem is the same in the momentaneous and the continuative. The other stems are all different. In all, there are eight different forms of this one stem, which would interact with affixation to express the full range of verbal inflectional categories. [Exercises 6 and 7]

■ 6.3.2 Apophony

So far we have seen affixation and stem alternations. In some cases affixation is supplemented or replaced by **apophony**, or vowel changes within a root, as shown below for English (14) and the Bernese dialect of Swiss German (15):

(14) a. sing, sang, sung
      b. drive, drove, driven

(15) a. suuffe [suːfə]   'drink (inf)'
          gsoffe [g̊sɔfːə]   'drunk (past part)'
      b. schwimme [ʃʊmːə]   'swim (inf)'
          gschwomme [g̊ʃʊʊmːə]   'swum'
      c. pfyffe [pfiːfə]   'whistle (inf)'
          pfiffe [pfɪfːə]   'whistled (past part)'

Other terms for apophony are **internal change** and, particularly when referring to English and other Germanic languages, ablaut. All three of these terms are sometimes applied to the vowel changes that apply to roots in Semitic languages, a topic that we address in the next section under the heading root-and-pattern morphology.

In the context of Germanic linguistics, ablaut is often reserved for apophony in verb paradigms, as in (14) and (15). A second term, **umlaut**, is used to describe the apophony found in singular–plural noun pairs like *goose~geese* or *foot~feet*. Umlaut is a phonologically conditioned alternation in which a vowel assimilates in part to a succeeding vowel. The term is used even when the succeeding vowel has been lost. For instance, the umlaut seen in the plural forms of the noun pairs *goose, geese* and *foot, feet* have resulted from vowel harmony with a high vowel in the plural suffix, which has since disappeared.

■ 6.3.3 Root–and–pattern morphology

In the Semitic language family, inflection often involves internal variations in vocalic and syllabic patterns, while the consonantal frame stays fairly stable. We call this root-and-pattern morphology, and it has already been discussed in chapter 3. Root-and-pattern is illustrated in (16) for the expression of number in certain Arabic nouns (examples from McCarthy and Prince 1990: 212, 217). The inclusion of the loanword 'bank' is to show that this particular way of forming the plural (referred to as the broken plural) is productive. What all of the plural forms in (16) have in common is that they begin with the syllable pattern CVCVV+:

(16)
Root	Singular	Plural	Gloss
jndb	jundub	janaadib	'locust'
slṭn	sulṭaan	salaaṭiin	'sultan'
ʕnb	ʕinab	ʕanaab	'grape'
nfs	nafs	nufuus	'soul'
bnk	bank	bunuuk	'bank'

Root-and-pattern morphology is yet another way of "bending" a form to fit a particular syntactic context. **[Exercises 8 and 9]**

▓ 6.3.4   Reduplication

Another means for expressing inflection that we find in certain languages is reduplication. Like root-and-pattern, reduplication has already been discussed, but from a phonological perspective, in chapter 3. We present examples of the Indonesian plural here. It is formed via full reduplication (examples are from Sneddon 1996: 16).

(17) kuda-kuda   'horses'
      rumah-rumah   'houses'
      singkatan-singkatan   'abbreviations'
      perubahan-perubahan   'changes'

When discussing Indonesian plural reduplication, it is important to note that it is not obligatory. Speakers of Indonesian have the option of using the unreduplicated form to refer to either singular or plural. So *kuda* not only means 'horse', but also 'horses'; *rumah* can refer to one house or more than one; and so on. The reduplicated plural is most likely to be used when the number of the noun is not clear from the context, as in the examples below (Sneddon 1996: 17):[9]

(18) a. Rumah-nya   dekat pohon-pohon mangga itu
          house- 3SG.POSS near tree- REDUP mango   that
          'His house is near those mango trees'
      b. Pada pinggang-nya   terikat bumbung-   bumbung
          LOC waist-   3SG.POSS PASS.tie water.container-REDUP
          kosong
          empty
          'At his waist are tied empty bamboo water containers'

Without reduplication of *pohon*, (18a) would be ambiguous between 'His house is near that mango tree' and 'His house is near those mango trees'; likewise, if *bumbung* were not reduplicated in (18b), the sentence could have the interpretation, 'At his waist is tied an empty bamboo water container', as well as the one given above.[10] Such ambiguity is not characteristic of plural reduplication cross-linguistically.

Children acquiring languages without plural reduplication sometimes spontaneously use reduplication to express the plural. An English-speaking child may say *shoe* for one shoe, but *shoe shoe* for two.

Reduplication can be used to express inflectional categories besides number. In section 6.1.1 we saw a few examples where partial reduplication is involved in the formation of the Latin perfective stem from the present stem, for example, *mordeo*: 'I bite', *momordi*: 'I bit'. Reduplication is also used in some languages as a derivational process. English has a derivational process of partial reduplication seen in *wishy washy*.

■ **6.3.5 Suppletion**

The last type of inflection that we will mention here is **suppletion**. Suppletion is said to take place when the syntax requires a form of a lexeme that is not morphologically predictable. In English, the paradigm for the verb *be* is characterized by suppletion. *Am, are, is, was, were,* and *be* have completely different phonological shapes, and they are not predictable on the basis of the paradigms of other English verbs. We also find suppletion with pronouns; compare *I* and *me* or *she* and *her*. Suppletion is most likely to be found in the paradigms of high-frequency words, as seen in the following table.

Examples of suppletion		
French	aller 'to go', être 'to be'	vais 'go (1sg)', suis 'am (1sg)'
Spanish	ir 'to go', ser 'to be'	fue 'went (1sg)', fue 'was (1sg)'
Finnish	hyvä 'good (nom. sg)'	parempi 'better', paras 'best'
Greek	[ɛnas] 'a, one (m.nom.sg)'	[mja] 'a, one (f.nom.sg)'
Swedish	ett 'one', två 'two'	första 'first', andra 'second'

We can look to historical linguistics for an explanation of why suppletive forms arise. Take, for example, the paradigm of the verb 'to go' in French. It comes from three different Latin sources. The infinitive, *aller*, and the first person and second person plural forms in the present, *allons* 'we go' and *allez* 'you (pl) go', come from Latin *ambulāre* 'to walk, to walk along'. The stem of future and conditional forms, such as *irai* 'will go (1sg)', has evolved from the Latin verb *ire* 'to go'. Finally, forms like *vais* 'go (1sg)' or *vont* 'go (3pl)' come from Latin *vadere* 'to go, to walk'. Thus we see that the idiosyncrasies of languages today can often be explained by looking at the languages of yesterday. **[Exercise 10]**

In certain cases, such as with *catch~caught* or *think~thought* and other verbs like them in English, it is most convenient to speak of **partial**

suppletion. In these cases, the initial phoneme or phonemes of the word remain the same, but there is both internal change and change to the end of the word (loss of segments and addition of a past tense indicator [t]). **[Exercises 11 and 12]**

Summary of inflection types

Affixation: accuse → accused, apply → applies
Apophony, a.k.a. internal change: foot → feet, see → saw
Reduplication: Indonesian **rumah** 'house', **rumah-rumah** 'houses'
Root-and-pattern: Hebrew **lomed** 'studies', **lamad** 'he studied'
Stem alternations: Latin **po:t-** (present), **po:ta:v-** (perfective) 'drink'
Suppletion: go → went, is → was
Partial suppletion: think → thought

■ 6.4 Syncretism

Having inventoried a variety of ways in which inflection is expressed cross-linguistically, we now turn to **syncretism**. We speak of syncretism when a single inflected form corresponds to more than one set of morphosyntactic features (this definition is paraphrased from Spencer 1991: 45). Syncretism is very common cross-linguistically. As Stump (2001: 212) notes, syncretism raises a number of questions relevant to morphological theory. In keeping with the non-theoretical approach of this book, we will not explore them here, but we refer the reader to Stump's book (pp. 212–41) for discussion. Here we limit ourselves to presenting a few examples of syncretism from that work.

The first examples that we present come from Bulgarian (these are from Stump 2001: 39, 213). In the Bulgarian imperfect and aorist paradigms, the second person singular and third person singular forms are identical. (The aorist is a past tense.) We show this in (19) for the verbs KRAD 'steal' and IGRÁJ 'play' (these are the citation forms of the lexemes):

(19) Imperfect 2sg krad-é-š-e   igrá-e-š-e
                3sg krad-é-š-e   igrá-e-š-e
      Aorist   2sg krád-e   igrá
                3sg krád-e   igrá

In (19), -š is a preterite suffix and -e is 3sg agreement. We see here that a single inflectional form such as *kráde* may express more than one set of morphosyntactic features: 2sg aorist or 3sg aorist.

Romanian also displays widespread syncretism. For many verbs, the first person singular in the present indicative paradigm is identical to the third person plural form. We show this in (20); both 1sg and 3pl forms are in boldface (data from Stump 2001: 213–14):

(20)   Romanian present indicative paradigms

	A UMPLEA 'to fill' 2	A FACE 'to do' 3	A STI 'to know' 4
1sg	**úmpl-u**	**fác**	**stí-u**
2sg	úmpl-i	fác-i	stí-i
3sg	úmpl-e	fác-e	stí-e
1pl	úmple-m	fáce-m	stí-m
2pl	úmple-ti	fáce-ti	stí-ti
3pl	**úmpl-u**	**fác**	**stí-u**

In (20), the infinitives are put in small caps because they are used as the citation forms of the lexeme. The numbers (2, 3, 4) under the glosses are the numbers of the conjugations these three verbs fall into. Syncretism in the present indicative does not take place in Romanian verbs of the first conjugation.

■ 6.5   Typology

The term **typology** refers to a classification based on the comparative study of types, and morphological typology was the first systematic method used by linguists in the nineteenth century to compare the structures of different languages. While other sorts of typology flourish today, especially syntactic typology, morphological typology has languished since it was criticized by the first American structuralists, especially Edward Sapir in his *Language* (1922). Still, the traditional terms are used often enough to warrant mention, and the distinctions, while they may not be valid for entire languages, are still quite useful for describing individual morphological phenomena.

The basic typology has to do with a scale running from **analytic** to **synthetic** languages, which encodes the degree to which the individual meaningful elements in a language are expressed separately. At the analytic end we have the **isolating** languages, of which Vietnamese is the prototypical example, because the only morphology it has is compounding. It has no derivational or inflectional processes of any kind. The next type is **inflective**, of which the more analytic subtype is **agglutinating**:

an agglutinating language like Turkish or Hungarian will have affixes, but they are strung out quite separately, each expressing a single notion, and easily identified. Consider the following simple table of Hungarian words:

		'house'	'river'
SINGULAR	NOMINATIVE	ház	folyó
	ACCUSATIVE	házat	folyót
PLURAL	NOMINATIVE	házak	folyók
	ACCUSATIVE	házakat	folyókat

The accusative case marker is -at (the vowel is deleted after a stem-final vowel), while the plural marker is -ak (with the vowel again deleting after a stem-final vowel). When a word is both accusative and plural, both affixes appear one after the other. Compare a **fusional** language, like Latin, shown in the next table:

		'lord'	'song'
SINGULAR	NOMINATIVE	dominus	cantus
	ACCUSATIVE	dominum	cantum
PLURAL	NOMINATIVE	domini	canti
	ACCUSATIVE	dominos	cantos

In these Latin forms, the same four slots, singular and plural nominative and accusative, are filled by four distinct suffixes: -s, -m, -i, and -os (here, the stem vowel deletes before the suffix vowel), so we say that the two morphosyntactic features in each of the cells of the table (e.g., NOMINATIVE SINGULAR) are fused. Latin is actually much more complicated, since these two nouns represent one of only five main types, each of which has a distinct set of forms.

The last stop on this continuum is **polysynthetic** languages, in which entire sentences are expressed in a single word. The languages most often cited as polysynthetic come from North America. The following discussion of the morphology of Nootka, a language spoken on Vancouver Island in British Columbia, follows closely that of Sapir (1922).

The Nootka root inikw- means 'fire' or 'burn'. Adding the suffix -ihl 'in the house' results in the word inikw-ihl, which means either 'fire in the house' or 'it burns in the house'. The addition of the article -'i serves to disambiguate this expression, so that *inikw-ihl-'i* can mean only 'the fire in the house', while adding the indicative suffix *-ma* will just as clearly show that the expression *inikw-ihl-ma* is verbal and means 'it burns in the house'. Returning to *inikw-ihl*, if we add the plural suffix *-'minih* to it, we get the expression *inikw-ihl-'minih*, which is still either 'fires in the house' or 'burn plurally in the house'.

We can diminutivize this plural by adding the suffix *-'is* to it: *inikw-ihl-'minih-'is* 'little fires in the house' or 'burn plurally and slightly in the house'. What if we add the preterit tense suffix *-it*? *inikw-ihl-'minih-'is-it* is not necessarily a verb meaning 'several small fires were burning in the house'. It may still be nominalized; *inikwihl'minih'isit-'i* means 'the former small fires in the house, the little fires that were once burning in the house'. It is not an unambiguous verb until it is given a form that excludes every other possibility, as in the indicative *inikwihl-minih'isit-a* 'several small fires were burning in the house'.

In all of these expressions, we see how a polysynthetic language like Nootka can build up complex expressions, indeed entire sentences, that consist of a single word. That is not to say that a language like English can't have one-word sentences. *Go!* is a perfectly well-formed such utterance. But one-word sentences are the exception in English, and the norm in Nootka.

■ 6.6 Summary

The term inflection – "bending" a lexeme – means changing its shape to meet the demands of its syntactic position or environment. Any change in form that is conditioned by syntactic factors counts as inflection, whether it involves affixation or not. So far in this chapter we have discussed various types of exponence (simple, cumulative, extended), distinguished between inherent and assigned inflection and between government and concord, and identified inflectional categories found cross-linguistically; we discussed ways to distinguish inflection from derivation; and we inventoried possible inflectional morphology types, which include affixation, stem alternations, apophony, root-and-pattern, reduplication, and suppletion. We looked at syncretism, and finally, morphological typology. In the Kujamaat Jóola portion of this chapter we will explore agreement (concord) in more detail by showing how it is realized in that language.

■ Agreement in Kujamaat Jóola

In chapter 2 we presented the Kujamaat Jóola noun classes. No discussion of noun class would be complete without also discussing agreement. While noun class, or gender, is a property of nouns, it can be reliably detected only by looking at those words with which the noun enters into an agreement relation. We got a hint of this in chapter 2 where we learned that certain Kujamaat Jóola words, such as *mbur* 'bread' and *dakar* 'Dakar', bear no noun class prefix, and others, such as *(e)jimukor* 'lion' and *(ε)bεkan* 'bicycle', bear one only optionally. Yet these nouns always have gender.

The set of words with which a noun enters into an agreement relation varies from language to language. In Kujamaat Jóola this set includes the categories in (1):

(1) a. Definite articles
     b. Pronouns
     c. Nominal modifiers (demonstratives, cardinal and ordinal numbers, particularizers, adjectives)
     d. Verbs
     e. Relative pronouns
     f. Genitive markers

In this section we present some of the forms that agreement in Kujamaat Jóola may take.

■ Definite article

The Kujamaat Jóola definite article has the form *-aC*, where C is identical to the consonant of the class prefix. Three noun classes have prefixes that consist of a single vowel: class 1 (*a-*), class 3 (*ε-*), and class 8 (*u-*). For these, the definite article has the form *-aw*, *-εy*, and *-aw*, respectively. Examples from Sapir (1965: 68) are given in (2):

(2) Cl. 1   a-ɲil-aw   'the child'
     Cl. 2   ku-ɲil-ak   'the children'
     Cl. 3   ε-yεn-εy   'the dog'
     Cl. 4   si-yεn-as   'the dogs'
     Cl. 5   fu-tiːk-af   'the war'
     Cl. 6   ku-tiːk-ak   'the wars'
     Cl. 7   ka-siːn-ak   'the horn'
     Cl. 8   u-siːn-aw   'the horns'

Cl. 9	bu̱-bəːr-əb	'the tree'
Cl. 10	ji-sɛk-aj	'the small woman'
Cl. 11	mu-sɛk-am	'the small women'
Cl. 12	ɲi-sɛk-aɲ	'the large women'
Cl. 13	ba-ɲil-ab	'the many small children'
Cl. 14	fa-kɔr-af	'the smoke'
Cl. 15	ma-kuk-am	'the brains'

▓ Pronouns

The form of first and second person pronouns do not depend on noun class. Third person pronouns do, however. Both subject and object pronouns have the shape Cɔ when free (as opposed to bound), with C corresponding to the consonant of the noun class prefix. The forms of third person pronouns for classes 1–15 are listed in (3):

(3)   Cl. 1:   ɔ-
      Cl. 2:   kɔ-
      Cl. 3:   yɔ-
      Cl. 4:   sɔ-
      Cl. 5:   fɔ-
      Cl. 6:   kɔ-
      Cl. 7:   kɔ-
      Cl. 8:   wɔ-
      Cl. 9:   bɔ-
      Cl. 10:   jɔ-
      Cl. 11:   mɔ-
      Cl. 12:   ɲɔ-
      Cl. 13:   bɔ-
      Cl. 14:   fɔ-
      Cl. 15:   mɔ-

▓ Nominal modifiers

While Kujamaat Jóola has a variety of nominal modifiers, including demonstratives, numbers, and particularizers (Sapir 1965: 27–8), there is no well-defined category that corresponds to Indo-European adjectives. This is not unusual among the world's languages. Throughout Africa, what might be considered canonical adjectives by speakers of Indo-European languages are rare (Welmers 1973). Instead, adjectival concepts like 'small', 'beautiful', or 'angry' are generally expressed by a verbal element. In Kujamaat Jóola, what at first glance appear to be adjectives are often formed with a verbal stem prefixed with a relativizer that agrees in noun class with the head noun:

(4) a.   ɛ-   yɛn-ɛy   ya-   gɔn-   ɔ-   ɛ
          3CL- dog-DEF3 3REL- be.mad- STAT- HAB
          'the mad dog' (lit. 'the dog which is mad')
     b.   si- bəː- s   sa-   jak-   as
          4CL-COW- DEF4 4REL- be.good- DEF4
          'the good cows' (lit. 'the cows which are good')

The relativizer takes the form Ca- when modifying a subject, and Can- when modifying an object. We see it again in the forms in (5), where the nature of the verb makes it more obvious that we are dealing with relative clauses. Note in (5b) that the object relativizer may stand on its own:

(5) a.   ku- ɲil- ak   ka-   riɲ-   ulɔm
          2CL-child- DEF2 2REL- arrive.from-SUBORD
          'the children who arrive'
     b.   ɛ- lɔːl-   ɛy   yan ndaw a- sɛk-   ɔ   ə- pur- en
          3CL-chicken- DEF3 3REL Ndaw 1CL-woman-POSS 1CL-leave-CAUS
          'the chicken that Ndaw's wife brought out'

A second way to form what appear to be adjectives is to attach a prefix of the form (C)V- to what Sapir calls a 'neutral theme' – that is, a stem that can be used as a noun, verb, adjective, or adverb depending on context. Again, the initial consonant of the prefix corresponds to the consonant of the noun class prefix. We see examples of neutral themes being used as adjectives in (6).

(6) a.   si- jamɛn-as   si- lulum-   əs
          4CL- goat- DEF4 4CL- European- DEF4
          'the European goats'
     b.   ɛ- yɛn e- lulum
          3CL- dog 3CL- European
          'a European dog'
     c.   e- be ɛ- narɛ
          3CL- cow 3CL-woman
          'a female cow'

Prefixes of the form Ca- (7 ka-; 13 ba-; 14 fa-; 15 ma-) take the form Cu- in this construction, perhaps to avoid confusion with the relative pronoun presented immediately above.

Demonstratives, which have the form $uC(\varepsilon)$, and particularizers, which have the forms $CV\text{-}k\varepsilon(n)$ (indefinite) and $CV\text{-}kila$ (definite), are illustrated in (7a–c). As we saw with neutral themes, prefixes of the form $Ca\text{-}$ surface as $Cu\text{-}$:

(7) a. si- jamɛn-as   use
         4CL-goat- DEF4 4DEM
         'these goats'

     b. ka- rɛg ku- kɛn
         7CL- story 7CL- PARTIC
         'a certain story'

     c. e- bə- y   ɛ- kila
         3CL-cow- DEF3 3CL- PARTIC
         'the cow (of which I am talking)'

Cardinal numbers up to 'four' and ordinals up to 'fifth' also agree with a head noun (8–9):

(8) a. ɛ- yɛn yə- kon
         3CL- dog 3CL- one
         'one dog'

     b. u̱- bəːr u- baːkir
         8CL- tree 8CL- four
         'four trees'

(9) a. ɛ- yɛn- ɛy ɛ- tɔŋɔndɛy
         3CL- dog- DEF3 3CL- first
         'the first dog'

     b. si- ɲaraː- s   si- tɔkɛn- as
         4CL- monkey- DEF4 4CL-fifth- DEF4
         'the fifth monkeys'

Higher numbers do not agree with a head noun (examples from Sapir 1970):

(10) *bu̱ti̱nken* 'fifteen' (class 9 invariable)
      kabanan 'twenty' (class 7 invariable)
      ceme 'one hundred' (invariable) < Mdk. *keme*

In languages where numbers agree with a head noun, it is typical for agreement marking to be limited to the lower numbers. In many modern European languages, for example, only the word for 'one' agrees in gender with its head noun.

■ Subject–verb agreement

Verbs in Kujamaat Jóola are generally marked for subject agreement. When the subject is expressed by a noun or noun phrase (or when a non-human subject noun phrase is understood), the corresponding noun class marker appears.[11] Markers of the form *Ca* prefix as *Cu* (cf. (11b–c)):

(11) a. e- munguno ɛ-   jum bɔ
          3CL- hyena   3CL- stop here
          'Hyena (a hyena) stopped here'
      b. ka- ɲɛn- ak ku- tuj- ut
          7CL- arm- DEF7 7CL- break- NEG
          'The arm didn't break'
      c. ba- suwaːb   bu- iit
          13CL- bird.DEF13 13CL- fly
          'The birds flew off'

A subject noun phrase does not have to be present in order for an agreement prefix to appear on the verb. Verbs may agree with implied subjects. In (12a), the verb *jɔl* 'come' agrees with the class 4 subject *si-jamɛn-as* 'the goats', as shown by the *si-* prefix. The verb appears with this prefix even when the implied subject 'goats' is left unstated (12b–e). **[Exercise 13]**

(12) a. si-jamɛn-as si-jɔl   'the goats came'
      b. si-gaba si-jɔl   'two came'
      c. s-ɔ si-jɔl   'they came'
      d. si-nifan-as si-jɔl   'the old ones came'
      e. s-cti alasan si-jɔl   'Alasanne's came'

Even this brief sketch of agreement in Kujamaat Jóola makes it clear that agreement is a pervasive part of its grammar. It is impossible to ignore. We close with the sentences in (13), which show how the repetition of agreement markers may give the impression of alliteration:

(13) a. fu- gɔl- af f-   umbə f- ɔ-   f-   ɛ
          5CL-stick-DEF5 5AGR-1POSS 5CL-here- DEF5- EMPH
          '_my_ stick is _here_ ~ _this_ is _my_ stick'
      b. si- jamɛn-as s-   umbə s- ɔ-   s-   ɛ
          4CL-goat- DEF4 4AGR-1POSS 4CL-here- DEF4- EMPH
          'these are _my_ goats'
      c. bu- bəːr- əb bə- mak- əb bu- lɔlɔ
          9CL-tree- DEF9 9REL- be.big- DEF9 9AGR- fall
          'the big tree fell'

Exercises

1. Italian verbs
    First, analyze the following data and identify all of the morphemes.
    Group suffixes denoting person into one set. Then determine whether
    each suffix or set of suffixes exemplifies simple or cumulative
    exponence.

parlo	'I speak'	parlavo	'I spoke'
parli	'you (sg) speak'	parlavi	'you (sg) spoke'
parla	'he speaks'	parlava	'he spoke'
parliamo	'we speak'	parlavamo	'we spoke'
parlate	'you (pl) speak'	parlavate	'you (pl) spoke'
parlano	'they speak'	parlavano	'they spoke'

2. Zapotec of the Isthmus, Mexico (Nida 1965: 38)
    Identify all the morphemes in the following set of data. List all
    morphemes that have allomorphs. Describe the distribution of all
    allomorphs having phonologically definable positions of occurrence.
    Finally, discuss the data in terms of exponence (simple, cumulative,
    or extended).

a. geta	'corncake'	sketabe	'his corncake'	sketalu?	'your corncake'
b. bere	'chicken'	sperebe	'his chicken'	sperelu?	'your chicken'
c. do?o	'rope'	sto?obe	'his rope'	sto?olu?	'your rope'
d. yaga	'wood'	syagabe	'his wood'	syagalu?	'your wood'
e. di?idʒa	'word'	sti?idʒabe	'his word'	sti?idʒalu?	'your word'
f. palu	'stick'	spalube	'his stick'	spalulu?	'your stick'
g. kuba	'dough'	skubabe	'his dough'	skubalu?	'your dough'
h. tapa	'four'	stapabe	'his four'	stapalu?	'your four'

3. The following data from Dixon (1994: 9–10) illustrate an important
    grammatical contrast, that between a nominative–accusative case
    system and an ergative one. Examine the data and explain how
    they illustrate the difference between an accusative language, exem-
    plified here by Latin, and an ergative language, exemplified by
    Dyribal, a language from northeast Australia. ABS stands for absolutive
    case and ERG stands for ergative case.

Latin

a. domin-us veni-t   'the master (NOM) comes'
b. serv-us veni-t   'the slave (NOM) comes'
c. domin-us serv-um audi-t 'the master (NOM) hears
                            the slave (ACC)'
d. serv-us domin-um audi-t 'the slave (NOM) hears
                            the master (ACC)'
e. domin-ī veni-unt   'the masters (NOM) come'
f. serv-ī domin-um audi-unt 'the slaves (NOM) hear
                            the master (ACC)'
g. serv-us domin-ōs audi-t 'the slave (NOM) hears
                            the masters (ACC)'

Dyribal

a. ŋuma   banaga-nʸu
   father+ABS   return-NONFUT
   'father returned'
b. yabu   banaga-nʸu
   mother+ABS   return-NONFUT
   'mother returned'
c. ŋuma   yabu-ŋgu   bura-n
   father+ABS   mother-ERG   see-NONFUT
   'mother saw father'
d. yabu   ŋuma-ŋgu   bura-n
   mother+ABS   father-ERG   see-NONFUT
   'father saw mother'

4. Should the relationship between the French words in the left and
   right columns of each example be characterized as inflection or
   derivation? Do each pair separately.

   a. saule   'willow (tree)'   saule pleureur 'weeping willow'
   b. aller   'to go'   allons   'go' (1pl)
   c. soûl [su]   'drunk' (m.adj)   soûle [sul]   'drunk' (f.adj)
   d. soûl   'drunk' (m.adj)   soûler   'to make
                                                       someone drunk'
   e. souris   'mouse'   souricière   'mousetrap'
   f. instituteur 'primary school   institutrice   'primary school
                   teacher' (m)   teacher' (f)
   g. le   'the' (m)   les   'the' (pl)
   h. racine   'root'   déraciner   'to uproot'
   i. aveugle   'blind'   aveuglément   'blindly'
   j. équilibre   'balance,   équilibriste   'tight-rope
                   equilibrium'   walker'

5. Examine the following data from Tzeltal, a language of Mexico (Nida 1965: 100). For each pair, indicate whether the formation is derivational or inflectional. Then list the characteristics that form the basis of your decision.

    a. h-čamel   'sick person'   čamel   'illness'
    b. šiwel   'fright'   šiw   'to be afraid'
    c. lumal   'land'   lum   'earth'
    d. mahk'il   'lid'   mahk'   'to close'
    e. awinam   'your wife'   ?inam   'wife'
    f. čenk'ultik   'bean patches'   čenk'ul   'bean patch'
    g. h-?u?el   'influential person'   ?u?el   'power'
    h. č'uunel   'offering'   č'uun   'to believe, obey'
    i. k'abal   'custody'   k'ab   'hand'

6. Sudan Colloquial Arabic (Nida 1965: 41)
    Identify as many morphemes as the data indicate. List all morphemes that have allomorphs. Describe the distribution of all allomorphs that have phonologically definable positions of occurrence. Although the nouns in the following problem exemplify root-and-pattern, you should treat the stems as single morphemic units for the purposes of this problem.

    a. kitabi   'my book'
    b. kitabak   'your (m.sg) book'
    c. kitabik   'your (f.sg) book'
    d. kitabu   'his book'
    e. kitaba   'her book'
    f. kitabna   'our book'
    g. kitabkum   'your (m.pl) book'
    h. kitabkan   'your (f.pl) book'
    i. kitabum   'their (m) book'
    j. kitabin   'their (f) book'
    k. axuy   'my brother'
    l. axuk   'your (m.sg) brother'
    m. axuki   'your (f.sg) brother'
    n. axuhu   'his brother'
    o. axuha   'her brother'
    p. axuna   'our brother'
    q. axukum   'your (m.pl) brother'
    r. axukan   'your (f.pl) brother'
    s. axuhum   'their (m) brother'
    t. axuhin   'their (f) brother'

7. Describe how the third person singular present indicative of *-er* verbs in Spanish is formed from the basic stem on the basis of the following forms. You should describe the types of allomorphy that you encounter (adapted from Nida 1965: 124–5).

	3sg present indicative			Basic stem	
a.	pide	/pide/	'asks for'	ped-	/ped-/
b.	sirve	/sirbe/	'serves'	serv-	/serv-/
c.	vende	/bende/	'sells'	vend-	/bend-/
d.	barre	/bare/	'sweeps'	barr-	/bar-/
e.	come	/kome/	'eats'	com-	/kom-/
f.	aprende	/aprende/	'learns'	aprend-	/aprend-/
g.	decide	/deside/	'decides'	decid-	/desid-/
h.	siente	/siente/	'feels'	sent-	/sent-/
i.	miente	/miente/	'lies'	ment-	/ment-/
j.	duerme	/duerme/	'sleeps'	dorm-	/dorm-/
k.	pierde	/pierde/	'loses'	perd-	/perd-/
l.	vuelve	/buelbe/	'returns'	volv-	/bolb-/
m.	mueve	/muebe/	'moves'	mov-	/mob-/

8. The following paradigms are from Hebrew. The root associated with the meaning 'sit' is Y-SH-V (in IPA, j-ʃ-v), and the root associated with the meaning 'write' is K-T-V. Analyze the formation of the following paradigms in the following manner: first, rewrite each form, replacing each consonant of the root with C, but retaining the value of the vowel and of any non-root consonants. Treat <sh> as one segment. For example, 'I sat' would be CaCaCti. Then describe the formation of the past and present tense for each person (1sg/pl, 2m/f.sg/pl, 3m/f.sg, 3pl). In the past tense, the stem before the second plural suffixes is different. Assume that this difference is for purely phonological reasons.

Past

a.	yashavti	'I sat'	katavti	'I wrote'
b.	yashavta	'you (m.sg) sat'	katavta	'you (m.sg) wrote'
c.	yashavt	'you (f.sg) sat'	katavt	'you (f.sg) wrote'
d.	yashav	'he sat'	katav	'he wrote'
e.	yashva	'she sat'	katva	'she wrote'
f.	yashavnu	'we sat'	katavnu	'we wrote'
g.	yshavtem	'you (m.pl) sat'	ktavtem	'you (m.pl) wrote'
h.	yshavten	'you (f.pl) sat'	ktavten	'you (f.pl) wrote'
i.	yasvu	'they sat'	katvu	'they wrote'

Present

a.	yoshev	'sit (m.sg)'	kotev	'write (m.sg)'
b.	yoshevet	'sit (f.sg)'	kotevet	'write (f.sg)'
c.	yoshvim	'sit (m.pl)'	kotvim	'write (m.pl)'
d.	yoshvot	'sit (f.pl)'	kotvot	'write (f.pl)'

9. Now add the following Hebrew data to those provided in the previous example. How can we express the formation of the future? How does its formation differ from that of the past and present? (Note that *x* alternates with *k* in Hebrew depending on position. You should assume that *x* in the forms below is the same underlying segment as *k* in the second column of Hebrew in the preceding problem, but you do not have to account for its distribution.)

a.	ʔextov	'I will write'
b.	tixtov	'you (m.sg) will write'
c.	tixtvi	'you (f.sg) will write'
d.	yixtov	'he will write'
e.	tixtov	'she will write'
f.	nixtov	'we will write'
g.	tixtvu	'you (m.pl) will write'
h.	tixtovna	'you (f.pl) will write'
i.	yixtvu	'they (m) will write'
j.	tixtovna	'they (f) will write'

10. Using an etymological dictionary, investigate the reasons for the following suppletive pairs in English:
   a. go/went
   b. good/better

11. Identify the morphological process at work in each set of words, and think of at least one more English example to add to each set.
   a. report/reported, grovel/groveled, purr/purred, saddle/saddled
   b. goose/geese, foot/feet, louse/lice, eat/ate, run/ran
   c. go/went, good/better, I/me, am/was

12. In the chapter we illustrated a number of different inflectional types, but they were not exhaustive. The following data are from the Congolese language Mongbandi (Nida 1965: 63). Determine the allomorphic alternation between the forms of the left and right columns. It consists solely of suprasegmental features.

All forms are in the completive aspect. The forms in the first column represent the basic forms of the roots. The tones on the forms in the first column are a fundamental part of the root.

	Forms with singular subjects	Forms with plural subjects	
a.	ŋgbò	ŋgbó	'swam'
b.	gwè	gwé	'went'
c.	mā	má	'heard'
d.	kpē	kpé	'fled'
e.	yó	yó	'carried'
f.	yé	yé	'agreed'
g.	bàtà	bātá	'guarded'
h.	hùlù	hūlú	'jumped'
i.	hākà	hāká	'taught'
j.	dīrì	dīrí	'answered'
k.	kōló	kōló	'pierced'
l.	sīgí	sīgí	'went out'
m.	díkò	dīkó	'read'
n.	gbíŋgà	gbīŋgá	'translated'

13. In his grammar of Kujamaat Jóola, Sapir states that there is sometimes a mismatch between the subject expressed by a noun phrase or freestanding pronoun and the subject expressed by agreement on the verb. We see below that a plural agreement marker (pronominal or noun class) can be used with a singular subject, implying that the subject is only partially expressed by the noun phrase.

a. injɛ nu- mịmịk di   suleman
    1   1PL- chat   with Souleymane
    'I was chatting with Souleymane'

b. e- mụngụn- ey si- lakɔ ɛ- jaw
    3CL-hyena- DEF3 4CL- PROG 3CL- go
    'The hyena (and some friends) were going'

In sentence (a), the verb bears 1pl agreement although the subject is 1sg; in (b) the verb bears class 4 agreement, although the subject is class 3.

Try to formulate a hypothesis about Kujamaat Jóola subject–verb agreement that accounts for these data, as well as the more general subject agreement facts presented in the chapter.

NOTES

1 The British and German spelling, *inflexion*, is even closer to *flex*.
2 In Modern English, a portmanteau is a briefcase, borrowed from the French for a carrying case for clothing. Carroll thought of blends like his own *slithy* as being two meanings packed together into one word, or carrying case. We first introduced the term *portmanteau* in section 4.2.4.1.
3 Note that the mapping is directional. We cannot work backwards and pair up every instance of /-ing/ with the feature [PRESENT PARTICIPLE] or [PROGRESSIVE], because there is more than one type of '-ing' in English (e.g., *babysitting* can be a present participle or a noun).
4 When speaking of default cases in morphology, it is often useful to invoke the Elsewhere Condition (Kiparsky 1982). We could have discussed the Elsewhere Condition here, but instead we have chosen to treat it in section 8.3.5 in the context of blocking.
5 The traditional notion of government gave rise to the Chomskian notion of government, used in certain theories of syntax, but the two are somewhat distinct.
6 An alternative is to say that the entire phrase receives accusative case under government and that the accusative case feature is distributed over all of its members.
7 The Latin term *accusativus* is a mistranslation of the Greek term *aitiatike* 'causal'. The problem is that the Greek word *aitia* means both 'cause' and 'accusation' and the Latin grammarians simply translated the wrong sense.
8 Regarding the morphemic breakdowns of example sentences, we have consistently put hyphens at the right edge of the leftmost element, rather than putting them at the right edge of prefixes and left edge of suffixes. Therefore, hyphenation in this book is not intended to provide information about direction of attachment of affixes.
9 Word-for-word glosses for Sneddon's examples were provided by Niken Adisasmito-Smith.
10 In Indonesian the picture is slightly more complicated. Expression of the category plural is ungrammatical in contexts like the following where plurality of the noun is explicit, in (i) because of the presence of the number *tiga* 'three', and in (ii) because shoes typically come in pairs (Sneddon 1996: 16–17):
   (i) Menteri mengunjungi tiga   negeri (*-negeri) asing
        minister visit.ACTIVE   three country (*-REDUP) foreign
        'The minister visited three foreign countries'
   (ii) Saya harus membeli   sepatu (*-sepatu) baru
        I   must buy.ACTIVE shoe   (*-REDUP) new
        'I must buy new shoes'
11 There is an exception: class markers consisting of a single vowel are optionally dropped in rapid speech when the subject directly precedes the verb.

7   Morphology and Syntax

We saw in the previous chapter that inflection and syntax are intimately related to one another. Inflection, we said, is the realization of morpho-syntactic features through morphological means. In this chapter we explore a variety of topics at the intersection of morphology and syntax, including morphologists' and syntacticians' definitions of inflection, structural constraints on morphological inflection, inflection and universal grammar, and grammatical-function-changing morphology. Since our target audience consists of students whose only exposure to syntax comes from an introductory course in general linguistics, we will avoid bringing in advanced syntactic analyses.

▪ 7.1 Morphological vs. Syntactic Inflection

We begin by distinguishing between two applications of the word *inflection*, one found chiefly in the morphological literature and the other in syntactic literature. For a morphologist, the presence of inflectional morphology in a language depends on the existence of multiple forms of a lexeme. If a lexeme has only one form, then there can be no morphological inflection. In syntax, there is no such requirement.

Chinese lexemes have only one form, abstracting away from phonologically determined alternations (mostly changes in tone). While Chinese has a few clitics or particles, including one that expresses past tense, these are generally not considered to be affixes. The same is true of Vietnamese, though the two languages are unrelated. For the morphologist, therefore, these two languages have no inflection.

From a syntactician's point of view, whether or not Chinese and Vietnamese have inflection is an entirely different matter. Even if a language does not express a particular notion such as number or case, it is typically assumed to be present in the syntax. Likewise, a syntactician may argue that a verb always agrees with its subject in an abstract sense. This abstract agreement is considered just as real in Chinese, where the verb form never depends on its subject, as in Russian, where the form of the verb changes depending on the person (first, second, third) and number (singular or plural) of the subject. In sum, morphological inflection is realized overtly, where syntactic inflection may or may not be.

Another difference between the morphological and syntactic usage of the term *inflection* is that morphologists speak of inflection only when dealing with bound forms. The reason for this is clear when you consider that in the previous chapter, we defined inflection informally as "bending" of a lexeme.

English has a syntactic category of modals, or modal auxiliaries. They are used to accompany other verbs and indicate that the action or state described by the sentence is something other than simple fact. *Alicia might go to the birthday party* isn't a simple fact about Alicia's going to a party; there is an element of uncertainty there. If we substitute other modals for *might*, the degree of uncertainly changes somewhat with each substitution: *Alicia **may** go to the birthday party*; *Alicia **can** go to the birthday* *party; Alicia **could** go to the birthday party; Alicia **must** go to the birthday party; Alicia **should** go to the birthday party; Alicia **would** go to the birthday party; Alicia **will** go to the birthday party.*

Should we consider these modals to be morphological inflection? The answer is no. In order to be classified as morphological inflection, a syntactic category must be expressed through bound forms. In the case of the English modals, we are not dealing with bound forms, but rather with separate words. Again, syntacticians differ from morphologists on this point. Most would treat auxiliaries as part of the inflectional system of a language. Morphologists are not denying the validity of this treatment, only distinguishing the full-word modals (i.e., syntactic inflection) from morphological inflection.

■ 7.2   Structural Constraints on Morphological Inflection

Cross-linguistically, we often find constraints on the realization of inflectional morphology. In Russian, for example, verbs show gender agreement with their subject (feminine, masculine, or neuter) only in the past tense. This fact about Russian has a historical explanation: the past tense form was originally an adjective and Russian adjectives agree in gender with the nouns that they modify. In Modern Hebrew, similarly, verbs agree in gender with their subjects, but only in the present tense (and hearing a Hebrew-speaking 3-year-old girl using correct feminine forms for all her present-tense verbs is a truly breathtaking experience). Again, this fact has a historical explanation: as with Russian past tense forms, Hebrew present forms were originally participles. Gender agreement is not optional in Hebrew and Russian. Instead, its morphological realization is context-dependent.

It is surprisingly easy to find languages where verb inflection is obligatory in some contexts, but impossible in others. We discuss a few such cases in the remainder of this section. All depend on syntactic context, rather than on tense, which is expressed as an inflectional part of the verb itself in Russian and Hebrew.

In the Kujamaat Jóola portion of this chapter, we will see that subject agreement is expressed obligatorily, except in the past subordinate and positive imperative forms of the verb. In some related languages, like Balanta, however, verbs agree with their subject only in certain syntactic contexts. In Balanta, verbs may be marked for subject agreement, but generally only in the absence of a subject noun phrase (1a). When a subject noun phrase is present, a subject prefix on the verb does not express agreement. Instead, it indicates that the subject is focused (1b) (data from N'Diaye-Corréard 1970: 30):

(1) a. bə- ɲāaŋ bēnte
         CL2-people come
         'The people came'

     b. bə- ɲāaŋ bə- dōoló bə- beeθa ma
         CL2-people CL2-few CL2-see   3SG.OBJ
         'A FEW PEOPLE saw him.'

Another example of a structural constraint on morphological inflection comes from the Central Khoisan language //Ani and its system of object agreement (Vossen 1985).[1] Finite verbs (except in the imperative) bear affixes that agree with a pronominal object in person, gender, and number (2a) or with a nominal object for number and gender (2b):

(2) a. tî   tsá mû-tì-tè
         me you see-1SG-PRES
         'You see me'

     b. gúénì=kʰòè-//ùà ≠xóà-   mà- ʔà !xóé=!xòè – m-
         hunter-   M.PL elephant-M.SG-OBJ run- REDUP/CAUS
                 tè
         -M.SG.OBJ-PRES
         'The hunters make the elephant run'

The catch is this: if a nominal object is not marked for gender and number, object agreement does not appear on the verb:

(3) gúénì=kʰòè-//ùà ≠xóà   !xóé-!xòè- tè
     hunter-   M.PL elephant run- REDUP -PRES
     'The hunters make the elephant run'

Here, in contrast to (2b), 'elephant' does not bear a gender–number suffix, and object agreement morphology fails to appear on the verb.

Finally, a well-known case is that of Arabic. Here the basic generalization is that subject–verb number agreement appears on the verb when the word order is SV (subject–verb) (4a) but not when it is VS (4b) (data from Ouhalla 1994: 43):

(4) a. l- tullaab- u   wasal- uu
         the-students-NOM arrived-3PL
         'The students have arrived'

     b. wasal- a l- tullaab- u
         arrived-3SG the-students-NOM
         'The students have arrived'

In (4b) third plural subject agreement is blocked, and instead we get default third person singular agreement.

In sum, in Balanta and Arabic subject agreement and //Ani object agreement, the realization of agreement is either obligatorily present or obligatorily absent, depending on the syntactic context. That this occurs in the world's languages is what we want you to take away from this section. If you have had extensive experience with syntax you might want to investigate in greater detail the structural analyses behind these facts.

■ 7.3 Inflection and Universal Grammar

Universal Grammar is the theory developed by Noam Chomsky that states that all languages are identical at some level of analysis. It has had a tremendous influence on the field of linguistics, and its validity is rarely questioned. A key phrase in the definition of Universal Grammar that we have provided is "at some level of analysis." What is the level of analysis at which languages are identical? At which levels do languages differ? More specifically, are inflectional categories universal?

In one sense, inflectional categories are universal. In the last chapter we gave an overview of inflectional categories that crop up over and over again in the world's languages. Yet it would be a mistake to say that the realizations of inflectional categories are stable cross-linguistically. To see what we mean, consider gender, a topic that we addressed in chapter 2.

Gender is highly problematic from a universalist point of view. As we noted in chapter 2, the number of noun classes in the languages of the Atlantic family vary widely. Kujamaat Jóola has 19, but Gombe Fula has 25, Serer 16, Wolof 10, Manjaku 14, and Balanta seven. Some Atlantic languages have multiple dialects, and dialects do not necessarily share the same number of noun classes. When we look past Atlantic to other language families of the world, we see that it is not only the number of genders that may vary from language to language; it is the entire organization of the gender system. However, despite differences between gender systems, some similarities do emerge.

German is a language that has three genders. They are called masculine, feminine, and neuter. Examples of nouns belonging to each gender are given in (5):

(5) | Masculine | | Feminine | | Neuter | |
|---|---|---|---|---|---|
| Mann | 'man' | Frau | 'woman' | Parlament | 'parliament' |
| Tag | 'day' | Lüge | 'lie' | Messer | 'knife' |
| Zuschlag | 'surcharge' | Erde | 'earth' | Mädchen | 'girl' |

Masculine, feminine, and neuter are obligatory inflectional categories of German. This means that every noun in the language, including borrowings like *Parlament* 'parliament', must belong to a gender. A noun cannot be genderless. Furthermore, gender is obligatory in that a noun cannot simply carry it around: its gender category must be expressed through agreement.

We can compare German to Ojibwa, an Algonquian language discussed by Corbett (1991: 20–2). Ojibwa has two genders, animate and inanimate (but note that some inanimate objects have grammatically animate forms):

(6)   Animate   Inanimate
      enini   'man'   essin   'stone'
      enim   'dog'   peka:n   'nut'
      mettikumi:šš   'oak'   pekkwe:šekan   'bread'
      a:kim   'snowshoe'   wa:wan   'egg'
      a:sso:kka:n   'sacred story'
      meskomin   'raspberry'

These function in the same way as the German genders in that they are obligatory and must be expressed.

How are the noun classification systems of German, Ojibwa, and Kujamaat Jóola related to one another? The obvious answer is that they are not related at all. The only thing they have in common is that for all of them gender is an obligatory inflectional category. Every noun must have a gender, and that gender must be expressed in the morphology.

If you look at many languages, you will discover that certain types of inflectional categories appear over and over again. For example, nouns are regularly inflected for case, number, and gender. Nouns in different languages will not necessarily inflect for the same cases – some languages will have two and others 20; nor will they inflect for the same genders. For verbs, the picture is similarly limited. Verbs might inflect for tense, aspect, mood, voice, or agreement, but you generally will not find languages where verbs inflect for other categories. Our brief overview of the German and Ojibwa gender systems, along with our more detailed treatment of the gender system of Kujamaat Jóola, should illustrate that inflectional categories themselves may not be universal, but there are universal principles governing what is inflectionally possible and what is not. **[Exercises 1 and 2]**

■ 7.4   Grammatical Function Change

In English we can say:

(7)   The governor broke the law

We can also say:

(8)   The law was broken by the governor

In grammatical terms, the sentence in (7) is active and the one in (8) is passive. *The law*, that which undergoes the action of breaking, occupies object position in (7), but in (8) it occupies subject position. The agent, *the governor*, occupies subject position in (7), but in (8) it surfaces as the object of the preposition *by*. It would have been equally grammatical not to mention the governor at all, as in (9):

(9)   The law was broken

There are times in life when the passive is very convenient. Perhaps the governor's administration needs to acknowledge that the law was broken but does not want to admit publicly that the governor was the one at fault.

In English we can also say:

(10)   Solomon made the governor break the law

I Iere, *the governor* is still the agent of the verb *break*, but it is not the subject of the sentence as a whole. Solomon has taken over that function. Sentences like the one in (10) are called causatives because they usually express the meaning 'cause to do something', or sometimes 'allow, persuade, help to do something'.

Finally, in English we can also say:

(11)   The governor broke the law for Susie

This sentence resembles the one in (7), but we have introduced another participant, *Susie*, the person for whom the governor broke the law.

We could discuss the morphology of *break* in the English sentences in (7–11), but its forms are fairly limited: *broke, broken, break*. None of these forms is limited to expressing a passive, causative, or 'for X' interpretation. (The *-en* of *broken* in (8–9) is sometimes considered a passive morpheme, but it is not limited to passive sentences. We could also say *The clock has finally broken*.) However, if we look at other languages, we often find that the passive, causative, and other types of grammatical-function-changing phenomena (we define the term *grammatical function change* immediately below) are associated with particular morphology. For example, we were introduced to the Kujamaat Jóola causative suffix in chapter 5.

Grammatical function change refers to "alternations in the grammatical encoding of referential expressions," to use the definition presented by Baker (1988: 1). In (7–8), for example, we saw that the agent can be encoded as a subject or object, depending on the form of the verb used: *broke* or *was broken*. Passive, causative, and other phenomena that we will illustrate in the remainder of this section are grammatical-function-changing phenomena because they can be seen as triggering the encoding change.

Our goal in this section is to help you recognize various types of grammatical-function-changing phenomena that are found cross-linguistically. We will not analyze them, beyond presenting basic definitions, because to do so would require us to go too deeply into syntax. Grammatical-function-changing phenomena involve morphology–syntax interactions at their most intimate.

■ 7.4.1 Passive

The active–passive distinction is traditionally considered one of voice.[2] (12a) represents the active voice, and (12b) the passive:

(12) a. Ashley wrote this article
      b. This article was written by Ashley

Ashley and *this article* are considered arguments of the verb. The arguments of a verb are individuals, entities, or items that are required to be present because of the verb's lexical entry. In its transitive use, WRITE has two arguments, an agent and a theme. In the active sentence (12a), the agent is in subject position, and the theme is in object position. (We have assumed throughout the book that readers have at least a passive understanding of thematic roles such as agent, instrument, and theme.)

Below we give an example of the passive contrasted with the active voice from Bajau, an Austronesian language (Donohue 1996: 784):[3]

(13) a. kita-ku uggo'
          see-1SG pig
          'I saw the pig'
      b. di-kita-ku   uggo'
          PASS-see-1SG pig
          'The pig was seen by me'

With these two sentences we see that although the passive entails a change in word order in English, it does not in all languages. In Bajau, the passive is formed via the affixation of a passive morpheme, *di-* to the verb.

Kujamaat Jóola also has a passive. It also looks very different from that of English. Note that the Kujamaat Jóola passive is used infrequently, and it is restricted for the most part to constructions with inanimate subjects. It is marked by the suffix *-i*:

(14) a. ni-   bɔɲ- i-   bɔɲ
         1SG.SUB-send-PASS-REDUP
         'I have been sent'
      b. w-af   wa-ri-ɛrit-i
         17CL-thing 17CL-eat-HAB.NEG-PASS
         'something uneatable'

Without the passive morpheme *-i*, (14a) would have the meaning 'I sent'.

We said that in Kujamaat Jóola, the passive is used less frequently than the active. Another way of saying this would be to call use of the active voice neutral, and use of the passive voice non-neutral. Whenever a situation like this arises in the world's languages, we call the neutral case the **unmarked** case and the non-neutral case the **marked** case. This is literally true in the examples we presented from Bajau and Kujamaat Jóola. In both cases, the passive is marked by a special morpheme, but the active requires no such marker. The terms marked and unmarked are frequently encountered in linguistics, and they are by no means limited to describing grammatical-function-changing phenomena.

■ 7.4.2 Antipassive

The antipassive occurs less frequently than the passive in the world's languages. It is one of the least well-known grammatical-function-changing phenomena. In the antipassive, an object of the verb is expressed instead in an oblique case or it becomes null. We illustrate it with a pair of sentences from Greenlandic Eskimo (Woodbury 1977, cited in Baker 1988: 9). In example (15a), the subject 'man' is expressed in ergative case, and the object 'children' is in absolutive case. In (15b), the subject 'man' instead bears absolutive case, and the object 'children' has been demoted, in a sense, to being expressed with instrumental case. There is a further difference. In (15a), the object 'children' triggers agreement on the verb; this is standard for objects in the language. In (15b), however, 'children', now in instrumental case, does not trigger agreement.

(15)   a.   Aŋut-ip miirqa-t   paar-ai
             man-ERG child-PL(ABS) care-INDIC/3SGSUB/3PLOBJ
             'The man takes care of the children'
       b.   Aŋut-∅   miirqa-nik   paar-si-vuq
             man(ABS) children-INSTR care-APASS-INDIC/3SGSUB
             'The man takes care of the children'

The antipassive morpheme in (15b) is -si. The two sentences given here express the same meaning, but they do so by different means.

■ 7.4.3   Causative

As we mentioned above, the causative typically expresses the meaning 'cause to do something' or sometimes 'allow, persuade, help to do something'. We illustrate it with an example from Kujamaat Jóola. On its own, the stem tɛy- means 'run'. When suffixed with the causative marker -ɛn, however, it means 'make run':

(16)   ba- laːb   bu- tɛy- ɛn- ɔla-   tɛy- ɛn
        13CL- sun.DEF13 13CL- run- CAUS- 1PL.INCL- run- CAUS
        'The sun made us run (seek shelter)'

■ 7.4.4   Applicative

The term applicative describes a number of different grammatical-function-changing phenomena cross-linguistically. They involve the addition of an applicative affix along with a change in function of an oblique object (e.g., locative, instrumental), indirect object, or null object. These come to be expressed as a main object of the verb, often called the applied object. Depending on the language and the particular construction, the applied object may be interpreted as beneficiary, maleficiary, goal, instrument, location, or motive. Most work on applicative constructions has involved the Bantu languages.

We illustrate the applicative construction with a pair of examples from the Kivunjo dialect of Kichaga, a Bantu language (Bresnan and Moshi 1990: 148):

(17)   a.   N-ɑ́-ɨ́-ly-à   k-élyà
             FOC-1S-PR-eat-FV   CL7-food
             'He/she is eating food'

b. N-ǎ-í-lyì-í-à   m̀-kà   k-élyà
    FOC-1S-PR-eat-APP-FV   CL1-wife   CL7-food
    'He/she is eating food for the benefit of the wife' or
    'He/she is eating food to the detriment of the wife (cheating
    on the wife)'

In the glosses for (17a–b), FOC is a focus morpheme; 1s is an agreement
morpheme for subject, class 1; PR is a present morpheme; APP is the
applicative morpheme; and FV is a final vowel. Diacritics on the Kichaga
words represent tones; they are not important here. We see that (17b) has
an additional object not found in (17a). The appearance of this object is
made possible by the addition of the applicative suffix -í to the verb.
(17b) has two possible interpretations, as we have shown. In the first, the
wife is considered the beneficiary; in the second a maleficiary.

In (18) we show that the same verb allows instrumental, locative, and
motive applied objects (Bresnan and Moshi 1990: 149):

(18) a. N-ǎ-í-lyì-í-à   mà-wòkő   k-êlyâ
          FOC-1S-PR-eat-APP-FV   CL6-hand   CL7-food
          'He/she is eating food with his/her hands' (instrument)
      b. N-ǎ-í-lyì-í-à   m̀-r̪ì-nyì   k-élyà
          FOC-1S-PR-eat-APP-FV   CL3-homestead-LOC   CL7-food
          'He/she is eating food at the homestead' (locative)
      c. N-ǎ-í-lyì-í-ˈá   njáá   k-êlyâ
          FOC-1S-PR-eat-APP-FV   CL9.hunger   CL7-food
          'He/she is eating the food because of hunger'

In (18b), r̪ is a retroflex r. You may ignore the diacritics here, including
the superscript exclamation point.

In their analysis of the Kichaga applicative construction, Bresnan and
Moshi write that the applicative construction is the only means by which
the semantic notions of beneficiary, maleficiary, instrumental, locative,
and motive can be expressed. There are no prepositions or case markers
in the language that might provide an alternative means. Languages
differ in this respect. In some languages with the applicative construction, paraphrases of it may be possible.

■ 7.4.5 Noun incorporation

The last type of grammatical-function-changing phenomenon that we illustrate here is noun incorporation. Gerdts (1998: 84) defines incorporation

as "the compounding of a word (typically a verb or preposition) with another element (typically a noun, pronoun, or adverb). The compound serves the combined syntactic function of both elements." Noun incorporation is the most common type. It involves the combination of a noun stem and a verb or adjective into a complex form that serves as a predicate. The following examples all illustrate noun incorporation. They are from Gerdts (1998: 84–5), who cites Sapir (1911), Woodbury (1975), and Comrie (1992), respectively. We have put the incorporated noun stems in boldface type.

(19)   Nahuatl, a Uto-Aztecan language of Mexico
  a.   ni-c-qua   in   nacatl
       I-it-eat   the   flesh
       'I eat the flesh'
  b.   ni-**naca**-qua
       I-**flesh**-eat
       'I eat flesh'

(20)   Onondaga, an Iroquoian language of Canada and the United States[4]
  a.   waʔhahninúʔ   neʔ   oyɛ́ʔkwaʔ
       TNS-he:it-buy-ASP   PRTC   it.tobacco
       'He bought the tobacco'
  b.   waʔha**yɛʔkwa**hní:nuʔ
       TNS-he:it-**tobacco**-buy-ASP
       'He bought (a kind of) tobacco'

(21)   Chukchee, a Paleo-Siberian language of eastern Russia
  a.   kupre-n   nantəvatgʔan
       net-ABS   set
       'They set the net'
  b.   **kopra**-ntəvatgʔat
       net-set
       'They set the net'

The noun stems in (19–21b) are clearly incorporated into the verb stem, as Gerdts notes, on the basis of positional and phonological criteria that we do not go into here. These examples also illustrate a general characteristic of noun incorporation cross-linguistically: incorporated noun stems do not take a determiner or bear case-marking morphology.

Our goal in this section has merely been to present the phenomenon of noun incorporation. There is much more that we could have discussed. Linguists have explored questions such as the following: when do speakers of languages with noun incorporation make use of it, and when do they use freestanding nouns? What restrictions are there on nouns that may be incorporated? Are there syntactic constraints on incorporation? We will leave you to explore these issues on your own. The article by Gerdts that we have referred to here would be a good place to start. [Exercises 3 and 4]

■ 7.5 Summary

Having read this chapter and chapter 6 on inflection you should have a better understanding of the ways in which morphology and syntax interact. Chapter 6 was primarily concerned with the expression of morphosyntactic features through inflection. This chapter has addressed a variety of different topics, including ways in which morphologists and syntacticians may approach inflection differently, structural constraints on the morphological realization of morphosyntactic features, and grammatical-function-changing morphology found cross-linguistically, including passive, antipassive, causative, applicative, and noun incorporation.

In the next section we finish our tour of Kujamaat Jóola morphology with an overview of its verbal morphology and interactions between morphology and syntax.

■ Kujamaat Jóola Verb Morphology

We begin by repeating the table given in chapter 5 that illustrates the basic structure of Kujamaat Jóola verbs.[5] Discussion of it can be found there. **[Exercise 5]**

The Kujamaat Jóola verb

2-	1-		-1	-2	-3
res	subject	STEM	aspect	object	subord
res neg	rel pronoun		mood	passive	redup
neg imper			past subord	noun	
past subord			negation	emphasis	
			directional		

■ Subject and object marking

We saw in chapter 6 that Kujamaat Jóola verbs agree with their subjects for noun class. The language also possesses a set of bound personal pronouns. Freestanding personal pronouns, which we won't present here, may be used in place of the bound ones to convey emphasis.

Bound subject pronouns

	Singular	Plural	
		Inclusive	Exclusive
1	ni- ~ i-	nu- ~ u- . . . -a ~ -al	nu- ~ a-
2	nu- ~ u-	ji-	
3	na- ~ a-	ku-	

Note that two forms are given for all but the second person plural and third person plural prefixes. In general, the full forms are used with the initial verb of a clause, in the absence of preceding prefixes or proclitics, and the shorter forms in other contexts. The alternation in the second portion of the first person plural inclusive suffix is morphophonemically determined, with the final /l/ surfacing before vowels but not consonants.

Somewhat surprisingly, the shorter form of the subject prefixes may substitute for the full form, as in the following example, to indicate an imperative or interrogative, or to emphasize the subject. *A priori*, we might have expected the longer form to convey greater emphasis. The explanation involves markedness (see section 7.4.1) and the relationship between context and form: the short form of the subject prefix is marked, and therefore more salient, when it occurs with a verb that is initial in its clause:

(1) u-   tigɛr fu- gɔl- af
     2SG- break 5CL- stick- DEF5
     'Did you break the stick?' or 'Break the stick!' or 'You broke the stick'

The Kujamaat Jóola bound object pronouns are presented below. These may be used for direct or indirect objects.

Bound object pronouns

	Singular	Plural	
		Inclusive	Exclusive
1	-ɔm ~ aːm ~ -an	-ɔla ~ -ɔlal	-uli ~ -oli̱
2	-i		-u ~ -ul
3	-ɔ ~ -ɔl		-iː ~ -il

As with the bound subject pronouns, the alternations shown in the table of bound object pronouns are morphophonemically determined, with the exception of the two first person plural exclusive pronominals, which are regional variants. As seen below, -ɔm is the basic form of the first person singular object marker (2). The variant -aːm appears when the verb includes a reduplicant or the simple subordinate marker -m/-mi (3), but is replaced by -an when immediately followed by a reduplicant that begins with a vowel (4). Notice that an indirect object pronoun always precedes a direct object pronoun. **[Exercise 6]**

(2) a. u-   saːf- ɔm-   iː
         2SG.SUB-greet- 1SG.OBJ- 3PL.OBJ
         'greet them for me'
     b. na-   sɛn- ɔm
         3SG.SUB-give- 1SG.OBJ
         'He gave me'

(3) a. ma- nu-   sɛl- aːm-   ɔ-   mi
         REL- 2SG.SUB-give- 1SG.OBJ-3SG.OBJ-SUBORD
         'this that caused you to give him to me'
     b. ku-   itɛn- aːm-   ɔ-   itɛn
         3PL.SUB-lift- 1SG.OBJ- 3SG.OBJ-REDUP
         'They lifted him for me'

(4) ku-   itɛn- an-   itɛn
     3PL.SUB-lift- 1SG.OBJ- REDUP
     'They lifted me'

▪ Aspect

Kujamaat Jóola does not have a tense system that expresses time-related notions like 'past' and 'present' directly.[6] Instead, it has an aspectual system. This means that it expresses notions such as duration, completeness, and doubt, which have more to do with the nature of the action of the verb or with the speaker's attitude than with time. The unmarked form of the verb can be interpreted either as present or past, as seen in (5):

(5) e- bəy   ni-   ŋar- ɛ
     3CL- cow.DEF3 1SG.SUB- take- NE
     'I take/took the cow'

The suffix -ɛːn, the so-called dubitive-incompletive, is used to indicate that an action has not been completed (much like the imperfect aspect familiar from English or the Romance languages) or that it is in doubt.[7] In (6), the final /n/ of the past absolute suffix assimilates in place with the following labial stop, surfacing as [m]:

(6) sunkɛn ni-   baj- ɛːm- baj bu̱- kori̱
     last.year 1SG.SUB-have- INC- REDUP 9CL-money
     'Last year I had money'

In (6), it is understood that the subject no longer has money. Sapir presents another example in Thomas and Sapir (1967): *Fuken nijɛɛnjaw kabaak, ɛmitɛy dɛsɔfɔm mənilə̃ñu* 'Yesterday I was going to Kabâk, but the rain overtook me (en route) and I returned (without getting there).' Here the verb *nijɛɛnjaw* (*jɛɛn* < -jaw-ɛːn 'go' + INC) 'was going' indicates that the action of going was not completed. Without the dubitive-incompletive marker, this sentence would mean instead that the subject went to Kabâk despite the rain.

The dubitive-incompletive marker -ɛːn may co-occur with other position-1 suffixes. It may precede or follow -ɛrit (habitual negative), -ut (negative), -ɔrut 'not yet', -ɔrulɔːt 'toward speaker' (negative), and -ulɔ 'toward speaker'. This fact tells us that they are in the same position. However, it always precedes the other variants of -ulɔ, -u̱, and -u̱l, as well as the habitual marker -ɛ and the second portion of the first person plural inclusive subject circumfix -a~-al.

Doubling the dubitive-incompletive marker emphasizes it. Such doubling occurs only in contrastive constructions. This is a good illustration of compositional semantics; it is as if each suffix contributes a degree of meaning:

(7) mantɛ a-   bɔɲ- ɛːn- ɛːn- ut   si- kor-   əs
     perhaps 3SG.SUB-send- INC- INC- NEG 4CL-money-DEF4
     a- ɲil- aw
     1CL-child- DEF1
     lɛt- a-   yɔk a-   kaɲ- ɔ
     RES.NEG-3SG.SUB-limit 3SG.SUB- hurt- REFL
     'If he had not sent the money the child would not have gotten into trouble'

We learned immediately above that there is some flexibility regarding the placement of the dubitive-incompletive suffix -ɛːn with respect to other first-position suffixes. The second member of the emphatic construction -ɛːn . . . -ɛːn is even more flexible: it may be placed anywhere with respect to the first-position suffixes except directly after the habitual -ɛ.[8] What's more, it can even follow an object pronoun.

Future in Kujamaat Jóola is expressed by using the resultative and resultative negative markers pan- and lɛ-~lɛt-, which appear outside of inflectional morphology for subject, as we see in the following examples (the /-n/ of pan- is dropped before nasals):

(8) a. pa- ni-   ŋar e-   bəy
         RES – 1SG.SUB-take 3CL- COW.DEF3
         'I will take the cow'
     b. lɛt-   i-   maŋ
         RES.NEG-1SG.SUB-want
         'I won't want'

In relative clauses, the future is expressed by a resultative clitic pi that combines with the marker agreeing with the relativized subject or object (Sapir 1965: 92). We see this in (9):

(9) a- ɲil- aw a- pi bakari a- pɔs- i
     1CL- child- DEF1 1CL- RES Bakari 1CL- wash- 2SG.OBJ
     'the child whom Bakari will wash for you'

Lastly, combining the dubitive-incompletive suffix with the resultative prefix lɛt-, a negative marker, results in a construction that indicates an action that missed taking place or that will not be accomplished. We might translate it as 'might have' or 'might not have'. **[Exercise 7]**

(10)   mantɛr basɛn nu-   ɲɛs- ɛːn- ɛ b- aː- b- ɛ,
       perhaps Bassen 2SG.SUB-look-INC- NE 9CL-here- 9CL- EMPH
       lɛt-   u-   juk- ɛːn- ɔl
       RES.NEG-2SG.SUB-see- INC- 3SG.OBJ
       'If you had been looking for Bassen, you might not have seen him'

The Kujamaat habitual marker is seen in (11). Gero and Levinsohn
(1993) point out that it has a progressive use as well, in which case
it occurs with the verb 'be' (12) (example from Gero and Levinsohn
1993: 82):

(11)   a.   ni-   maŋ- ɛ-   maŋ
            1SG – want- HAB- REDUP
            'I always want'

       b.   nu-   boɲ- e- u- ə-   boɲ
            1PL.EXCL.SUB-send- HAB- DIR- 1PL.EXCL.SUB-REDUP
            'we always send from'

(12)   ɔːm- b- ɔ ə-   siil- e
       be- 15CL- INAN 3SG.SUB- cook-HAB
       'She is cooking'

The habitual marker combines with the negative marker in a single
morpheme, -ɛrit:

(13)   i-   ŋar- ɛːn- ɛrit
       1SG.SUB-take- INC- HAB.NEG
       'I did not always take'

■ Negative

The negative is generally indicated by the suffix -ut, but as seen in the
last section, the resultative and negative are expressed by a single morpheme, lɛ-~lɛt- (cf. (8b)), and the habitual and negative are also expressed
by a single morpheme, -ɛrit (cf. (13)). Similarly, -ulɔ 'toward speaker' and
-ɔrut 'not yet' combine to produce -ɔrulɔːt:

(14)   a.   i-   maŋ
            1SG.SUB-want
            'I want'

       b.   i-   maŋ- ut
            1SG.SUB-want-NEG
            'I don't want'

■ Emphasis and subordination

We have seen two forms of emphasis in the Kujamaat Jóola verb system already. The short form of the subject pronoun can be used where the full form is expected (e.g., in the first verb in a clause) to emphasize the subject. The dubitive-incompletive marker itself can be emphasized by reduplication.

Reduplication serves to create emphasis of the Kujamaat Jóola verb stem as well. This process highlights its action, in contrast to its arguments:

(15) ba- laːb   bu- tɛy- ɛn- ɔla-   tɛy- ɛn
      13CL- sun.DEF13 13CL- run- CAUS- 1PL.INCL- run- CAUS
      'The sun made us run (seek shelter)'

The noun emphasis (NE) suffix -ɛ places emphasis on either the subject or a complement that precedes the verb:

(16) e-   be   ni-   ŋar- ɛ
      3CL- cow 1SG.SUB-take-NE
      'I took a cow'

As might be expected, the use of this marker interacts with word order in complex ways, as we will see at the end of this chapter.

One property of the noun emphasis marker is that it occupies the same position class as the object and passive markers. This could be accidental, and the fact that they never co-occur could be explained as a logical impossibility. A second, more enticing possibility, however, is that they share the same position because they contribute the same sort of information. The discussion in Sapir (1965: 101–2), together with an examination of the sentences in the grammar and other published texts, indicates that the presence of either the object or the noun emphasis marker prevents a corresponding noun phrase from occurring in postverbal position. It is possible that the presence of an object or noun emphasis marker in the morphology eliminates the need for the corresponding noun phrase in the syntax. The same can be said, of course, for the passive marker. If this hypothesis is on the right track, the positional similarity between the object, noun emphasis, and passive markers may correspond to a functional similarity.

Sapir (1965) presents the simple subordinate -m~-mi with emphasis markers because it "shifts emphasis from the verb to its immediate, usually post-verb, environment" (p. 35). It occurs most often in relative clause constructions or verb strings (the /u/ in (17a) is epenthetic):

(17) a. wa   nu-   rεg- u- m
          17cl-thing 2sg.sub-say- V- subord
          'What did you say?'

      b. ə- nin- əw a-   kεt-mi   na-   sεn- aːn-   sεn
          1cl-man-def1 who-die subord 3sg.sub – give-1sg.obj-redup
          e- bəːy
          3cl-cow.def3
          'the man who died gave me the cow'

The actual use of -mi is more complicated than what is presented here,
and in many ways it is akin to the noun emphasis marker (whose usage
is also more complex than our discussion would indicate), as is brought
out by Gero and Levinsohn (1993). We refer the reader to that paper, as
well as to Hopkins (1990), for further information.

The past subordinate (ps), marked by the circumfix ba . . . er, sets off
a subordinate clause (18a–c). As its name indicates, the information
within the subordinate clause typically refers to an event or state that
precedes the action described by the main verb, although the opposite
is true when the subordinated verb bears the suffix -ɔrut 'not yet' (18b).
In negative constructions, the second element of the circumfix, -εr, is
dropped (18a–b). What does this suggest about the true nature of this
circumfix?

(18) a. a- mpa- ɔm   na-   sεn- ɔm,   injε ba- baj- ut
          1cl-father- 1sg.poss 3sg.sub-give-1sg.obj I   ps- have- neg
          waf
          thing
          'when my father gave (it) to me, I had nothing'

      b. bεy nu-   lakɔ-ε aw ba-jaw-ɔrut   dakar
          where 2sg.sub-stay-ne you ps- go- not.yet Dakar
          'where were you before you went to Dakar?'

      c. ba-rεg- εr-ul
          ps-speak-ps-2pl.obj
          'having spoken to you'

Note that although we classify the second portion of the past subordinate
as a position-1 suffix, following Sapir (1965), it may co-occur with the
dubitive-incompletive marker, which it always follows, and the 'towards
speaker' marker -u~-ul, which it precedes. It does not co-occur with any
other first-position suffix.

■ Summary

The facts present here highlight the need for a morphological component in any theory of grammar. The Kujamaat Jóola verb is complex, yet highly structured, and cannot be accounted for in purely syntactic (or phonological) terms, a fact that is highlighted by exercises 5–7. We have also seen that in semantic terms, the Kujamaat Jóola verb system is based on aspect, rather than tense. This is not at all unusual. It has been determined, for example, that Proto-Indo-European also had an aspectual system. Note that we have not presented every Kujamaat Jóola verbal affix here. Sapir describes others, including obligative and indefinite markers (see Thomas and Sapir 1967). [Exercises 8 and 9]

■ A Brief Survey of Kujamaat Jóola Syntax

We have spent a great deal of space in this book discussing Kujamaat Jóola morphology. It seems appropriate to conclude with a brief presentation of a few syntactic facts, ones that are related to its morphological analysis. We take as our starting point the basic word order, which is SVO (Sapir 1965: 100; example from Hopkins 1990: 82–3):

(19) ñaa fú- tut-   af   fu- sumbo-   e- sumbo
      now 7CL-small.one-DEF7 7CL-chew.tobacco-HAB-REDUP
      sumba-ay
      tobacco-DEF10
      'The small one always chews tobacco'

As shown in (20), the subject of a finite clause always precedes the verb:

(20) a.   ə- nine na- juk- ɛ
           1CL- man 3SG- see- HAB
           'A man sees'
           *na-juk-ɛ ə-nine
      b.   ɔ   na- juk- ɛ
           3SG 3SG- see- HAB
           'He sees'

The order of verbal complements, however, is generally free. Any permutation of the sentence in (21a) is permitted, but they vary in terms of what is emphasized:

(21) a. ε- jamεn- εy fu- ri- af ni- sεn- ε
          5CL- goat-   DEF3 5CL- food- DEF5 1SG- give-NE
          'I gave the food to the goat'
      b. furiaf εjamεnεy nisεnε
      c. εjamεnεy nisεnε furiaf
      d. furiaf nisεnε εjamεnεy
      e. nisεnε furiaf εjamεnεy
      f. nisεnε εjamεnεy furiaf

If there is a possibility of ambiguity, speakers will always place the direct object closest to the verb. In the case of postverbal complements, the direct object directly follows the verb; in the case of preverbal complements, it directly precedes:

(22) a. ni- sεn- ε a- kamban- aw a- jaŋ- aw
          1SG-give- NE 1CL-boy-   DEF1 1CL-girl- DEF1
          'I gave the boy to the girl'
      b. a- jaŋ- aw a- kamban- aw ni- sεn- ε
          1CL-girl- DEF1 1CL-boy-   DEF1 1SG-give- NE
          'I gave the boy to the girl'

According to Sapir, if a verb is not marked for noun emphasis, a preverbal complement must then be restated via a bound person marker or postverbal object pronoun. Restatement of the NP object with a pronoun, bound or freestanding, is obligatory if it is [+ human] (23). Non-human preverbal objects are preferably, but not obligatorily, restated (24):

(23) alasan ni-   sεn- ɔ-   sεn bə- kor- əb
      Alasan 1SG.SUB-give- 3SG.OBJ- REDUP 13CL- money- DEF13
      'I gave Alasanne the money'

(24) a. bə- kor- əb ni- sεn- sεn (bɔ) alasan
          13CL- money- DEF13 1SG- give- REDUP (13CL) Alasan
          'I gave the money to Alasanne'
      b. e- bəːy   i- sεn (yɔ)   ja fu- ri-af
          3CL-cow.DEF3 1SG-give (3CL.3SG) if 5CL-food-DEF5
          'If I give the food to the cow'

If both the direct and indirect object occur preverbally, both may be restated by bound pronominals. According to Sapir, only one is obligatorily restated, but he does not specify the indirect or direct object (25). The bound indirect object pronoun precedes the direct object pronoun:

(25) a. a- ɲil- aw   ku- sɛk-   ak   ni- sɛn- il- ɔ- sɛn
         1CL-child-DEF1 5CL-woman-DEF5 1SG-give-3PL-3SG-REDUP
         'I gave the child to the woman'

     b. a- ɲil- aw   ku- sɛk-   ak   ni- sɛn- ɔ- iː- sɛn
         1CL-child-DEF1 5CL-woman-DEF5 1SG-give-3SG-3PL-REDUP
         'I gave the women to the child'

If two [–human] objects precede the verb, one – preferably the indirect object – is restated:

(26) ɛ – jamɛn-ɛy   fu- ri-   af   ni- sɛn- sɛn   yɔ
      3CL-goat- DEF3 5CL-food-DEF5 1SG-give-REDUP 3CL.it
      'I gave the food to the goat'

Exercises

1. Discuss the ways in which the section of this chapter on morphology and Universal Grammar relates to the foundational belief we gave in chapter one: *languages*, which we can write with a small *l*, are different from *Language*, with a capital *L*.

2. Can you think of phenomena besides gender that are potentially problematic from an extreme universalist point of view? Is there any way to reconcile them with Universal Grammar, as we have done for gender?

3. Ganja Balanta (Senegal)
   Identify the derivational morpheme which is common to the italicized verb in (b–d). (Hint: it participates in vowel harmony with the root.) Then use the data provided to describe its meaning (data from Fudeman 1999).
   a. *insogma*   '1 will call him'
   b. *insogudma* Sibow   '1 will call Sibow for him'
   c. anin ma *wusud*   'The woman bought Segou a tunic
      ndundugi Segu   (*ndundugi*)'
   d. *aweetid* Segu biti ma 'She/he found Segou the dog (*biti ma*)'
   e. *aweet* Segu   'She/he found Segou'

4. On the basis of the meaning of the following clauses, identify the grammatical-function-changing phenomena at work (data from Bajau, an Austronesian language described by Donohue 1996). The grammatical-function-changing morpheme is in boldface. Interlinear glosses have been omitted on purpose.
   a. *Meoh **di**-daka asu*   'The cat was caught by some dogs'
   b. *Pa'Harun ukir-**ang**-ku surat*   '1 wrote a letter for Mr Harun's benefit'
   c. *Pa-kang-ku kareo ana'*   '1 fed the child some shark' or '1 fed the child to the shark' (Hint: 'feed' bears what relation to 'eat'?)
   Note that *Pa'Harun* in (b) means 'Mr Harun'.

5. The advantage of the table given at the beginning of the section on Kujamaat Jóola verb morphology is that it lays out the position classes of Kujamaat Jóola verbal morphemes clearly. However, it simplifies matters, as a close reading of the remainder of the section reveals.

Use the data in this chapter to draw up a new diagram of the Kujamaat Jóola verb that expresses the complexity of morpheme positioning.[9]

6. Here are some examples of Kujamaat Jóola bound object pronouns in context. These examples show that, unlike derivational suffixes, bound object pronouns do not participate in verb stem reduplication. On the basis of what you have learned in this and the previous chapter, why might this be? (It may also help to look at the discussion of Kujamaat Jóola stems in chapter 5.)

a. ku-   buburɛn-   ɔla-   buburɛn
   3PL.SUB-grind-   1PL.INCL.OBJ–REDUP
   'they ground us (incl.) into the sand'

b. ku-   sɛn- aːm- i-   sɛn
   3PL.SUB-give- 1SG.OBJ–2SG.OBJ–REDUP
   'They gave you to me'

c. na-   sɛn- uli-   ɔ-   sɛn
   3SG.SUB-give- 1PL.EXCL.OBJ–3SG.OBJ–REDUP
   'He gave him to us (excl.)'

7. Discuss the dubitive-incompletive suffix -ɛːn in terms of compositional semantics. (You may want to refer back to chapters 4 and 5.) Be sure to discuss both doubling of the dubitive-incompletive suffix and its co-occurrence with the resultative prefix -lɛt. Are these unambiguous examples of compositional semantics, or do they raise any problems?

8. Find as many examples in the Kujamaat Jóola section of this chapter as you can that exemplify:
   a. simple exponence
   b. cumulative exponence
   c. extended exponence

9. How does the division of labor between morphology and syntax in Kujamaat Jóola compare to that of English and other languages you know?

NOTES

1 // represents a lateral click, ! a palatal retroflex click, and ? an alveolar click.
2 Some people make the mistake of referring to the passive or active as tenses. Tense, as we noted earlier in this book, indicates time: past, present, future.

3   The active may be expressed in two different ways in Bajau. There is what Donohue calls the actor voice and what he calls the object voice. We present the object voice here because passives do not occur with the actor voice.

4   We have simplified the morpheme-by-morpheme gloss of the Onondaga phrases somewhat.

5   This section on Kujamaat Jóola verb morphology, based on Sapir (1965) and Sapir's revised view of the system in Thomas and Sapir (1967), is the longest in the book, and also the densest. We recommend that instructors lead students through it, but then have students digest the data by exercising their understanding of it creatively. They can begin with the exercises provided at the end of this chapter. In order to fully benefit from this section, instructors will want to spend two or more classes on it. We believe that what students will gain in skills of morphological analysis will be well worth the time and effort.

6   Neither does English, in fact.

7   In Sapir (1965), the suffix -ɛːn is considered a past marker, and its reduplicated form, which we learn below is emphatic dubitive-incompletive, is considered an indicator of remote past. He revises this analysis in his 1967 paper.

8   This is probably due to a phonological constraint against superlong vowels, which we would have if the habitual ɛ were to merge with ɛːn. Furthermore, if the illicit sequence */ɛ + ɛːn/ were to be reduced to /ɛːn/, the habitual meaning would be unrecoverable.

9   Instructors should be aware that this task will be time-consuming.

8 Morphological Productivity

This chapter is based on two observations about morphology:

(1) a. Though many things are possible in morphology, some are more possible than others.
     b. Though there are infinitely many potential words in a language, some are more likely to become actual words than others.

These two statements, while similar, express slightly different ideas. The first (1a) is a general statement about morphological processes. We have seen that morphology can take many forms. Limiting ourselves to English, regular derivation and inflection might involve affixation, internal change (ablaut and umlaut), and category change without any overt morphological marking, to name just a few. But some of these processes are more possible than others. In the realm of verb inflection, a randomly selected verb is more likely to make its past tense by affixation than by ablaut. The second statement (1b) deals specifically with individual words. On a very basic level, words such as *pfug*, *ngu*, or *yawelelulitopikuro* are much less likely to become actual words of English than *fug*, *ung*, or *yawel*. On another level, a word like *mini-burger* 'little burger' is more likely than *burgerlet* (and may, in fact, already exist), even though *-let*, like *mini-*, means 'small' (cf. *booklet*, *piglet*). More subtle differences among forms and how likely they are to become actual words can be tested only through carefully designed experiments. Issues like these fall under the rubric of **morphological productivity**, the topic of this chapter.

■ 8.1   What is Morphological Productivity?

To say that a given morphological pattern is more **productive** than another is to say that there is a higher probability of a potential word in the first pattern being accepted in the language than there is of a potential word in the second pattern. We can illustrate this with a simple example from English: plural formation. English nouns make their plural in a number of different ways, as can be seen in the following set of words (Bauer 2001: 2):

(2)   cats, dogs, horses, oxen, deer, mice, hippopotami, cherubim

In light of all of these ways to mark nouns as plural, what does a speaker of English do when confronted with novel words, such as those in (3)?

(3)   argaz   'crate of specific style'
       smick   'type of cracker biscuit'
       brox   'piece of computer hardware'
       ceratopus   'type of dinosaur'
       cheppie   'type of antelope'

Chances are that, despite the existence of other plural formations, an English speaker will mark all of these words as plural by suffixation of /z/: *argazes*, *smicks*, *broxes*, *ceratopuses*, and *cheppies*. The only likely exception is *ceratopus*, which could plausibly be given the plural *ceratopi*, on the basis of Latin borrowings such as *alumni*, *foci*, and *nuclei*.[1]

Bauer (2001: 3), to whom we owe the set of words in (3), selected them very carefully. The word *argaz* 'crate', for example, is in fact a Hebrew noun. It would therefore be possible to pluralize it as *argazim*, on the pattern of *cherubim, seraphim,* and *kibbutzim.* But this special plural would require that the speaker be familiar with the Hebrew plural and that this type of crate be connected somehow with Israel or Judaism. Bauer chose the word *brox* 'piece of computer hardware' because it rhymes with *ox* and because for some, the computer called a *Vax* (manufactured in the 1970s) was pluralized as *Vaxen* (presumably on analogy to *oxen*). Thus, there would be a precedent for pluralizing *brox* as *broxen*. Even so, the layperson would almost certainly pluralize both of these words as *broxes* and *Vaxes.* To return to our first statement at the beginning of this section, the English /z/ plural is more productive than other existing plural formations because there is a higher probability that speakers will accept and create forms like *argazes* and *broxes* (and *prouses, meers,* and *vilds*) than *argazim* and *broxen* (and *price, meer,* and *vildren,* cf. *mice, deer,* and *children*). **[Exercise 1]**

One term that we will be using a lot is **potential word**. A potential word could be a word, but isn't. One example is *Mugglehood* 'the state of being a non-wizard', which we created from *Muggle* 'non-wizard', a word found in J. K. Rowling's Harry Potter books, and the English suffix *-hood. Mugglehood* isn't defined in the dictionary, and it probably is not in your working vocabulary. But when we did an online search for it, we found not only three instances of *Mugglehood,* but also numerous instances of *Muggledom* and *Muggleness.* Apparently we are not alone in thinking that *Mugglehood* is a potential word. Perhaps someday it will be included in the dictionary.[2]

The suffix *-th* creates nouns from adjectives (e.g., *deep* → *depth, wide* → *width*). It has a meaning that is similar to *-ness: length* means the same thing that *longness* would mean if it were a word; if you could say *decidedth,* it would mean the same thing as *decidedness.* But only *-ness* can be called productive. In fact, no word in *-th* has successfully been integrated into standard written English since the coining of *width* in 1627. People have certainly tried, coming up with words like *greenth, illth,* and *lowth.* But they have not been very successful. Speakers of standard English simply don't accept new coinages in *-th.* **[Exercise 2]**

When we study productivity, we study phenomena and distinctions like these. One question we need to ask about productivity is whether it is part of linguistic **competence**. Competence is Chomsky's (1965) term for the knowledge that speakers and hearers have of their language. It contrasts with **performance**, or how the language is actually used in concrete situations. In actual performance, a speaker may hesitate, stop in mid-sentence, or commit one or another sort of slip of the tongue. But a linguist, in studying the language, would not regard such hesitations, half-sentences, and speech errors as part of the language. That is not to say that these phenomena should be ignored. Slips of the tongue, for example, have provided great insights into the general structure of language. And code mixing, a type of linguistic performance in which fluent speakers of two or more languages may mix these languages freely in mid-sentence in conversation, is an area of active research. Though slips of the tongue and code mixing are not linguistic competence, but rather linguistic performance, both can still be studied fruitfully for what they tell us about language.

Some people would say that productivity is not part of linguistic competence either, because, in order for something to be considered part of competence, it must be structural and 'all or none'. Productivity is a probabilistic notion, as we will see, and some linguists believe that if something is probabilistic it is not structural, and hence is not part of the grammar. Under this view, productivity would have to be treated as a phenomenon that is related to a speaker's competence, but that is not part of it.

The alternative position, and the one we take here, is that if speakers are sensitive to productivity, and if it is part of what they do with language, not just a factor that influences language, then it is part of their linguistic competence. The question of whether it is structural is simply not important. If we let ideology get in the way of linguistic investigation, then we will miss out on important generalizations. Moreover, while productivity itself is not structural, it is very easy to show that it has structural effects that may turn out to be relevant to structural theories of language.

■ 8.2 Productivity and Structure: Negative Prefixes in English

One reason that it is likely that productivity can tell us something about language structure is that the more productive a morphological derivational process is, the more likely it is to have a compositional output, one whose meaning is transparently predictable from the meaning of its input. The converse is also true: the less productive a derivational process, the more likely it is to result in a non-compositional, semantically idiosyncratic, non-transparent output.

To illustrate this point, consider negative prefixes in English. Zimmer (1964) looked at three of them, *non-*, *un-*, and *in-*, and discovered that the most productive of the set, *non-*, also has the most semantically transparent derivatives. This is shown by the contrast between the two columns in (4):

(4) non-Christian   unchristian
     non-human   inhuman

What's the difference? *Non-Christian* means 'not Christian'. While *unchristian* can mean that, too, more often than not it means something like 'not behaving in a Christian manner' or even 'uncivilized and barbaric'. Likewise, *non-human* simply means 'not human', while *inhuman* refers to the absence of human qualities like pity or kindness. A person can be both human and inhuman, but not human and non-human. Thus, while the *non*-words in general simply negate their bases, the *in*- and *un*- words have the meaning 'completely opposite to X', where X is the meaning of their bases, in the way that *east* and *west* or *long* and *short* are opposed. To put it in a more technical way, *non*- is a **logical** or **contrary negator**. Using logical notation, we could represent *non-Christian* as in (5), where $\neg$ means 'not':

(5) $\neg$ Christian

Un- and *in*- are examples of **contradictory negators**, whose addition to a word X results in a new word meaning 'opposite of X'.

Zimmer's observation extends to other derivational affixes. Overall, *-ness* is more productive in English than *-ity* (Aronoff 1976). Consider the pair *collectivity~collectiveness*. While both may mean 'the quality or condition of being collective', only *collectivity* has the additional meaning 'the people considered as a body or a whole'. Overall, when we compare many such pairs, it is the *-ness* derivative that has more transparent semantics. Sometimes, the *-ity* derivative sounds or looks odd, while the *-ness* derivative is pretty much always acceptable. Compare *conduciveness* with *conducivity*. The former is fine, but the latter is so unacceptable that our spelling checker kept on correcting it to *conductivity*. And we can go beyond morphology to make the observation that syntax, which is always productive, is by definition compositional.[3]

■ 8.3   Degrees of Productivity

We began this chapter with two observations, repeated below:

(6) a. Though many things are possible in morphology, some are more possible than others.
     b. Though there are infinitely many potential words in a language, some are more likely to become actual words than others.

Implicit in these two observations is the belief that productivity is not absolute. Morphological processes do not fall into two neat categories, productive and unproductive. They are best seen as being spread out along a scale, with some being more productive than others. This is the view of the majority of scholars (see Bauer 2001: 126), and we will not consider the alternative view here.

There are a number of types of constraints that limit productivity and that can be seen as contributing to or even determining to what degree a particular formation is productive. We will outline some of those constraints here, following Bauer's (2001: 126–39) discussion.

■ 8.3.1 Phonological constraints

The first type of constraint on morphological productivity is phonological. We have already seen that phonology is a factor in the distribution of allomorphs (see chapter 3). It is therefore not surprising that phonology constrains morphology in other ways. Bauer identifies three types of phonological constraints on productivity. At times it is the segmental make-up of the base that is important. At others, it is the suprasegmental make-up of the base, such as stress placement. In the last case, it is the number of syllables in the base that matters.

An example of the first type discussed by Bauer is the Modern Hebrew pet-name suffix -le, borrowed from Yiddish. It can only attach to bases ending in a vowel (Glinert 1989: 437):

(7)   ába 'father' > ábale 'daddy'

As an example of the second type, where it is the suprasegmental make-up of the base that matters, Bauer presents -al suffixation in English. This suffix may only attach to verbs that are stressed on the final syllable, as seen in the examples in (8). (Bauer notes that the apparent exception *burial* should not be considered a counterexample, because it has a different etymological source.)

(8)   acquittal, arrival, denial, dismissal, rebuttal, referral, revival

Bauer illustrates the last type, instances where the number of syllables in the base is important, with Tzutujil (Dayley 1985: 212), where the suffix -C_1oj '-ish' may only attach to monosyllabic adjectives, as in *rax-roj* 'greenish'. **[Exercises 3 and 4]**

■ 8.3.2   Morphological constraints

Another way in which productivity can be constrained is by morphological constraints. It might be the case that the base must have a certain structure, belong to a certain morphologically or syntactically defined class, such as a gender, or terminate in a particular affix. In chapter 4 we encountered a morphological constraint of the first type: certain English suffixes may only attach to unsuffixed bases. As an illustration of the second type, we find affixes that attach only to bases that have a particular etymological origin. Bauer, citing Mackridge (1985: 320), gives the example of Modern Greek, where the suffix -adoros may only attach to words of Romance origin. Thus we find *kombinadoros* 'trickster' from *kombina* 'trick' (< French *combine* 'trick').

■ 8.3.3   Syntactic constraints

A very basic type of syntactic constraint on word formation that has been cited by linguists is the lexical category of the base. Many affixes attach only to nouns, verbs, or adjectives. English *re-*, for example, attaches to verbs. *React, reapply, relocate, reread*, and *rewrite* are all possible words of English, while **represident* 'someone who is elected president for the second time' or **rewhite* 'white (adj.; used of something that was once white and is now white again)' are not. In chapter 3 we saw another type of syntactic constraint. The English secondary affix #able may attach only to transitive verbs.

■ 8.3.4   Semantic constraints

Productivity can also be constrained by semantic factors. Barker (1998) studies the English suffix *-ee* found in words like *advisee, addressee, enlistee*, or *employee* using a large set of naturally occurring examples such as the following (p. 720):

(9) a. There was the Asian influenza casualty . . . who was replaced gallantly by an influenza **recoveree**, Mr Robert Harben.
    b. [experiment involving shining lights into the subject's eyes] The **adaptee** then cannot tell the difference between yellow and white, i.e., is yellow-blind.

  c. These young musicians were chosen from over 200 **auditionees**.
  d. The ground rules were simple: to find ways to relax that required absolutely no effort on the part of the **relaxee**.
  e. The paella didn't turn out very well, but fortunately my **dinees** were quite understanding.

Barker finds that -*ee* suffixation is constrained by three semantic factors. First, the referent of the newly derived noun must be sentient. Second, the referent of the -*ee* noun is typically characterized by a relative lack of volitional control: the *dinees* in (9e) have no control over the paella they are served, and the *adaptee* (9b) does not manipulate the lights. Finally, the -*ee* noun and the stem must be episodically linked. Barker (1998: 712) gives the example of the noun *lessee*, from the verb *lease*: "every leasing qualifies some individual as a lessee, and for every lessee, there must be a leasing event which qualifies them as a lessee." He continues by pointing out that it is not the case that all deverbal nouns must be episodically linked to their stems. We can *dump* a pencil sharpener into a wastebasket without the wastebasket qualifying as a *dump*. Someone who *consorts* does not automatically become a *consort*, and so on.

■ 8.3.5 Blocking

The last type of constraint we would like to mention here is **blocking**. Blocking involves two expressions, one potential and one actual. We say that a potential expression is prevented from occurring because another expression with the same meaning and function already exists. In the context of inflection, forms like **childs*, **oxes*, **mouses*, and **foots* are blocked by the existence of *children*, *oxen*, *mice*, and *feet*. In fact, wherever we find irregular inflectional morphology, it is best to say that the irregular forms block the application of the regular, or default, rule. This has been formally articulated in work on Lexical Phonology (Kiparsky 1982), and is related to the Elsewhere Condition, which states that a more specific rule or process (e.g., to make *child* plural, add the suffix [rən] and change the vowel of the root to [ɪ]) will apply before a more general rule (e.g., to make plural, add /z/). The Elsewhere Condition is important in many areas of morphology, not just productivity.

We also find blocking of derivational formations. In chapter 5 we observed that the existence of the verb *mail* prevents speakers from using a zero-derived verb **mailbox* 'to put a letter or package in a mailbox in order to send it to a recipient'. It would be odd to refer to a piece of silverware that is used to cut food as a *cutter* because the word *knife* already exists, unless the new utensil is somehow special. And **corresponder* doesn't occur, presumably because we already have the word *correspondent* (Barker 1998: 703).

The example *cutter* is particularly informative, because that word does exist, but in different senses – many of them. There are a number of agentive meanings to the word *cutter*, used for occupations that involve cutting. Someone who castrates animals is a *cutter*, as is one who cuts fur or cloth to make garments. We also use the word *cutter* to refer to someone who edits and cuts motion picture shots and assembles them into a finished sequence, someone who pulverizes ore samples so that they may be subjected to chemical analysis, or someone who cuts gems, monumental or building stones, or glass. There are boats and sleighs called cutters. Incisors (which are distinguished from the teeth called *grinders*) are called *cutters*. So are particularly incisive comments. Of particular relevance here is the fact that a number of cutting instruments go by the name *cutter*, including rotary cutters and the sapphire or diamond point of a stylus.[4] The meaning 'piece of silverware used for cutting' is conspicuous by its absence. This shows that true semantic blocking is exactly what is going on here.

Blocking is an economy principle that can be thought of informally as an injunction to avoid coining synonyms: if you already have a perfectly good expression for something, don't invent another one. Very clear evidence that blocking is based on the avoidance of creating synonyms comes from syntax, where it operates just as it does in morphology. Why, for example, do we say *this morning, this afternoon, this evening*, but not **this night*? The answer is that this *expression* is blocked by *tonight*. Remember that blocking does not constrain forming words, but rather forming words with particular meanings, which means that a word may be blocked in one sense but not in another. And indeed, *this night* is perfectly acceptable with a different sense from the blocked one, as in the phrase "*Why is this night different from all other nights?*" where *this* is used in a more purely demonstrative way. Similarly, while *the day before yesterday* or *the day after tomorrow* are both common expressions, we cannot say **the day before today* or **the day after today*, because we already have the perfectly good words *yesterday* and *tomorrow* with these exact meanings. French, by contrast, has the expression *avant hier* for the equivalent of *the day before yesterday* and *après demain* for the equivalent of *the day after tomorrow*, so French also blocks the translationally equivalent expression of these phrases, which are perfectly acceptable in English, because we have no word for them. The constraint is thus the same across all languages, but its results depend on the individual existing words of each one. **[Exercises 5–9]**

■ 8.4   Salience and Productivity

We next tackle the oxymoron of productive unproductivity (this last a term we coined just now), or the evidence that speakers have unproductive rules or processes at their disposal. For simplicity, we will refer simply to rules, since the difference between the two terms is more one of personal preference. The fact that speakers use both unproductive and productive rules is a major reason for including productivity in speakers' competence. As we will show, speakers can take advantage of the unproductivity of a rule, just as they take advantage of productivity, but to different ends. Do unproductive rules serve any function? We will show that they do.

When a word is formed from an unproductive rule, that word is more salient than its productively formed counterpart. If I were to use the word *coolth* in conversation instead of the equivalent productively formed *coolness*, people would notice, and in some contexts, that could be a useful thing. This brings us back to the novel words we discussed in chapter 1, and the fascinating observation that many of them apparently break morphological rules. For example, Latin or Greek suffixes are sometimes attached to Germanic stems, as in *smorgsaphobia* (heard in an episode of *Frasier*) or *denogginize* (from an episode of *Seinfeld*), and the adjectival prefix *un-* is sometimes affixed to nouns. Some of our older readers may remember a past *7-Up* advertising campaign, where it was referred to as the *uncola*.

Novel words are called nonce forms or hapax legomenona (we encountered both of these terms in section 4.2.1). Evidence of the value of novel words comes from the fact that novel words are more common in contexts where salience counts, such as advertising or journalism. One way, for example, to create a catchy headline is to include a recognizably novel word. The following examples are all from *The Economist* (emphasis ours):

(10) a.   "Subsidized **cow chow**"
           [noun–noun compound; vol. 362(8263), March 9, 2002, p. 39]
      b.   "**Enronitis** delights local auditors"
           [*Enron*, an oil company, plus *-itis*; vol. 362(8265), March 23, 2002, p. 69]
      c.   "George Bush, **McCainiac**"
           [blend of *McCain* and *maniac*; vol. 362(8266), March 30, 2002, p. 30]
      d.   "Farewell **eurosclerosis**"
           [*euro-* plus *sclerosis*; *The World in 2002*, p. 102]

All of these words stand out, because speakers immediately recognize that they have never seen them before. Words formed by unproductive processes, like *uncola*, are even more salient. People who hear them stop in their tracks for a moment, trying to put a finger on why they don't sound quite right.

The relationship between unproductive rules and contexts where there is a need for saliency holds in other languages, too. In Modern Hebrew, many blends (see discussion in chapter 4) are brand names, and are less likely to be created in normal speech (Bat-El 1996). In French, blending is fairly rare, but it can be found in contexts where it is important to stand out: a flyer advertising Belfort's *Eurockéennes*, a blend of *Européen* 'European' and *rock*, is more eye-catching than one that simply proclaims "European Rock Festival." The same goes for *Irrockuptibles*, which happens to be both the title of a French magazine and a rock festival in Spanish-speaking Buenos Aires.

In addition to salience, words formed by unproductive rules have another function: they are useful for coining technical terms, which need to have a distinctive meaning. Take a word from the title of this chapter, *productivity*. Why don't we say *productiveness*? Research on the two suffixes involved has shown that technical terms are more likely to be formed with *-ity* than *-ness*. We don't talk about Einstein's theory of *relativeness* or say to somebody that his analysis lacks *objectiveness*; we say *relativity* and *objectivity*. In pottery, one method of firing is called *reduction firing*. Reduction involves removing oxygen from the firing atmosphere and results in more interesting colors in the glazing. In order to do reduction firing, you have to use special, reductive clays that will not explode under reduction. What do potters call this property? They call it *reductivity*, rather than *reductiveness*.

In summary, if a language has two ways of doing something, one of which is less productive, the less productive rule or process has a linguistic purpose. It may be that the less productive rule will result in a word that stands out, useful in newspapers, magazines, and advertisements, or it may be that it will result in a form that sounds more technical or learned.

■ 8.5 Testing Productivity

In chapter 1, we said that we take a "no holds barred" approach to linguistics. If we can use a tool, no matter how unconventional, to come to a better understanding of how speakers and hearers use and process language, we are all for it. Morphological productivity offers many opportunities for researchers with this kind of philosophy, and in recent years, linguists have used many different tools to come to a better understanding of how we produce complex words. These include studies that use standard dictionaries, rhyming dictionaries, and large corpora, on the one hand, and technologically sophisticated techniques such as positron emission tomography (PET), on the other. In this section we report on some of these studies.

■ 8.5.1   English suffixes

Aronoff and Schvaneveldt (1978) conducted an experiment to verify that productivity figures in individuals' linguistic competence and to judge its consistency across speakers and words. The experiment focused on -*ness*, a native English suffix, and -*ity*, of Latin-Romance origin, which often attach to the same morphological and semantic classes of words. We see this in triplets like the following, where all three members can be found in a dictionary:

(11)   immense   immenseness   immensity
       scarce   scarceness   scarcity
       exclusive   exclusiveness   exclusivity
       porous   porousness   porosity

The two suffixes differ, however, in that -*ness* is more productive overall, especially with certain types of stems like those of the shape *X-ive*.

Aronoff and Schvaneveldt presented speakers with three sets of words: (i) actual words, like *activity* or *assertiveness*, where *actual* means listed in *Webster's Collegiate Dictionary*; (ii) possible words, like *effervescivity* or *affirmativeness*, where *X-ive* occurs in the dictionary, but not the -*ness* or -*ity* suffixed form; and (iii) non-words. Here not only is *X-ive* not listed in the dictionary – neither is *X*. Examples of non-words are *remortiveness* and *lugativity*.

In the course of the experiment, 141 subjects were asked to judge 40 words, 100 possible words, and 40 non-words, which were presented in randomized lists. For each subject, half of the words were suffixed in -*ity* and half in -*ness*. The 40 actual words were the same across all subjects, but possible words and non-words were counterbalanced so that half of the subjects would get, for example, *effervesciveness* and *elaborativity*, and the other half would get *elaborativeness* and *effervescivity*. This was done to ensure that judgments would be based on the felicity of the suffix and not some peculiarity of the stem it attached to.

The final variable in the study involved the instructions given to the subjects, who were divided into three groups of 47 each. One group was asked to judge whether the items were in their vocabulary; the second group was asked whether the items were English words; and the third group was asked whether the words were meaningful. As it happened, the instructions had little effect on the subjects' judgments.

It turned out that English speakers preferred the actual words in -ity (they were balanced for frequency). When it came to the non-words, they didn't care, and on the potential words, they preferred the -ness words. This shows that speakers can tell the difference between a more productive and less productive rule.

Another experiment yielded even more interesting results. Anshen and Aronoff (1988) tested the productivity of the patterns X-iveness, X-ivity; X-ibility, X-ibleness; and X-ional, X-ionary. We follow them in ignoring the last two, since the most interesting results have to do with the contrast between the behavior of -ity and -ness. Anshen and Aronoff asked their subjects, all native English speakers, to list on paper all of the words that they could think of that ended in these strings. They expected that speakers would come up with more forms in the more acceptable, and therefore more productive, patterns (X-iveness, X-ibility). In fact, speakers listed more forms for both the X-ibility and X-ivity patterns than for the other two, as shown in the following table (Anshen and Aronoff 1988: 644).

Number of words cited by respondents

	-ness	-ity
X-ible	30	101
X-ive	61	86

Just as interesting was the observation that the number of nonce words in the subjects' lists was much higher for the patterns ending in -ness than those ending in -ity, as shown in the following table.

Extant versus nonce words

	Extant	Nonce
X-ibleness	9	12
X-ibility	38	8
X-iveness	17	16
X-ivity	19	9

On the basis of their experiment, Anshen and Aronoff hypothesize that *-ity* forms are stored in the lexicon, but that *-ness* forms are built by rule as they are needed (on the fly, as psychologists say). In other words, there are two ways in which speakers access words: they may find them in the lexicon, or they may create them from existing bases. If speakers create *-ness* words on the fly, there is nothing to prevent them from using novel forms. If, on the other hand, *-ity* words are memorized, the forms that the subjects retrieve are likely to exist in other people's lexicons, as well. This explains the results in the second table on p. 223. It is also reasonable to expect a greater variety in the *-ness* words than in the *-ity* words, because speakers choose the latter from a defined stored set, but make the former up as they need them. This also turned out to be the case (Anshen and Aronoff 1988: 645).

Another hypothesis that came out of Anshen and Aronoff's study is that the observation that speakers build words in *-ness* on the fly can explain why rules that were extremely productive historically leave few or no traces in the modern language. Words in *-ness* are not stored in the lexicon, so if the productive rule disappears, so will the many forms ending in *-ness*. Anshen and Aronoff cite Broselow (1977), who notes that the Old English deadjectival nominalizer *u-* was the most productive such affix in Old English, yet has left no reflex in Modern English. Broselow explains this fact by hypothesizing that *u-* forms were never stored in the lexicon, but were instead built by rule when needed. Once the rule is lost, all the forms disappear almost instantaneously.

Anshen and Aronoff propose that *-ibleness* is like *u-* in that it was once very productive, but is now quite marginal. Other affixes that seem to have gone the same way include *be-*, as in *beware* and *bedevil*, and prepositional prefixes, like *with-* or *at-*. Some of these, like *at-*, have left no trace at all. We only have a few words in *with-* left: *withdraw, withhold, withstand*. These affixes all serve as evidence for the notion that if a rule dies, then people will not remember any of the words that were formed with the rule.

The prediction that, if an affix was once highly productive, then it will have disappeared with hardly a trace is something that can be demonstrated quite easily, particularly for prefixes, by using a dictionary. The *Oxford English Dictionary* is particularly useful for this type of investigation because it lists not only the first recorded time a word appeared, but also the last.

In the second section of their article, Anshen and Aronoff (1988) discuss a theory of how speakers of a language find words. Put yourself in the position of someone who has to find a word. Let's say that during a conversation, you need to use a noun that expresses an abstract quality having to do with retaining.

There is a theory that says that when speakers are zeroing in on the stem of a word, they have three ways in which they can find the word they are looking for. The first way is to search the mental lexicon for words that the speaker has memorized by rote. The second is to build a word by rule. And the last way is to create a word by analogy. The three methods are then rote, rule, and analogy. (For evidence that this goes on, see Kuczaj 1977 and Bybee and Slobin 1982.) Crucially, Anshen and Aronoff claim that speakers do all three at the same time. If a word is very frequent, it has been reinforced in their memories and so speakers will find it easily. This may be why irregularities tend to persist in the most frequently used words of a language, for example, the paradigm 'to be' in English. If speakers do not find a word in the lexicon very quickly, then rule or analogy will win out, depending on how quickly each operates, which may vary in a given case, depending on complex factors.

This theory sheds some light on *-ibleness* words and why English speakers tend not to like them. While the *-ness* rule is very productive overall, in this particular environment it is dead. Speakers can retrieve an *-ibility* word from their mental lexicons more quickly than they can create a new word in *-ibleness*.

8.5.2 The importance of hapax legomena

According to Baayen (1992), if you want to study morphological productivity, then it is important to study hapax legomena, words that appear only once in a given corpus, preferably a large one. Why? If you adhere to the theory discussed immediately above, then a productive rule is like a machine that spins out words, throws them into the air, and doesn't bother to keep track of them. Words that appear only once in a large corpus are more likely than words that are used repeatedly to have been formed by a productive rule.

If this seems counterintuitive to you, then think of it in terms of concrete examples. An acquaintance of ours recently said of her infant son, "He's my *handsome-dandsome* little boy." If you look in the dictionary, you won't find *handsome-dandsome*. But it does not sound at all odd. Semi-reduplicatives like this one are common in English: *chitchat*, *jingle-jangle*, *flip-flop*, *zigzag*. *Handsome-dandsome* would fall out as a hapax legomenon if it were part of a large corpus precisely because it follows a productive pattern, and the woman who uttered it created it on the fly.

Memorized words, ones that are not created on the fly but are stored in the lexicon, are more likely to recur in a large corpus. So in a large corpus, we would expect to find multiple examples of words like *monitor*, *third*, *argues*, or *get*. Of these four words, *argues* follows a productive pattern – suffixation of /s/ to form the third person singular present. But we are not claiming that words that follow a productive pattern have to be hapax legomena. We are saying that if a word is a hapax legomenon, then it is more likely to have been formed by a productive rule.

If you take a huge corpus – say, 30, 50, or 100 million words – and look for words that occur only once, this will be a very good indicator of productivity. The formula that Baayen proposes is quite simple: productivity $\mathcal{P}$ is equal to the number of words occurring only once in a corpus divided by the total number of tokens of words of the same morphological type:

(12) $\mathcal{P} = n_1/N.$

For example, if we are considering the type *X-ness* (e.g., *redness*), then we look for words that occur only once in our corpus (perhaps *decidedness*), and we divide the total number of such once-only words by the total number of occurrences of the type *X-ness* in our corpus. This will be our measure of the productivity of the type *X-ness* in our corpus. The larger and more representative of the language the corpus is, the closer this $\mathcal{P}$ number comes to the actual productivity of the pattern in the language.

Baayen's formula does not take into consideration how many different types of words there are, only the ratio of hapax legomena to actual words. If you find a high ratio of words that occur only once in a given pattern to the total number of words in the pattern, you demonstrate productivity. This is a formula with reasonable predictability. Again we have found a technique for indirectly gaining access to what kind of linguistic knowledge speakers possess.

There are some caveats to Baayen's formula, as pointed out by Bauer (2001), who applied the formula to the Wellington Corpus of Written New Zealand English. In that corpus, the suffix *-iana* occurs only once, in the word *Victoriana*. If we apply the formula, the number of hapax legomena is one and the total number of tokens in the corpus is also one, so *-iana* appears to be totally productive – an apparently absurd result. This doesn't reflect a problem with Baayen's formula, as Bauer notes. Instead, the problem lies with the relatively small sample size. The Wellington Corpus of Written New Zealand English contains not much more than a million words. While that may seem like a large number, it is not big enough for our purposes. (Baayen's original corpus was about 18 times larger.) It's also important to keep in mind that the numbers we get by applying Baayen's formula cannot be compared across corpora of different sizes. The same affix might garner different $\mathcal{P}$ results depending on the corpora used. This doesn't invalidate the formula. It comes about because the $\mathcal{P}$ value produced is relative to the size of the corpus.

■ 8.5.3 Regular and irregular English past tense verb forms

The last study we would like to mention here was conducted by Jaeger et al. (1996) using **positron emission tomography (PET)**. Positron emission tomography is a brain imaging technique that takes advantage of the fact that the brain is extremely hungry for glucose and oxygen, both of which are transported by the blood. Radioactive isotopes and glucose are injected into the arteries before subjects engage in specific cognitive activities. The radioactive glucose allows maps of brain activity, based on blood flow, to be produced. Jaeger et al. were interested in the brain activity associated with the processing of regular and irregular past tense verb forms in English. Should regular and irregular verbs be treated as one and the same by linguistic theories and processing models of language, or are they intrinsically different?

Early generative theories hypothesized that all past tense verbs, whether regular or irregular, are generated by rule (Chomsky and Halle 1968). This approach can also be found in some more recent work (for example, Halle and Mohanan 1985). A problem with it, however, is that the rules needed to generate the wealth of possible forms in English can result in very abstract underlying representations and few constraints on the actual rules themselves. Aronoff (1976) and Hooper (1976) argued that only rules formed by productive processes belong in the morphological component. Irregular words and words formed by unproductive processes are stored in the lexicon. When multiple words formed by unproductive processes exist, speakers are able to see the patterns that relate them, but this does not mean that the rule itself is present in the mental grammar. Although none of these theories claimed to be processing models, all of them were based on beliefs about the workings of the human mind. Rule-based approaches to irregular and regular verb morphology assume that storage space for memorized forms in the brain is at a premium. Words are therefore argued to be stored in as economical a form as possible, with redundant properties eliminated. The second type of approach assumes that the brain is capable of memorizing enormous numbers of words, and also that it is more efficient or economical to simply retrieve memorized lexical forms than to create them anew via a plethora of different rules (which, in the first approach, must also be stored).

Processing models fall into the same two general types. Some treat regular and irregular past tense verb forms as being processed by the same system. Some treat them as being processed differently from each other. More discussion can be found in Jaeger et al. (1996).

Jaeger et al. set out to shed some light on these competing types of models, which they call single-system theories and dual-system theories. Nine subjects viewed five lists of words or nonce forms. They were required to give a spoken response to each form, one at a time. The five lists were as follows:

(13)   List contents   Required task
    1:    English verb forms   Read them aloud
          Ex: *hit, clean, change, dance*
    2:    Nonce forms   Read them aloud
          Ex: *mab, gruck, prane, krent*
    3:    Verb stems with regular past tenses   Speak the past tense
          Ex: *pull, place, love, count*
    4:    Verb stems with irregular past tenses Speak the past tense
          Ex: *fall, build, shoot, dig*
    5:    Nonce verbs   Speak the past tense
          Ex. *baff, pode, gloan, plem*

The researchers collected data on the regions and levels of brain activity, the subjects' responses, and their reaction time. The idea was that patterns of brain activity recorded in the PET scan would be similar for all lists if regular and irregular past tense forms are indeed created by the same process. If, however, they are generated by different processes, the results of the PET scan would be different for the regular and irregular past tense formations.

When the study was completed, Jaeger and the others found that subjects spoke aloud the past tense forms of regular verbs significantly faster than irregular verbs. Response times for the past tense of nonce forms were closest to those of regular verbs. When subjects were asked to give the past tense of irregular verb forms, their brains showed larger areas of brain activity. Finally, while there was overlap in the areas of the brain activated by each activity, it was also the case that the regular verb task and the irregular verb task each activated different areas of the brain, as well. These results support dual-system theories that claim that regular and irregular past tense verb forms are generated by different mechanisms.

Seidenberg and Hoeffner (1998) criticize Jaeger and her colleagues for presenting regular verb forms and irregular verb forms in completely separate lists. Since the regular verb forms all work the same way, it could be that the subjects predicted the process they had to apply and therefore computed them faster than the irregular verbs, which fell into no such pattern. Jaeger et al. (1998) disagree with the criticism. This contention, however, highlights the care with which experiments must be designed. Researchers must try to predict criticisms of their experimental design and correct them prior to executing the study. It also underscores the need for more studies of this type before we draw hard conclusions about the mechanisms of morphological productivity. A design error may or may not influence a given set of results. We can only decide that after conducting a number of different experiments. **[Exercise 10]**

■ 8.6   Conclusion

You should now have a general understanding of morphological productivity and the phonological, morphological, syntactic, and semantic factors that constrain it. We have also introduced you to various ways in which morphological productivity can be tested. This is one of the newest and fastest-developing areas of linguistics.

This chapter departs from previous ones in not having a section on Kujamaat Jóola. The reason for the lacuna is simply that we do not have access to the sort of data that would allow us to discuss productivity in Kujamaat Jóola. We hope, though, that the small window that we have opened will inspire a student to make the journey to Basse Casamance that we have not been able to undertake and to begin the study of morphological productivity in Kujamaat Jóola.

Our hope is not entirely baseless. One of us once published a couple of articles on Arapesh, a language of Papua New Guinea, based entirely on data from the one grammar of the language, published by Reo Fortune in the 1940s. Lise Dobrin, then a graduate student in Chicago, read the articles and became so fascinated that she went off to Papua New Guinea and spent 18 months studying and analyzing the language. She wrote her dissertation on Arapesh and continues to do research on the language and the community. So keep us posted.

Exercises

1. Ask two native English speakers who do not study linguistics to conjugate the following novel verbs. In class, discuss the results. Were all informants in agreement on the conjugation of each verb? If not, what explains the variation? What do the results of the experiment tell you about productive English verbal inflection?
   e.g.: present: *I become, she becomes*; past: *I/she became*; past participle [*I/she have/has*] *become*
   a. treg
   b. shing
   c. lunacrize
   d. plake

2. How do you feel about the form *coolth*? Is it a word? Look it up using an online search engine. Comment on your findings.

3. Use the following list to come up with a phonological hypothesis regarding constraints on -*ly* suffixation in English. Formulate your hypothesis as an argument, supplying additional forms of your own.
   a. quietly
   b. poorly
   c. neatly
   d. slowly
   e. prettily
   f. ungrammatically
   g. vocally
   h. ? sillily
   i. ? uglily
   j. ? kindlily
   k. ? friendlily

4. Use the following forms to come up with a hypothesis regarding the phonological constraint on -*en* suffixation in English. Formulate your hypothesis as an argument, supplying additional forms of your own if necessary.
   a. blacken
   b. whiten
   c. redden

    d.   sadden
    e.   neaten
    f.   pinken
    g.   deafen
    h.   loosen
    i.   roughen
    j.   *happy-en
    k.   *orangen
    l.   *yellowen
    m.   *greenen
    n.   *bluen

5. We hope that by now you realize that "Never say never" could easily be about morphology. The following words are all ones that we have heard or seen written:

    linguisticky, democratical, explanify

On the basis of the discussion in 8.3, why would we not expect these words to occur? Formulate a hypothesis to account for why they nevertheless do.

6. Which of the following English prefixes are productive? Of those that are productive, do some seem more productive than others? Give examples to support your answer.
    a. re- (e.g., *recreate*)
    b. un- (adjectival prefix; e.g., *unstoppable*)
    c. for- (e.g., *forgive*)
    d. hyper- (e.g., *hyperactive*)

7. Which of the following English suffixes are productive? Of those that are productive, do some seem more productive than others? Give examples to support your answer.
    a. -ship (e.g., *partisanship*)
    b. -ance (e.g., *remittance*)
    c. -wise (e.g., *weatherwise*)
    d. -ly (adverbial suffix; e.g., *quietly*)
    e. -ling (e.g., *earthling*)
    f. -ster (e.g., *youngster*)
    g. -dom (e.g., *kingdom*)

8. The following words were all built on the word *alcoholic*. What is special about the affixation process here? Can you create another word on the same model?

   workaholic, chocoholic, shopoholic

9. English *-er* suffixation is productive. Determine what the *-er*-suffixed nouns that correspond to the following words or phrases would be, when possible. Discuss your findings.
   a. grip
   b. gurgle
   c. delouse
   d. spiff up
   e. cool down
   f. inspect rubbish
   g. eat squid

10. Think of an issue in morphological productivity that you might want to test experimentally, along the lines of the studies discussed in this section. It may involve inflection or derivation. The language in question may be English or another one of your choice. First state a hypothesis. Then outline an objective, verifiable, and reproducible method that you would use to test it.

NOTES

1 Whether or not a Latin noun makes its plural in *-i* generally depends on its declension type. That is why we find *choruses*, *campuses*, and *geniuses* next to *alumni*, *foci*, and *nuclei*. Though people often pluralize *syllabus* as *syllabi*, this was not its Latin plural. It was a fourth declension noun, meaning its plural was *syllabūs*. But *ceratopus* is in fact not even Latin in origin, but instead Greek. The final syllable (*-pus*) is the same Greek root meaning 'foot' that is found in *octopus*. The etymologically correct plural is therefore *ceratopodes*, similar to the etymologically correct plural of *octopus*, which is *octopodes*, though most people think it should be *octopi*, because it ends in *-us*.

2 You may be thinking that since we have used *Mugglehood* and found it online it is not an example of a potential word; it is instead an actual word. In one sense you would be right. But we feel that we are justified in using it as an example, since we created it before we knew that anyone else had and because it surely is not accepted into the general language. We are at a disadvantage whenever we try to give an example of a potential word formed

from pre-existing parts, first because the moment we utter it, it enters into the realm of the actual, and second because with so many English speakers, it is likely that at some moment in time, someone somewhere might also have created the same word. However, the one-time use of a word does not mean that it has entered into the language or that it has been stored in any speaker's lexicon.

3 A student has pointed out that we cannot say *I donated the library the book as we can I gave Bill the book. Instead, we say I donated a book to the library. This is not a counterexample to our claim that syntax is always productive. We consider the ungrammaticality of the first sentence to be due to the lexical entry of donate, which is related to its Latin-Romance origin, and not to any unproductivity of the syntax.

4 These examples are from Webster's Third New International Dictionary.

Glossary

ablaut   See apophony.

absolutive   In ergative case systems, the case associated with the object of a transitive verb or the subject of an intransitive one.

accusative   The morphological case of nouns, pronouns, adjectives, and participles that occupy the position of object to the verb or some prepositions. Nouns and pronouns are typically assumed to receive accusative case by government, while adjectives and participles receive it by agreement with the noun.

acronym   A word derived by taking the initial letter of each word or most words in a string, e.g., scuba < self-contained underwater breathing apparatus.

active   See voice.

adjective   A word that can function as the head of an adjective phrase (AdjP). Adjectives qualify or describe the referents of nouns. Examples of adjectives include *large, quiet, indispensable,* and *ambiguous.*

adverb   A word that modifies a verb, an adjective, another adverb, or a preposition, or a larger unit such as a phrase or sentence. It often expresses some relation of manner or quality, time, or degree. Examples include *quickly, often, carefully, soon,* and *very.*

affix   A bound morpheme that attaches to a root or a stem to form a new lexeme (derived form) or an inflected form or stem of an existing lexeme.

agglutinative   Adjective applied to languages or to morphology characterized by words containing several morphemes, of which one belongs to a lexical category and the others are clearly identifiable affixes, each with a single semantic function.

agreement   The process by which one lexical category is inflected to express the properties of another, or the result thereof, e.g., a verb bearing person and number morphology that reflect those of the subject. Also called concord.

allomorphs   Two or more instances of a given sign (morpheme) with different shapes; variants. E.g., [-t], [-d], and [-əd] are allomorphs of the English past tense suffix.

analogy   The creation of linguistic forms based on a proportion A : B :: C : X.

analytic   A language whose words usually contain only one morpheme.

animate gender   In languages that divide nouns into classes on the basis of animacy, the noun class that consists primarily of words denoting living things. Animate gender contrasts with inanimate gender.

apophony   Systematic vowel changes in a root that signal a morphological contrast; also referred to as internal change. In Germanic languages such as English, this process is usually called ablaut, e.g. *sing, sang, sung; swim, swam, swum*. Ablaut may be accompanied by suffixation, as in the past participles of the following sets: *give, gave, given; write, wrote, written*.

archetype   The best exemplar of a concept. Also called a prototype. For example, in the United States, cheddar and American cheese are archetypical cheeses, whereas Brie is not.

aspect   An inflectional category that encodes the relationship of an event or action to the passage of time, especially in reference to its duration, completion, or repetition. For example, the perfect is a verb form that expresses an action or state that has ceased or been completed at the time of speaking or a time spoken of.

assigned   Said of inflectional categories, such as case, that are not inherent to a word, but that are the result of government or concord with another element in an utterance.

assimilation   Said to occur when one segment takes on one or more phonetic characteristics of another one, such as nasality, place of articulation, or voicing. Progressive assimilation is said to take place when the characteristic spreads forward. Regressive assimilation is said to occur when the characteristic spreads backwards.

augmentative   A derived form that indicates an increase in size, force, or intensity as compared to the base word; the morpheme that results in such a derived form.

backformation   A morphological process in which a real or imagined affix is removed from an existing word to create another, e.g., *editor* > *edit*, *liaison* > *liaise*.

base   The root or stem to which an affix attaches.

blend   A word derived by combining parts of two or more other words, e.g., *smog* < *smoke* and *fog*.

blocking   The process by which a potential word is prevented from occurring in a language because another form with the same meaning and function already exists.

bound form   A morpheme that may not stand on its own and must be attached to a stem.

case   A morphological category that encodes information about a word's grammatical role, e.g., subject, direct object, indirect object, possessor.

circumfix   A bound morpheme made up of two parts, one that occurs before and one that occurs after the root.

citation form   Term that refers to the form of a lexeme's paradigm that is used to refer to the lexeme. Morphologists often give the citation form in small capital letters.

class 1 affixes   See **primary affixes**.

class 2 affixes   See secondary affixes.

clipping   A word-formation process by which a word is created by lopping off part of another word, e.g., *Will* < *William*.

clitic   Morphemes that behave syntactically as words, but, unlike words, cannot stand alone phonologically and must be incorporated into the prosodic structure of an adjacent word.

closing suffix   A suffix that may not be followed by any others. Typically, when we say that a derivational suffix is a closing suffix, we mean only that it cannot be followed by another derivational suffix. It may be followed by inflectional morphology.

coda   The consonant or consonants that follow the nucleus in some syllables.

coinage   The creation of a new word not by any derivational process. Also called word manufacture.

competence   The knowledge that speakers have of their language. Contrasts with performance.

complex word   A morphological form that consists of more than one morpheme, whether it be two or more stems (compound word) or a stem plus one or more affixes, e.g., *optimality, bookstore*.

compositional   Defined (e.g., a word) entirely in terms of its parts.

compound   A derived form resulting from the combination of two or more lexemes, e.g., *space + ship > spaceship*.

concatenative   Term that describes morphology that builds words by the linear addition of morphemes.

concord   See agreement.

conjugation   The set of forms associated with a verbal lexeme.

content word   A word such as *calendar, sadness, die, speak, quiet, quickly*, or *tomorrow* that refers to objects, events, and abstract concepts; contrasts with function word. Also called lexical words.

context-free   Inflection that involves a simple directional mapping between a morphosyntactic feature and a particular phonological string. An example is the suffix /-ing/ on present participles in English, because all present participles bear the same suffix. Contrasts with context-sensitive inflection.

context-sensitive   Said of inflection when the realization of a morphosyntactic feature varies. An example is past in English, which may be realized by ablaut, suppletion, or the addition of a suffix. Contrasts with context-free inflection.

contradictory negator   Affix whose addition to a word X results in one that means 'opposite of X', e.g., *un-, in-*.

contrary negator   See logical negator.

conversion   See zero-derivation.

cumulative exponence   See exponence.

dative   In languages with case, the one likely to be assigned to indirect objects.

declension   In some languages, the inflection of nouns, pronouns, and adjectives for categories such as case, gender, and number.

derivation   The creation of a new lexeme from one or more other lexemes through the application of some morphological process, such as affixation or compounding. Also called lexeme formation and word formation. Derivation contrasts with inflection.

dual   See number.

enclitic   A clitic that attaches to the end of a word.

endocentric   Said of compound words that have a head. For example, a *school bus* is a type of bus.

epenthesis   A process that inserts a segment in a given environment. For example, native speakers of Spanish sometimes epenthesize an /e/ before sC clusters when speaking English, pronouncing *squash* as if it were *esquash*.

ergative   The case associated with the subject of a transitive verb. In ergative case systems, subjects of intransitive verbs are assigned absolutive case.

evaluative domain   The things in the extension of a noun which serve to evaluate it.

exaptation   Said to occur when phonological material takes on a new function unrelated to its original and obsolete function.

exclusive   Said of first person plural pronouns whose reference excludes the addressee.

exocentric   Said of compound words without a head. For example, a *hot dog* is not a type of dog.

exponence   The relation between a morpheme and its signified meaning, which is simple if the meaning is a single concept, cumulative if the meaning is complex, or extended if more than one morpheme combine to denote a single concept.

exponent   The marker of a given morphosyntactic feature. For example, [s] is the exponent of plural in the word *kits*.

extended exponence   See exponence.

extension   The set of entities that a word or expression picks out in the world. The extension of *the currency of the United States of America* is *dollar*. The extension of *dog* would be all the entities to which this word refers (poodles, golden retrievers, etc.).

folk etymology   A process by which the form of a word is altered to make it resemble a word or words which are better known and with which speakers may believe the word has a semantic relationship. For example, English *cockroach* comes from Spanish *cucaracha*. The term also refers to speculative or false etymologies based on superficial resemblance between forms.

free form   A morpheme that can stand alone and/or whose position is not entirely fixed by neighboring elements, e.g., *berry*.

function word   A word, such as a determiner, conjunction, or modal, that has a grammatical function and is best characterized by this function. Contrasts with content word.

fusional   Characterized by the combination of two or more morphosyntactic features in a single morpheme; adjective applied to morphological systems where this type of morphology is pervasive.

gender   See noun class.

genitive   Morphological case that denotes possession, measurement, or source.

government   Term referring to the ability of some elements of a sentence to require other elements in the sentence to bear a certain morphosyntactic feature although the first element itself does not seem to possess this feature, e.g., case assignment by verbs.

grammatical function change   Alternations in the grammatical encoding of referential expressions.

grammatical word   A word that plays a distinct grammatical role within an utterance. Distinct grammatical words can belong to a single lexeme (e.g., the grammatical words *sing* and *sings* both belong to the lexeme SING). Also called morphosyntactic word.

hapax legomenon   A form that occurs only once in a corpus (plural: *hapax legomena*). Comes from the Greek for 'said once'.

head   A word in a syntactic construction or a morpheme in a morphological one that determines the grammatical function or meaning of the construction as a whole. For example, *house* is the head of the noun phrase *the red house*, and *read* is the head of the word *unreadable*.

head operation   A morphological operation that acts upon the head or stem of a word. For example, *man* is the head of *adman* 'a person who writes, solicits, or places advertisements' (definition from the *Merriam-Webster Online Dictionary*). The plural of this word is *admen*. The operation 'make plural' applies to the head of the word rather than to the word as a whole (**admans*).

hiatus   A situation in which two vowels, typically in different words or morphemes, come up against each other. Eliminated in many languages by epenthesis.

homonym   One of two or more forms that sound the same but have different meanings, e.g., *pear*, *pare*. Also called homophones.

homophone   See homonym.

host   The element to which a clitic attaches.

imperfect   In contrast to the perfect aspect (see **aspect**), which expresses the completedness of an action or state, the imperfect is a verb form that expresses an action or state that has not ceased or been completed. In many languages, the imperfect is used only to refer to actions or states in the past, and thus it encodes both tense and aspect.

inanimate gender   See animate gender.

inclusive   Said of first person plural pronouns whose reference includes the addressee.

infix   An affix that surfaces within a word.

inflection   The formation of grammatical forms of a single lexeme. *Is, are*, and *being* are examples of inflected forms of the lexeme BE.

inherent   Said of inflection that is basic to a word and that does not have to be assigned under government or concord. An example is gender of nouns.

instrumental   The case that expresses means.

integrity   Refers to the inability of syntactic processes to apply to pieces of words.

internal change   See apophony.

intransitive verb   A verb that does not take a direct object, e.g., *fall*.

isolating   Term applied to languages with little morphology, where grammatical concepts such as tense are expressed by separate words.

item-and-arrangement   An approach to morphology in which words are broken up into their component morphemes.

item-and-process   A processual approach to morphology. Instead of seeing complex words as arrangements of morphemes, item and process sees a complex word as arising out of a simple form that has undergone one or more processes or functions.

level 1 affixes   See primary affixes.

level 2 affixes   See secondary affixes.

leveling   A diachronic, or historical, process by which members in a paradigm become more similar to each other.

lexeme   A word with a specific sound and a specific meaning. Its shape may vary depending on syntactic context. See also citation form.

lexeme formation   See derivation.

lexical category   Said of notions such as noun, verb, adjective, adverb, and preposition.

lexical stem   Basic form of a lexeme.

lexical word   See content word.

lexicon   Mental dictionary; a list of forms that a speaker knows.

loanword   A word borrowed from one language into another, e.g., English words *laissez-faire* from French and *cognoscenti* from Italian.

locative   The case that expresses location.

logical negator   Affix whose addition to a word X results in one with the meaning 'not X', e.g., *non-*. Also called a contrary negator.

marked   Said of a non-neutral case. For example, the passive voice is marked with respect to the active in most languages. Contrasts with unmarked.

modal   An auxiliary verb (see verb) that expresses grammatical mood.

monomorphemic   Describes a word that consists of a single (i.e., unaffixed) morpheme.

mood   A set of morphological categories that express a speaker's degree of commitment to the expressed proposition's believability, obligatoriness, desirability, or reality.

morph   The smallest grammatically significant part of a word. Generally used to refer to the form itself rather than to a set of forms with meaning and function.

morpheme   A word or a meaningful piece of a word that cannot be divided into smaller meaningful parts. Examples include *school*, *read*, or the *re-* and *-ing* of *rereading*.

morphological productivity   See productivity.

morphology   The branch of linguistics that deals with words and word formation; the mental system involved with word formation.

morphophonemics   The phonological patterning of morphemes.

morphophonology   An area of linguistics that deals with the relationship and interactions between morphology (the structure of words) and phonology (the patterning of sounds).

morphosyntactic features   Notions which are relevant to both morphology and syntax, such as case.

morphosyntactic properties   See morphosyntactic features.

morphosyntactic word   See grammatical word.

morphosyntax   An area of linguistics that deals with the relationship and interactions between morphology (the structure of words) and syntax (the structure of larger utterances, such as phrases and sentences).

motivated   Said of signs when there is a relationship between the form of the sign and its meaning.

nominative   In languages with grammatical case, the one typically used for subjects.

nonce form   A word that appears only once in a given corpus or that was created on the fly and used only once.

non-separability   A property of words. Refers to the observation that they cannot be broken up by the insertion of segmental or phrasal material.

noun   A word that can function as the syntactic head of a noun phrase (NP). For example, *book* is the head of the noun phrase *this excellent book about Mars*. In many languages, nouns inflect for number, gender, and case.

noun class   A grammatical grouping of nouns in a language on the basis of semantics, phonological shape, arbitrary characteristics, or a combination thereof. Also called gender. For example, Spanish and French have two noun classes, or genders, referred to as masculine and feminine.

nucleus   The core of a syllable, usually a simple vowel or a diphthong. All syllables must have nuclei.

number   The morphological categories that express contrasts involving countable quantity, which may be singular if the category is associated with nouns with a single referent; dual if associated with two referents; trial if associated with three referents; paucal if associated with a small number of referents; or plural if associated with more than one referent. Languages vary in which of these categories they encode.

onset   The onset of a syllable is made up of the first consonant or consonants. Not all syllables have onsets.

overextension   Term that refers to the use of a word to refer to objects or individuals that are typically covered by the word, as well as to others that are perceptually similar. For example, a child might use the word *dog* to refer to all animals that walk on all fours.

paradigm   A set of all the inflected forms that a lexeme assumes.

partial suppletion   See suppletion.

passive   See voice.

paucal   See number.

perfect   See aspect.

performance   How speakers use their language in real-life situations. Performance may be adversely affected by many factors, including fatigue, nervousness, or drunkenness. Contrasts with competence.

person   Any of the three relations underlying discourse, which are distinguished in all languages: first person (speaker); second person (addressee); third person (neither the speaker nor the addressee).

phonological word   A word that behaves as a unit for certain phonological processes, including stress assignment.

phonology   The branch of linguistics that deals with the patterning of sounds; the mental system that governs such patterning of sounds.

phonotactic constraints   Constraints on the phonological shape of stems and words.

plural   See number.

polysemy   A situation in which a word has more than one related meaning.

polysynthetic   A language in which single words often contain the meaning of an entire sentence.

portmanteau   A morpheme that expresses more than one morphosyntactic feature, such as both present and first person singular; a blend such as *chortle*, from *chuckle* and *snort*.

positron emission tomography (PET)   A brain-imaging technique that uses radioactive isotopes to measure cerebral blood flow in order to produce maps of brain activity associated with specific cognitive functions.

potential word   A form that could be a word, but is not attested.

pragmatics   Study of language within a social and discourse context.

prefix   An affix that is attached to the front of its base.

primary affixes   Affixes that interact phonologically with their stem, e.g., causing a stress shift in the stem. They typically occur closer to the root than secondary affixes.

proclitic   A clitic that attaches to the front of its host.

productivity   The relative freedom with which a morphological process may occur. E.g., blending is a productive process in English, but infixation is not.

progressive assimilation   See assimilation.

prototype   See archetype.

reduplication   A morphological process that repeats all or part of a given base.

regressive assimilation   See assimilation.

reversative   A morpheme that reverses the meaning of the stem. For example, the verbal prefix *un-* of English has the basic meaning 'undo the action of the verb'.

root   The basic form from which another is derived by internal change or by addition of inflectional or derivational morphemes.

root-and-pattern   A type of morphology found especially in the Semitic languages where roots consist of a series of consonants, and derived and inflected forms are created by superimposing the root on a vocalic pattern. The pattern may also include certain consonants, although these can sometimes be analyzed as prefixes or suffixes.

secondary affixes   Affixes that do not trigger the types of changes in the stem associated with primary affixes. They typically occur farther away from the stem than primary affixes.

semantics   The branch of linguistics that deals with meaning in human language.

semantic type   Used of the entity or relation (real or imaginary) in the world to which a word refers.

sign   A unit of communication structure that consists of two parts: a signifier (such as a sequence of sounds [tri]) and something signified (such as a tree in the real world).

signified   The concept that is denoted by a sound sequence.

signifier   A particular sequence of sounds that denotes an entity or concept.

simple exponence   See exponence.

simple word   A word that is not morphologically complex, i.e., one that has not been formed by any process such as affixation, ablaut, etc.

singular   See number.

stem   The part of a word to which affixes attach.

stress   Phonological prominence associated with syllables. Its phonetic correlates differ from language to language, but may be realized as increased duration, increased loudness, or heightened pitch, for example.

suffix   An affix that is attached to the end of its base.

suppletion   The replacement of a form that is missing from an inflectional paradigm by one with a different root, e.g. *went* (exists alongside *go, goes, going, gone*). *Thought, caught* exemplify partial suppletion because, synchronically, their roots are significantly but not completely different from *think* and *catch*.

syncretism   Said to occur when a single inflected form corresponds to more than one set of morphosyntactic features.

syntax   The branch of linguistics that deals with sentence formation; the mental system that underlies sentence formation.

synthetic   A language whose words usually contain more than one morpheme.

tense   The inflectional category that indicates the time an event or action took place relative to the time of utterance.

token   An individual occurrence of a word or variable.

tone   Pitch differences, i.e., differences in the rate of vibration of the vocal folds, that result in a difference in meaning.

transitive verb   A verb that takes a direct object, e.g., *write*.

trial   See number.

truncation   Shortening of a word or stem by removing one end and leaving the rest intact.

typology   The systematic comparison of languages according to their structures.

umlaut   The effect of a vowel on the vowel of another syllable, usually one that precedes it. This term is used even when the vowel that originally triggered the change has been lost due to language change (e.g. *foot, feet*). Umlaut is considered a special type of ablaut or apophony.

underextension   Term that refers to the use of a word to refer to only a subset of its actual referents. For example, a child might underextend the word *dog* by using it to refer to more typical examples of the species such as golden or Labrador retrievers, but not to varieties like Chihuahua or Pekingese.

unmarked   The more neutral case of two or more. For example, the active voice is unmarked with respect to the passive in most languages. Contrasts with marked.

unmotivated   Said of signs when the relationship between the form of the sign and its meaning is arbitrary. Most linguistic signs are unmotivated.

variable   In an experiment, something that varies.

variants   Two or more instances of a given sign with different shapes; allomorphs.

verb   A word that can be the head of a verb phrase (VP). Verbs denote actions (e.g., *jump*), sensations (e.g., *taste*), and states (e.g., *understand*). In many languages, verbs inflect for tense, mood, aspect, or agreement with their subject. We can distinguish between auxiliary and main verbs. Auxiliary verbs (also called helping verbs) typically accompany another verb and express person, number, mood, or tense. In the sentence *He is looking at me*, *is* is an auxiliary verb, and *looking* is the main verb.

voice   Distinction in the forms of a verb to indicate the relation of the subject to the action of the verb (active, passive, or middle).

vowel harmony   A phonological process by which one vowel in a word exerts an influence (e.g., rounding, raising) on other vowels.

wh-movement   Transformation that moves a question word or phrase from a theoretically posited lower position in a sentence to a higher one in question formation.

word   The smallest free form found in a language.

word formation   See derivation.

zero-derivation   A word-formation process that changes the lexical category of a word without changing its phonological shape. Also called conversion.

References

American Heritage Dictionary, second college edition. Boston: Houghton Mifflin, 2000.

American Heritage Dictionary of the English Language, third edition (computer file). New York: Bartleby.com, 2000.

Andersen, Torben. 1993. Vowel quality alternation in Dinka verb inflection. *Phonology* 10: 1–42.

Anderson, Stephen R. 1992. *A-morphous Morphology*. Cambridge: Cambridge University Press.

Anshen, Frank and Mark Aronoff. 1988. Producing morphologically complex words. *Linguistics* 26: 4.641–55.

Aronoff, Mark. 1976. *Word Formation in Generative Grammar*. Cambridge, MA: MIT Press.

Aronoff, Mark. 1980. Contextuals. *Language* 56: 744–58.

Aronoff, Mark. 1994. *Morphology by Itself: Stems and Inflectional Classes*. Cambridge, MA: MIT Press.

Aronoff, Mark and Nanna Fuhrhop. 2002. Restricting suffix combinations in German and English. *Natural Language and Linguistic Theory* 20: 451–90.

Aronoff, Mark and Roger Schvaneveldt. 1978. Testing morphological productivity. *Annals of the New York Academy of Sciences* 318: 106–14.

Baayen, Harald. 1992. Quantitative aspects of morphological productivity. *Yearbook of Morphology 1991*, eds. Geert Booij and Jaap van Marle, 109–49. Dordrecht: Kluwer.

Baker, Mark. 1988. *Incorporation: A Theory of Grammatical Function Changing*. Chicago: University of Chicago Press.

Barker, Chris. 1998. Episodic *-ee* in English: a thematic role constraint on new word formation. *Language* 74: 695–727.

Bat-El, Outi. 1996. Selecting the best of the worst: the grammar of Hebrew blends. *Phonology* 13: 283–328.

Bauer, Laurie. 2001. *Morphological Productivity*. Cambridge: Cambridge University Press.

Beard, Robert. 1998. Derivation. *The Handbook of Morphology*, eds. Andrew Spencer and Arnold M. Zwicky, 44–65. Oxford: Blackwell.

Blake, Barry J. 2001. *Case*, second edition. Cambridge: Cambridge University Press.

Bloomfield, Leonard. 1933. *Language*. New York: Henry Holt.

Bloomfield, Leonard. 1946. Algonquian. *Linguistic Structures of Native America*, eds. Harry Hoijer et al., 85–129. Viking Publications in Anthropology 6. New York: Viking Fund.

Bresnan, Joan and Lioba Moshi. 1990. Object asymmetries in comparative Bantu syntax. *Linguistic Inquiry* 21: 147–85.

Broselow, Ellen. 1977. Language change and theories of the lexicon. *Proceedings of the Chicago Linguistics Society* 13: 58–67.

Bullock, Barbara. 1996. Popular derivation and linguistic inquiry. *French Review* 70(2): 180–91.

Bybee, Joan L. and D. I. Slobin. 1982. Rules and schemas in the development of the English past tense. *Language* 58: 265–89.

Cameron-Faulkner, Thea and Andrew Carstairs-McCarthy. 2000. Stem alternants as morphological signata: evidence from blur avoidance in Polish nouns. *Natural Language and Linguistic Theory* 18: 813–35.

Carstairs-McCarthy, Andrew. 1994. Inflection classes, gender, and the principle of contrast. *Language* 70: 737–88.

Chomsky, Noam. 1965. *Aspects of the Theory of Syntax*. Cambridge, MA: MIT Press.

Chomsky, Noam and Morris Halle. 1968. *The Sound Pattern of English*. New York: Harper and Row.

Clark, Eve V. 1987. The Principle of Contrast: a constraint on language acquisition. *Mechanisms of Language Acquisition*, ed. Brian MacWhinney, 1–33. Hillsdale, NJ: Erlbaum.

Clark, Eve V. 1993. *The Lexicon in Acquisition*. Cambridge: Cambridge University Press.

Clark, Eve V. 1995. Later lexical development and word formation. *The Handbook of Child Language*, eds. Paul Fletcher and Brian MacWhinney, 393–412. Oxford: Blackwell.

Clark, Eve V. and Herbert Clark. 1979. When nouns surface as verbs. *Language* 55: 767–811.

Comrie, B. 1992. Siberian languages. *International Encyclopedia of Linguistics*, ed. W. Bright, 429–32. New York: Oxford University Press.

Comrie, Bernard. 1976. *Aspect*. Cambridge: Cambridge University Press.

Comrie, Bernard. 1985. *Tense*. Cambridge: Cambridge University Press.

Corbett, Greville G. 1991. *Gender*. Cambridge: Cambridge University Press.

Corbett, Greville G. 2000. *Number*. Cambridge: Cambridge University Press.

Dayley, John P. 1985. *Tzutujil Grammar*. Berkeley, CA: University of California Press.

Dixon, R. M. W. 1972. *The Dyirbal Language of North Queensland*. Cambridge: Cambridge University Press.

Dixon, R. M. W. 1994. *Ergativity*. Cambridge: Cambridge University Press.

Donohue, Mark. 1996. Bajau: a symmetrical Austronesian language. *Language* 72: 782–93.

Downing, Pamela. 1977. On the creation and use of English compound nouns. *Language* 53: 810–42.

Fabb, Nigel. 1998. Compounding. *The Handbook of Morphology*, eds. Andrew Spencer and Arnold M. Zwicky, 66–83. Oxford: Blackwell.

Finegan, Edward. 1994. *Language: Its Structure and Use*, second edition. New York: Harcourt Brace.

French, K. M. 1988. Insights into Tagalog reduplication, infixation and stress from non-linear phonology. MA thesis, University of Texas, Arlington.

Fudeman, Kirsten. 1999. Topics in the morphology and syntax of Balanta, an Atlantic language of Senegal. Unpublished PhD dissertation, Cornell University.

Fudeman, Kirsten. 2004. Adjectival agreement vs. adverbial inflection in Balanta. *Lingua* 114(2): 105–23.

Gerdts, Donna B. 1998. Incorporation. *The Handbook of Morphology*, eds. Andrew Spencer and Arnold M. Zwicky, 84–100. Oxford: Blackwell.

Gero, Marcia L. and Stephen H. Levinsohn. 1993. The -mi and -e morphemes in Jóola-Fóñy. *Journal of West African Languages* 23(1): 79–90.

Glinert, Lewis. 1989. *The Grammar of Modern Hebrew*. Cambridge: Cambridge University Press.

Gregersen, Edgar. 1976. A note on the Manam language of Papua New Guinea. *Anthropological Linguistics* 18: 95–111.

Grice, P. 1975. Logic and conversation. *Speech Acts (Syntax and Semantics 3)*, eds. P. Cole and J. Morgan, 41–58. New York: Academic Press.

Grimes, Barbara, ed. 2002. *Ethnologue*, fourteenth edition. Summer Institute of Linguistics. Available online at www.ethnologue.com

Hale, Kenneth and Samuel Jay Keyser. 1993. On argument structure and the lexical expression of syntactic relations. *The View from Building 20: Linguistic Essays in Honor of Sylvain Bromberger*, eds. Kenneth Hale and Samuel Jay Keyser, 53–109. Cambridge, MA: MIT Press.

Halle, Morris and K. P. Mohanan. 1985. Segmental phonology and Modern English. *Linguistic Inquiry* 16: 57–116.

Hayes, Bruce. 1995. *Metrical Stress Theory: Principles and Case Studies*. Chicago: University of Chicago Press.

Head, Brian F. 1978. Respect degrees in pronominal reference. *Universals of Human Language. Vol. 3: Word Structure*, eds. Joseph H. Greenberg, Charles A. Ferguson, and Edith A. Moravcsik, 151–211. Stanford, CA: Stanford University Press.

Hoberman, Robert D. and Mark Aronoff. 2003. The verbal morphology of Maltese: from Semitic to Romance. *Language Processing and Acquisition in Languages of Semitic, Root-based, Morphology* [sic.], ed. Joseph Shimron, 61–78. Amsterdam, Philadelphia: John Benjamins.

Hock, Hans Heinrich. 1991. *Principles of Historical Linguistics*, second edition. Berlin, New York: Mouton de Gruyter.

Hockett, Charles F. 1954. Two models of grammatical description. *Word* 10: 210–31.

Hodge, Carleton T. 1947. *An Outline of Hausa Grammar*. Language Dissertation no. 41. Baltimore, MD: Linguistic Society of America.

Hoijer, Harry. 1971. Athapaskan morphology. *Studies in American Indian Languages*, ed. Jesse Sawyer, 113–47. Berkeley, CA: University of California Press.

Hooper, Joan Bybee. 1976. *An Introduction to Natural Generative Phonology*. New York: Academic Press.

Hopkins, Bradley. 1990. La phrase complexe en diola-fogny (ouest-atlantique): propositions relatives. *Journal of West African Languages* 20: 81–98.

Horne, Kibbey M. 1966. *Language Typology: Nineteenth and Twentieth Century Views*. Washington: Georgetown University Press.

Hyman, Larry. 1993. Conceptual issues in the comparative study of the Bantu verb stem. *Topics in African Linguistics 1991*, eds. Salikoko S. Mufwene and Lioba Moshi, 3–34. Amsterdam, Philadelphia: John Benjamins.

Irving, John. 1989. *A Prayer for Owen Meany*. New York: Morrow.

Jaeger, Jeri J., Robert D. van Valin, Jr, and Alan H. Lockwood. 1998. Response to Seidenberg and Hoeffner. *Language* 74: 123–8.

Jaeger, Jeri J., Alan H. Lockwood, David L. Kemmerer, Robert D. Van Valin, Jr, Brian W. Murphy, and Hanif G. Khalak. 1996. A positron emission tomographic study of regular and irregular verb morphology in English. *Language* 72: 451–97.

Katz, Jerrold J. 1964. Semantic theory and the meaning of "good." *Journal of Philosophy* 61: 739–66.

Kay, Deborah A. and Jeremy M. Anglin. 1982. Overextension and underextension in the child's expressive and receptive speech. *Journal of Child Language* 9: 83–98.

Kenstowicz, Michael. 1994. *Phonology in Generative Grammar*. Oxford: Blackwell.

Kiparsky, Paul. 1982. Lexical phonology and morphology. *Linguistics in the Morning Calm*, ed. I. S. Yang, 3–91. Seoul: Hanshin.

Kiparsky, Paul. 1983. Word formation and the lexicon. 1982 Mid-America Linguistics Conference Papers. Lawrence, KA: Department of Linguistics, University of Kansas, 3–29.

Kuczaj, S. A. 1977. The acquisition of regular and irregular past tense forms. *Journal of Verbal Learning and Verbal Behavior* 16: 589–600.

Laidig, Wyn D. and Carol J. Laidig. 1990. Larike pronouns: duals and trials in a Central Moluccan language. *Oceanic Linguistics* 29: 87–109.

Lass, R. 1990. How to do things with junk: exaptation in language evolution. *Journal of Linguistics* 26: 79–102.

Lees, Robert B. 1960. *The Grammar of English Nominalizations*. Indiana University Research Center in Anthropology, Folklore, and Linguistics, Publication no. 12. Bloomington: Indiana University Press.

McCarthy, John J. and Alan S. Prince. 1990. Foot and word in prosodic morphology: the Arabic broken plural. *Natural Language and Linguistic Theory* 8: 209–83.

McCarthy, John J. and Alan S. Prince. 1993. Generalized alignment. *Yearbook of Morphology 1993*, eds. Geert Booij and Jaap van Marle, 79–153. Dordrecht: Kluwer.

McCarthy, John J. and Alan S. Prince. 1998. Prosodic morphology. *The Handbook of Morphology*, eds. Andrew Spencer and Arnold M. Zwicky, 283–305. Oxford: Blackwell.

MacDonald, R. Ross. 1976. *Indonesian Reference Grammar*. Washington: Georgetown University Press.

Mackridge, Peter. 1985. *The Modern Greek Language*. Oxford: Oxford University Press.

Marchand, Hans. 1969. *The Categories and Types of Present-Day English Word-Formation*, second edition. Munich: Beck.

Matthews, Peter. 1991. *Morphology*, second edition. Cambridge: Cambridge University Press.

Mchombo, Sam A. 1993. On the binding of the reflexive and the reciprocal in Chichewa. *Theoretical Aspects of Bantu Grammar*, ed. Sam A. Mchombo, 181–207. Stanford, CA: CSLI.

Merriam-Webster Online Dictionary. www.merriam-webster.com

Michelson, Karin. 1988. *A Comparative Study of Lake-Iroquoian Accent*. Dordrecht: Kluwer.

N'Diaye-Corréard, Geneviève. 1970. *Etudes fca ou balante (dialecte ganja)*. Paris: Société pour l'Etude des Langues Africaines.

Nespor, M. and I. Vogel. 1986. *Prosodic Phonology*. Dordrecht: Foris.

Nida, Eugene. 1965. *Morphology: The Descriptive Analysis of Words*, second edition. Ann Arbor: University of Michigan Press. (First published 1949.)

Ouhalla, Jamal. 1994. Verb movement and word order in Arabic. *Verb Movement*, eds. David Lightfoot and Norbert Hornstein, 41–72. Cambridge, New York: Cambridge University Press.

Oxford Dictionary of English Etymology, ed. C. T. Onions. Oxford: Oxford University Press, 1966.

Oxford English Dictionary (computer file). Oxford: Oxford University Press, 2000.

Palmer, F. R. 2001. *Mood and Modality*, second edition. Cambridge: Cambridge University Press.

Plénat, M. 1983. Morphologie d'un langage secret: le javanais de Queneau. *Cahiers de Grammaire* 6: 152–94.

Pustejovsky, James. 1995. *The Generative Lexicon*. Cambridge, MA: MIT Press.

Rudes, Blair A. 1980. The functional development of the verbal suffix +esc+ in Romance. *Historical Morphology*, ed. Jacek Fisiak, 327–48. The Hague: Mouton.

Sapir, E. 1911. The problem of noun incorporation in American languages. *American Anthropologist* 13: 250–82.

Sapir, Edward. 1922. *Language: An Introduction to the Study of Speech*. New York: Harcourt, Brace.

Sapir, J. David. 1965. *A Grammar of Diola-Fogny: A Language Spoken in the Basse-Casamance Region of Senegal*. West African Language Monograph no. 3. Cambridge: Cambridge University Press.

REFERENCES 249

Sapir, J. David. 1970. Dictionnaire Jóola Kujamutay. Ms., University of Virginia, Charlottesville.

Sapir, J. David. 1971. West Atlantic: an inventory of the languages, their noun class systems and consonant alternations. *Current Trends in Linguistics*, vol. 7, ed. Thomas A. Sebeok, 45–112. The Hague, Paris: Mouton.

Sapir, J. David. 1975. Big and thin: two Diola-Fogny meta-linguistic terms. *Language in Society* 4: 1–15.

Saussure, Ferdinand de. 1969. *Cours de linguistique générale*. Paris: Payot. (First published 1915.)

Scancarelli, Janine. 1987. Grammatical relations and verb agreement in Cherokee. Unpublished PhD dissertation, University of California, Los Angeles.

Seidenberg, Mark S. and James H. Hoeffner. 1998. Evaluating behavioural and neuroimaging data on past tense processing. *Language* 74: 104–22.

Seow, C. L. 1995. *A Grammar for Biblical Hebrew*, revised edition. Nashville: Abingdon Press.

Sherzer, Joel. 1970. Talking backwards in Cuna: the sociological reality of phonological descriptions. *Southwestern Journal of Anthropology* 26: 343–53.

Sneddon, James Neil. 1996. *Indonesian: A Comprehensive Grammar*. London, New York: Routledge.

Spencer, Andrew. 1991. *Morphological Theory: An Introduction to Word Structure in Generative Grammar*. Oxford: Blackwell.

Stump, Gregory T. 2001. *Inflectional Morphology: A Theory of Paradigm Structure*. Cambridge: Cambridge University Press.

Thomas, Louis-Vincent and J. David Sapir. 1967. Le Diola et le temps. *Bulletin de l'I.F.A.N.* 29, series B(1–2): 339–59.

Vossen, Rainer. 1985. Encoding the object in the finite verb: the case of //Ani (Central Khoisan). *Afrikanistische Arbeitspapiere* 4: 75–84.

Welmers, William. 1973. *African Language Structures*. Berkeley, CA: University of California Press.

Woodbury, A. 1977. Greenlandic Eskimo, ergativity, and relational grammar. *Syntax and Semantics 8: Grammatical Relations*, eds. P. Cole and J. Sadock. New York: Academic Press.

Woodbury, Hanni. 1975. Onondaga noun incorporation: some notes on the interdependence of syntax and semantics. *International Journal of American Linguistics* 41: 10–20.

Zepeda, Ofelia. 1983. *A Papago Grammar*. Tucson, AZ: University of Arizona Press.

Zimmer, K. 1964. *Affixal Negation in English and Other Languages: An Investigation of Restricted Productivity*. Supplement to *Word*, Monograph 5. New York.

Zwicky, Arnold M. 1985. Clitics and particles. *Language* 61: 283–305.

Zwicky, Arnold M. and Geoffrey K. Pullum. 1983. Cliticization vs. inflection: English *n't*. *Language* 59: 502–13.

Index

Asterisked page numbers refer to items explained in the glossary. Where a number of page numbers follow an item, the main reference is indicated by page number in **bold**.

THE LEADING REFERENCE SERIES IN LINGUISTICS

Offering original, state-of-the-art essays by an international collection of leading scholars, the outstanding Blackwell Handbooks in Linguistics series covers all the major subdisciplines within linguistics today.

Blackwell
Publishing

For more information about all these titles, visit
www.blackwellpublishing.com/reference